Dear Friends,

My wish is to help you navigate through *Life's Little Emergencies*. Whether you need plastic organizers for all of your fabulous jewelry, that perfect little black dress, an amazing set of dishes for your holiday feasts, outfits for work, dates, and lounging around the house, have no fear, JCPenney has got it all inside!

I hope you enjoy reading *Life's Little Emergencies* and remember, it's all about True Beauty™ inside and out, find yours!

Peace, passion, and always fashion,

also by Emme

True Beauty

ST. MARTIN'S PRESS
NEW YORK

life's little emergencies

[*Everyday Rescue for Beauty, Fashion, Relationships, and Life*]

Emme ®

AND NATASHA STOYNOFF

Library of Congress Cataloging-in-Publication Data
Emme.
Life's little emergencies : everyday rescue for beauty, fashion,
relationships, and life / Emme and Natasha Stoynoff.
p.cm.
ISBN 0-312-28682-1
1. Clothing and dress. 2. Fashion. 3. Beauty, Personal.
4. Women—Life skills guides. I. Stoynoff, Natasha. II. Title
TT507 .E47 2003
646.7'0082—dc21
2002033285

First Edition: March 2003

10 9 8 7 6 5 4 3 2 1

To my sweet, gutsy gal,

Toby Cole

Jonathan, you are such

an inspiration

For beautiful Maria and

The Bear . . .

A Note to Readers

The health, nutrition, beauty, and other tips in this book are for informational purposes only. They are not intended to take the place of individual advice from a physician or other trained professionals. These tips have worked for us in tackling some of life's little emergencies. But everyone is different. So, as they say, read labels and warnings carefully, avoid excessive use, and always listen to your body. Don't turn little emergencies into bigger ones.

Contents

Acknowledgments

We couldn't have asked for a more encouraging editor than Jennifer Enderlin. Thank you for pushing us forward and loving bath and beauty products like we do. Kim, Elizabeth, Michael, and Fran, thank you for tying it all together. John and Greg, you kept me laughing.

For a wonderful team; without them, it would be impossible to do what I do: To Dan Strone, my literary agent, and Sara—thank you for always believing in me every step of the way.

My dear friend and office manager, eagle-eye Amy Fierro, whose passion and untiring editing and administrative efforts helped make this book complete.

Sarah Hall and her incredible troupe, including Haasan and Elise, for always working hard and making me look so good; and Mark Koehn and Larry Tedesco, for going the extra mile and always being there for the big questions.

Phil Aronson, my husband and business partner, who happily took over bathing duty and clean-up patrol of our toddler, fed me

when I needed to meet deadlines, and understood when I needed to go into hibernation and get this book done . . . thank you for your never-ending support and love.

Melanie, for being an incredible sister, friend, and major help in and around this project. A great big hug of thanks to all of our wonderful and diversified contributors: Marc Allen, Judy and Herman Aronson, Seth and Liora Aronson, Bradley Bayou, David Beahm, Sarah Bouissou, Bobbi Brown, Dr. Kelly Brownell, Kim Cattrall, Sally and Walter Clark, Gad Cohen, Fran Cooper, Jennifer Lyles Crawford, Jennifer Morgan Crawford, Wendy Derby, Melanie Dunea, Linda Ellerbee, Chip and Jen Entwistle, Kristen Ericksen, Caroleigh Evarts, Kendall Farr, grillmeister Mark Fierro, Kim France, Dawn Gallagher, Ellen Goodman, Dr. Jane Greer, Mariska Hargitay, the ever-adventurous Sue Hendrickson, Dr. David B. Herzog, Holly Hoff, Andrea Jovine, Mary Jo Keeble, Kerri, take-charge Cindi Leive, Mavis Leno, Nancy Lublin, Kevin Mancuso, Camryn Manheim, Lenard Matias, Nora McAniff, Dr. Diane Mickley, Elinor Morris, Elayne Moss, Chris Noth, Patricia O'Brien, Dave Paladino, Lillian Papp, Julie Payette, Mauri Pioppo, wiz Greg Prato, music masters Jill Garfunkel and Nick Robinson, Jacci Rosa, Leah Rozen, Dr. Ira Sacker, tante Patty Sicular, Antonio Sini, Basil Stevens, Tara, Cheryl Tiegs, nutritional goddess Evelyn Tribole, Aida Turturro, David Tutera, Karen Valenti, Maria Verel, Nicole Weedon, Dr. Bonnie Eaker Weil, Naomi Wolf, Dr. Jan Yager, and Trisha Yearwood, and to all of our female on-line friends, your heart and generosity of spirit are felt in these pages.

Not to forget, Cirsten "remain calm" Carle, Hal Upbin and the entire past and present Emme Collection and True Beauty gang, Brian Dubin, Andrew, Jeff G., Mark Itkin, Krista from WMA, Dorothy and Gavin, Linda G., Sherri and Monica, Wayne Ferguson, Diana B., Ayfer and Selima, the wild F. E. Team from E!, Brad and Michelle, and Nathalie S. for all you do with Toby.

To all the gang at *People* magazine, who fed and watered Natabella after her all-night writing sessions. To the boys at Starbucks, who brought her espressos on the hour. And especially, thanks to Natasha's husband, Steve, who did all the chores at home and gave Tashka chocolate when she had writer's block.

A truly grateful thank you goes out to our wonderfully eclectic circle of women friends without whom I would be a fish out of water. Over the years we have shared our finest moments, worst pitfalls, best tips, and exhibited varying degrees of forgiveness over hour-long phone calls, drawn-out dinners, and precious *girls-only* weekends. To be unguarded, exposed, and naked with our point of view (without too much ridicule) is always as refreshing as a plunge in the ocean on a hot summer's day.

Bella, what a slice of life we've shared together over the last two years! I am blessed to have had someone so fun to share it with. Thank you for your ever-present good nature, humor, and continual search for the perfect bath while juggling rewrites, interviews, and squeezing specifics from me!

Introduction

It's the Little Things...

Life is full of little emergencies.

No matter how cool, young, and hip you are, sooner or later they're going to get you, girl!

Some will knock the wind out of you and leave you sitting on your butt with your skirt over your head, wondering what happened to your perfect life. Others will just tick you off and leave you biting your lip, staring hard at your broken nail.

They may not seem like much in the big scheme of things, especially in a world that sometimes looks as though it's gone completely mad. But let's face it—if you are a gutsy girl on-the-go, these *little* emergencies can get in your way, trip you up, and have *big* consequences.

Think of how a day, a year, or a career can hinge on the smallest thing.

Did the too-tight blouse cost you the job interview? Were you denied that credit card because you didn't pay the phone bill? Is your boyfriend a sweet guy but a catastrophe in the kissing

department? These are all little emergencies that loom large in every young woman's life.

Don't sweat it, you're not alone! True, a girl's life can be filled with daily dilemmas that can grow into minor disasters. But help is at hand.

Life's Little Emergencies . . . Everyday Rescue for Beauty, Fashion, Relationships, and Life is the on-the-go girl's guide to solving pesky problems in a fun and female-friendly way.

You're not going to get lectured in these pages. No sermons, judgments, or criticisms allowed . . . just straight, from-the-lip, girl-talk advice.

Think of this book as a best girlfriend who's always there with tidbits of good information when you need her. That's why I sat down to write it with my buddy, Natasha. We both know from experience that no emergency is so big or so small that it can't be solved with a heart-to-heart between trusted girlfriends.

Like me, Natasha is a great believer in the power of gal-pal bonding and the sacredness of female wisdom.

I first met Natasha three years ago when we were both reaching into a huge bowl of M&Ms at a ritzy Park Avenue hotel. She was a big, strapping blonde, just like me—and a chocolate lover to boot. We hit it off instantly.

Over countless pasta dinners and I won't mention how many glasses of fine red wine, we spilled our guts—sharing our ups and downs, victories and tragedies, flirtations and failures. We bonded over our love of long, lingering baths, lofty career goals, and the fact that we had both lost our beautiful mothers at far too early an age.

Sometimes we came away from these dinners with our mascara running down our cheeks. Other times our ribs would ache from laughing so hard. But we always left feeling cared for, confident, and inspired.

We wondered how we could share this wonderful sense of sisterhood and camaraderie with other women—especially those setting out on paths similar to those we had stumbled along just a few years before.

Well—this book was the answer. We pooled our experiences and asked our friends—women from all walks of life and all very wise in their own wonderful ways—to share their stories and give advice. We even asked some of you young women surfing the Net to chip in your two cents' worth. And we threw in a few wise guys, too, for good measure and a dash of testosterone.

On these pages we offer a glimpse of how others, just like you, have not only gotten through life's little emergencies but have learned to embrace them and turn them into life's little triumphs.

So kick off your shoes, curl up on the couch, and get good and comfy.

It's time for some straight-from-the-heart girl talk.

life's little
emergencies

beauty emergency!

Wow. Now *that's* a mouthful. To hear the poets tell it, beauty is this unreachable, all-consuming, mind-boggling panacea to which we all aspire . . . but fall woefully short. Me? I ascribe to the simpler, grassroots, Forrest Gump school of philosophy: Beauty is as beauty does.

To me the word *beauty* covers a vast, colorful spectrum. It can be the smile my daughter gives me when I least expect it. It can be the bare nape of a woman's neck when her hair is twisted up and tiny tendrils fall softly. It can be a pair of men's strong hands in motion—veins popping. It can be a rose blooming. I see beauty everywhere I look and sometimes in the oddest places.

My mom taught me that beauty is simplicity. There was nothing overdone or forced when she "made" herself beautiful every morning before work or at night before a party. She put on a dab of color here, a spritz of scent there, and a lot of charm. She showed me that each person is attractive in her or his own way and praised people's unique physical qualities—a warm speaking

voice; a rosy complexion; a great smile. It wasn't about looking like someone else, I learned, it was about appreciating what you have and who you are.

Even in the modeling world, where "beauty" can be a changeable, unattainable ideal, the models I know understand the ultimate, constant beauty secret that never goes out of style: confidence. And then, for polish, they trade about a zillion makeup, hair, and skin tips for the *outside* of the package. Because there's nothing wrong with a little plucking and pruning. If putting on a bit of mascara or curling your hair or giving yourself a facial makes you feel good about yourself, why not? If you *feel* beautiful, you *are* beautiful.

And why not be proud of it? In the past, when people told me I looked great, I'd feel a little uncomfortable and I'd say, "Oh thanks, I just lost some weight," or "Yeah, I just bought this

WISE WOMAN

Cheryl Tiegs, supermodel

Beauty Is Growth

To say that beauty comes from within us is a cliché, but it's true. If you keep yourself happy it shows on your face. When I started out in New York as a young model, my agent said to me, "The key to beauty is to always learn and grow and educate yourself and have new experiences." I never forgot that. When you are learning something new or experiencing adventures for the first time it brings excitement to your eyes, to your face, to your whole being. Once when I was going through a troubled time, a therapist told me, "Cheryl, take up a new hobby . . . take up needlepoint . . . plant a rose garden . . . do something you've never done before." You start off wobbly at first but soon you get good at it and it makes you feel so great. Keep exploring. It brings a contentedness to you and helps with self-esteem. And that's what makes you "beautiful."

dress." I'd make excuses or apologies and my appraiser would look deflated like I just shoved a gift back into her face. I don't do that anymore. Now I say, "Thank you!"—and I mean it!

About Face!

Natasha's cool friend, Rachel, who wears only red and black, is obsessed with finding the perfect red lipstick. She has at least twenty tubes in shades of scarlet, crimson, ruby, burgundy, and cherry in her purse at any one time.

My beauty obsession is of a more architectural nature.

Yes, okay, anybody who knows me already knows this: I have an eyebrow fetish. I admit it. It's almost as bad as my shoe fetish. Tweezerman tweezers are God!

And it just so happens that Natasha has those bushy, Slavic eyebrows that are tough to tame so we're kind of eyebrow codependent on each other. She hates to pluck. I *live* to pluck! At my annual summer barbecue last year, I noticed she was overdue for a little pruning. I beckoned her over to the grassy knoll in the backyard, took out my instrument of torture (I never leave home without it, even if I'm only going to the backyard), and pointed to the grass.

"Here?" she asked.

"Here," I answered sternly. My tweezer finger was itchy.

Hiking up my blue-jean skirt, I crouched over Natasha as she lay on her back on the grass and I plucked, plucked, plucked. It was cause for small alarm among my party guests who thought Natasha was having some sort of attack, she was yelping a bit (I would have put on some baby-teething stuff first to numb the area but hadn't had Toby yet to know what a lifesaver Oragel is to numb pain), or that I was giving her mouth-to-mouth resuscitation.

"Okay, okay, show's over, folks," Natasha said finally, as she got up and smoothed her fingers over her newly smooth and tamed brows.

Well, it was an emergency as I saw it. Natasha's brows were criminally out of control; and it was my job to subdue them!

I can't help myself. After you've sat in the chair of some of the world's most famous makeup artists, you learn a thing or two about the tweezing, contouring, and tinting of the female face and you want to try what you've learned on your girlfriends.

For example, my friend, makeup artist Maria Verel, who has worked on such beautiful faces as Diana Drall, Diane Sawyer, and Nora Ephron, taught me these all-important tweezing "never" tips that have made me mistress of the tweezers in my peer group:

> Never tweeze when you're angry or bored.
> Never take too much at one time; go for a few hairs at a time and step away from the mirror.
> Never oversnip with scissors or hairs will look stubby and harsh.
> Never forget symmetry.
> Never tweeze from the top.
> Never shave your eyebrows.
> The thin arch is *over* so don't go there.

But I didn't learn everything at once. My education in primping was a slow process. Don't forget, I'm a tomboy at heart.

For the longest time, I was guilty of making the number-one mistake a makeup novice is guilty of: TOO MUCH. I used to pile it on, layer after layer, before a modeling shoot. As an athlete who was forever in the water or at the gym, I was so used to being barefaced that when I finally got my fingers into those colored pots and lipsticks and powders, I went a little girl crazy. At my early modeling shoots, I'd arrive with my face already painted to the max.

"There's just too much of it," the makeup artists would *tsk, tsk, tsk*, over and over again, as they wiped and sponged and powdered it off.

"Where?" I'd ask.

"Um, all over the place."

Time after time, makeup artists would tell me: "If you're wear-ing a strong lip color, go light on the eye makeup and vice versa. Make one part of the face the focal point."

My friend Maria would drill that one home to me: "When you wear bright red lipstick, it stands out like a fine piece of jewelry. Your lips will shine more brilliantly if they don't have to compete for attention with other intensely made-up features."

So heed these words of wisdom: LESS IS MORE.

Here are some of her emergency tips:

MARIA SAYS . . .

☑ **To make eyes wider:** Always curl your lashes before putting on mascara; it makes your eyes appear bigger and brighter, which automatically narrows your face.

☑ **To open your eyes:** Curl the lashes, color in between the lash roots with a soft eyeliner pencil, then apply a lot of mascara. Only do this to the top lashes because doing the bottom too will be overkill.

☑ **To cover zits:** Use allergy eye drops that you can buy from a drugstore to take the redness out of a blemish. Dab a few drops on the spot, or hold a piece of cotton saturat-ed with the drops on the pimple for two minutes, then allow the area to dry. Top with a thin layer of concealer and set with translucent powder.

☑ **To keep lipstick off your teeth:** Line and fill lips with a lip pencil that matches your lipstick. Next, apply lipstick over the liner but avoid the inner edges of your lips—that's the trouble zone. Then blot lips with a tissue and apply a color sealer to set your lipstick until you wash it off. Try

BeneFit She Laq ($24) or Lip Last by English Ideas Cosmetics ($18). If your lips are chapped, however, you might find a sealer drying, so use a lip stain that blots on like ink and top it with a gloss for extra shine. Try Stila Lip Rouge ($26) with Prestige Aromatherapy Lipgloss in clear ($2.95).

☑ **To save money on products:** Buy from the drugstore! I've been using drugstore makeup forever. They perform equally as well as department-store brands. In fact, many are made in the same factories. Read labels for ingredients, noting those first in the list are the highest concentrations. Sometimes all that differs is the fragrance added (or not added), and/or the packaging.

Open the door again to the Avon Lady! Seriously, their products are great and so are their prices. Take a closer look. Their performance is on par with the leading brands. So when Avon comes calling, answer the door!

Some of Maria's Favorite Drugstore Items:

☑ Wet 'n' Wild #666 lip pencil
☑ L'Oreal Colour Riche lipstick in Tawny and Cornsilk Classic Translucent Powder
☑ Maybelline Illegal Lengths Mascara

▶ **TAKE NOTE:** *Out in the sun a lot? I concocted a great makeup/sunscreen potion that makes you look great and protects you from the rays. My friend, makeup artist* **Fran Cooper,** *was testing a variety of makeup bases under the spray of a shower to see if they could stand enormous amounts of sweat without sliding off the face (she was preparing to do makeup for Janet Jackson for her* Live in Hawaii *TV special). She told me that just wearing makeup base alone did a good job of blocking* *out harmful burning rays. That got me thinking . . . what if I were to mix a high SPF nongreasy sunscreen like my favorite Coppertone Sport 30 with a Colorstay base by my old buddies at Revlon? (Once this stuff goes on, it stays on.) I beach tested this idea in St. Maarten and WOW, what a find. Five days in the sun and not a freckle or burn in sight. And the makeup didn't smear all over my clothes. Just one word of warning: If your skin is sensitive and you're not used to wearing makeup, you might be prone to breaking out. Make sure you clean your face thoroughly before bed!*

Learn What's Best for You

After lots of trial and error, you'll know your face like the back of your hand, so to speak. You'll know what works for you and what doesn't.

I learned that birch-brown eye shadow makes my eyes bluer. I learned to use shimmer below my brow bone and above my cheeks to add a nice contrast in pictures. Taupe eye shadow became my friend for instant cheekbones. I learned not to use heavy powder—especially under the eyes—because it gets crepe-like on me and it screams, LOOK, I'M WEARING MAKEUP!

I learned to fix my ruddy complexion with a yellow-tinted base and concealer. I learned to define my eyes with a kohl pencil in dark blue or black underneath the inside of my upper lid (*not* on the bottom, like we did in the 1970s). I learned to blend, blend, *blend*.

But most of all, I learned that I know my face better than anyone else and not to let anyone mess with it.

Think of Brooke Shields and her famous thick eyebrows (*again with the eyebrows!*). For years makeup artists wanted to pluck them, but she resisted. She knew they fit her face and were a signature look for her.

On one TV appearance when I worked with a new makeup artist, I asked her to pump up my eyes with a few false eyelashes and she said, "Oh, I just ran out of my regular eyelash glue . . . but I have this other stuff they use for mustaches."

I was hesitant. I knew my eyes could be sensitive and told her so.

"Oh, don't worry," she said, "it'll be *fine*."

As she liberally applied the stuff, my eyes started to water from the fumes.

I went out to do my appearance with the eyes of America on me, and my eyelids started to tighten and close up. My eyes turned bloodshot. Everything became like putty. Seems this mustache glue was crystallizing on my lids and jagged bits of it were falling into my eyes.

It took me a week to get those lashes off my eyes. After that I never again let anyone put a product on me that I hadn't already tried myself.

I Stick to What I Know and My Daily Routine Goes Like This:

- ☑ Clean face with Aveda gel cleanser.
- ☑ Moisturize with Kiehl's Ultra facial moisturizer SPF 15. (spring and summertime)
- ☑ Moisturize with Sundāri Neem and Tamanu Corrective Moisturizer for dry skin (fall and wintertime)
- ☑ Blend light base in Bobbi Brown Protective Face Lotion SPF 15 moisturizer in sand.
- ☑ A bit of color on my brows, Laura Mercier in topaz.
- ☑ A little contour under my cheekbones, taupe by Bobbi Brown.
- ☑ Dab the apples of my cheeks with MAC HUSH frost or STYLE frost.
- ☑ Curl my lashes with my Shu Uemura curler.

☑ Draw on the upper inside lid with my Laura Mercier black liner pencil.

☑ Maybelline Great Lash Mascara in black.

☑ Lip gloss, Bobbi Brown in petal.

Ten minutes, *total*.
(applause, applause)

And here's my favorite trick for keeping lipstick off the teeth throughout the day: Before you leave the house in the morning or after you reapply at lunch or dinner, put your index finger in your mouth and pull it out. Once you close your lips around your finger and pull it out, all the lipstick from the inside of your lips comes off and you have no more lipstick worries. Works every time and a tip you should tell all your girlfriends. (Caution: Do not do this in public in mixed company. It could be taken in the wrong way. . . .)

The Mane Event: After-Work Hair That Won't Let You Down

What to do when you plan a special night on the town with your girlfriends and your hair loses its oomph right at 5 P.M.? I knew if I asked Kevin Mancuso, celebrity stylist, hair expert, and author of *The Mane Thing*, he would know how to help.

"Any day-into-evening hairstyle is best achieved with a strong start! Take the time to build a strong foundation with your morning blow-dry, natural air-dry, or set. This will help give your hairstyle the strength to make it through the day and then some. So plan ahead as to what your evening look will be. Up or down, your hair will work the best if the texture is set from the start. There are no rules; evening hair can be controlled or loose. It depends on how you feel, what you're wearing, or where you're going."

FINE HAIR: For lasting volume, use a volume spray concentrating mainly on the roots. Blow-dry with a smaller than usual round brush. (Choose your brush according to the length of your hair. In this case, your hair should be able to wrap around the brush at least two times.) Using a blow-dryer, smooth hair onto the brush when hair is almost dry. Roll it down the scalp, heat it up thoroughly, and then switch to cool. Cool it down entirely and release. You can roll the section back up without the brush and use a clip to hold it in place. This will give it more strength and holding power. When you're finished, brush it and go! If you lose volume through the day, take all of your hair into your hands in an upward direction and twist loosely up and into a high soft bun. Don't twist too hard or tight. Pin high up on your head (so it looks pretty). Continue your day and in the evening, let it down. It will have more movement and volume and whether you wear it up or down, it will be voluminous and pliable enough to style.

CURLY HAIR: Curls that last all day! For naturally curly hair, it's best to air dry gently. Don't touch it too much while it's drying. Start to air dry with an application of leave-in conditioner or styling products. There are many types of curly hair and many products to choose from. Read the labels of the products and experiment with different ones until you come across the combination that works for you. I have found that using a straightening gel that is designed to blow out curl can actually be useful to leave in curly hair. Let it dry naturally or twist loosely into a bun. Let it dry, and when you take it down it will be a looser, softer curl.

For straight looks, again start with a good strong blow out in the morning. I like to use styling spray with a little straightening gel on the ends. The styling spray has hold so your blow-dry will last longer and the straightening gel will make hair easier to glide through with your brush. In the evening, you can quickly go over the hair with a flat iron for a super-straight, glossy-finished look. Again, up or down, you will be working with the best-prepared texture.

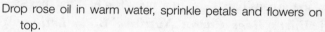

WISE WOMAN

Dawn Gallagher, purist, author of *Naturally Beautiful*

Natural is a somewhat ambiguous term in the cosmetics industry. When a label says "natural" this may not necessarily mean what the average consumer supposes. It has been calculated that over a lifetime the average woman's complexion will absorb over three pounds of chemicals from cosmetic products. For example, many soaps and shampoos contain sodium lauryl sulfate. This compound can be obtained from a natural source, like coconut. After a decade of obscurity, the art of making natural beauty treatments at home is becoming popular again.

DAWN'S ROSE PETAL BATH

1–3 fresh rose petals
1 tablespoon dried lavender flowers
1–2 drops rose oil
Drop rose oil in warm water, sprinkle petals and flowers on
    top.

For a groomed, simple look (sort of Ralph Lauren), side part your hair and pull it into a low ponytail. Put a band around the hair then wrap the ponytail with a strand of your own hair around the base where you just put the band. Pin it in, leaving a few random strands loose. Great with a simple black dress.

For more great ideas check out *www.themanething.com.*

Scrub-A-Dub-Dub . . . What's in Emme's Tub?

I'm addicted to beauty products. My outdoor, wooden shower at the summer house I rent on the Jersey Shore has two giant racks of scrubbing, smoothing, bubbly stuff that smells good enough to eat.

Emme

Have products, will travel. If you came to my home in New Jersey and peeked behind my shower curtain, here's what you'd find:

- ☑ *Tara Ayurveda Aromatherapy Candles in Vata and Pitta:* These candles are amazing because a lot of care has gone into the ingredients (all natural). They smell so darn good and make your room or home smell like a place of calm.
- ☑ *Aveda Gel Cleanser in a pump:* I do not go anywhere without it—it's been my trusty facial cleanser for years. The toughest grime (layers and layers of makeup) comes off quickly with out drying my skin.
- ☑ *Body Shop Nut Butter:* Softens my rough spots quickly and minimizes stretch marks.
- ☑ *Kiehl's Creme de Corps:* Learned from my days as a model, this always makes my skin look dewy right after shaving. Keeps hands soft in winter. The best for shaved legs!
- ☑ *Burt's Bees Carrot Nutritive Body Lotion:* When I have sunburn, this makes it feel better.
- ☑ *Clairol Herbal Essences Shampoo:* I am a sucker for a good ad: Orgasms from a hair product? I'll try it!
- ☑ *Charles Worthington Dream Hair Definite Difference Instant Repair Treatment:* The best conditioner after I get my hair highlighted. It gives back the moisture lost in the dyeing process.
- ☑ *Kiehl's Hair Conditioner and Grooming Aid Formula 133:* I just love this easy leave-in that doesn't make my hair limp after it dries. A little goes a long way for fine hair.
- ☑ *Origins Salt Butter Body Scrub:* Goodbye dead skin cells.
- ☑ *Aubrey Organics Herbal Liquid Body Soap:* A little goes a long way and it washes off the toughest makeup job in a jiffy.

☑ ***Lush Back for Breakfast Shower Gel:*** It pops you out of bed. I buy three at a time.

☑ ***Lush Bath Bombs:*** For extraordinary, long soaks. I get these for those who travel with me for various book signings, fashion shows, or other personal appearances. Everyone needs a little break after a long day away from home or on the selling floor!

☑ ***Essentiel Elements Wake Up Rosemary Bath Salts:*** Another good product to keep you awake or get you out of bed.

☑ ***Crabtree & Evelyn Sweet Almond Massage Oil:*** This is a good example of a simple yet gratifying reward. After my nighttime bath, I massage my legs, arms, torso, and feet with this oil. It's a truly lavish treat for myself.

☑ ***Fresh Lavender Oil from Tuscany and the South of France:*** If you have any friends traveling to either of these places, put in your order. I wear it as a perfume and use it as a sleeping aid.

☑ ***Dr. Hauschka Blackthorn Body Oil:*** This is a real treat for a body that needs some serious TLC. I have used the lavender oil as well and either one will do the trick after a long, hard day. Massage on skin after bath or use as a bath oil.

So Ya Wanna Be in Pictures?

The question I'm asked most often by women I meet in the street, in the grocery store, at the gym, in airports, on college campuses (I think you get my drift) is: "How can I become a model?"

My advice:

1. Go to your favorite local department stores and specialty shops and ask if you can do some informal modeling

WISE GUY

Gad Cohen, hair stylist for *Glamour, Vogue, GQ, Marie Claire,* and *ELLE.*

If hair is your crowning glory but your tiara's looking a tad tarnished, here's a crash course on keeping it shiny and healthy:

The Three Rules of Hair
1. Have a great cut four times a year.
2. Let your color enhance, not detract from, your face.
3. Keep your hair in good condition.

Color Coordinate
Be careful when doing home hair color. Remember: It's permanent! Don't go too far out of range from your natural hue. Never do highlights at home—they should always be done professionally. Single process will give you better chances out of a box.

What's Your Condition?
Curly, wavy, or coarse hair needs more conditioning than other types. For fine hair, condition only the ends. Flat hair? Use a product like Progaine, from the makers of Rogaine. It pumps up your hair and lifts your roots. For curly hair, instead of shampooing frequently like the other hair types, shampoo less often but wet hair daily as more of a rinse and then add a leave-in conditioner to get "wake-up hair" under control.

for them. This is a great way to find out if modeling is something you really want to pursue and if you like it.

2. Check your phone book for the top three modeling agencies listings if you must. Personal referrals really are the way to go because there are many movers and shakers waiting to take your hard-earned money.

3. I can't stress this enough: Don't fall for modeling agency scams. Top agencies will ask you to show them personal

photos of yourself, but they will never ask you to do a shoot and pay thousands of dollars. Show up with clean hair and a close-to-bare face. Show only snapshots that you already have. Believe me, if they are interested, they will guide you to a professional photographer who will not charge more than $150–$300 to get your portfolio started.

4. Most agencies look for women who are five-eight to six feet, fit, and well proportioned. For "straight" modeling, you must be sizes 4 to 8. Plus-size models range from sizes 14 to 16 for print work and sizes 14 to 22 for runway work.

5. Keep in mind that the road to modeling is very difficult. Knowing that, thousands of young women write, call, and show up at agencies around the country to try their luck at being picked. Only two or three out of thousands have the goods. That is a fact.

6. If you get rejected, do not take it personally. There are many things you are meant to do in this life. Think about what they are and move on!

Skin Deep (Pantry Lifesavers)

Even models have beauty emergencies. *Especially* models.

On the morning of a big Clairol shoot, I woke up and felt a little bump on my lip. Uh-oh. Of all days. (Like there's ever a *good* day for a cold sore?)

I tried to calm myself: Hey, babe, it's only a bump. It's not a huge, festering boil hanging off the side of your face. You'll live. Now, cover the darn thing up!

I stole my husband Phil's styptic stick, which he uses when he cuts himself shaving, and dabbed some on. Then I put on a layer of calendula ointment. The third and fourth layers were concealer, which I took with me as I ran out the door and crossed my fingers.

At the shoot, my makeup artist could not be fooled. She took one look at my lip and took pity on me.

"Gonna have to cover *that* up," she mumbled, and got busy painting. She was grateful I had brought my own lip brush and lipsticks. She worked her magic with powder concealer and dark lipstick. Picture perfect. The camera never picked up on my little secret.

Ahh, *saved*—once again—from beauty disaster.

(P.S.: That night I took some vitamin C, garlic, lots of water, a zinc tablet, and slept eight hours. By morning, the darn thing was gone.)

T he vitamin C and garlic that zapped my little beauty emergency into nothingness were just two of the many age-old, natural beauty secrets lurking in your kitchen. Our grandmas knew best when they mixed up their own pretty potions of herbs and whatever else they could pull from the ground. I hear Cleopatra used to bathe in milk and wax her legs using a sticky, cooked, sugar-water-lemon mixture.

I remember my mom making her own beauty remedies from whatever she found in the fridge. One time, before a date, I saw her crack a few eggs into a bowl and take the bowl into the bathroom. What was she gonna do with them? I wondered.

I went to investigate, and saw her leaning in close to the bathroom mirror.

"It takes years off," she explained, as she dabbed the raw egg whites on the corners of her eyes with her fingertips, smoothing out the skin there, *"for about three hours."*

I soon found out the fridge held a lot of other miracle, magical elixirs in the name of beauty. Avocados (for a moisturizing mask), oils (ditto), oatmeal (to exfoliate dry, sensitive skin), and strawberries (brightens skin); they weren't just for eating anymore.

When I'm out of cold cream or want relief from a sunburn, I

rummage through the refrigerator for plain yogurt, slather it on, and rinse it off. And on mornings when I wake up—but my face *doesn't*—I fill a giant pasta bowl with cold water, ice, and lemon juice and plunge my face in it. Homemade beauty remedies have been around since the first cavewoman accidentally covered her face with wet mud (whoa! a facial!) and saw her zits disappear.

Mother Nature was here long before Aveda. And she's a heck of a lot cheaper.

EMERGENCY 1: *Pimples*

You've got a date and you've also got a gigantic zit. Dab on some toothpaste, tea-tree oil, or unfiltered honey to dry the sucker up.

EMERGENCY 2: *Hair Like Straw*

If your hair feels like you washed it with Ajax, get out the mayonnaise or olive oil. Slather it on, stick on a shower cap for thirty minutes, shampoo off. Jerry Hall, the former Mrs. Mick Jagger, swears by this treatment.

EMERGENCY 3: *Puffy Eyes*

Sometimes, it hurts to be beautiful. So when I tell you the best way to get rid of puffiness under the eyes is with that old hemorrhoid staple, Preparation H, just trust me and don't get any in your eyes. A lot of models swear by this. The kinder, gentler route is to put tea bags soaked in icy water on your closed eyelids or slices of cucumber soaked in cold milk. Also, Mom's trick: beaten egg whites on the surrounding skin (thanks, Mom).

EMERGENCY 4: *Depressed Hair*

Give it a beer! Douse your hair in Aussie brew and rinse off. It will give you fluffiness. And no one would be the wiser if you take a little sip during the rinse cycle. Also, mayonnaise as a conditioner. Slather it on your hair before you shampoo and let it sink in for ten minutes. Wash out.

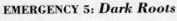

EMERGENCY 5: *Dark Roots*

Boost your blond with some vodka and lemon juice. Pour it on, sit out in the sun, then wash off. Your colorist will give you hell, but, hey, it works when you don't have the dough for touch-ups. Do a little mayo conditioning after this to combat the drying effects of the lemon.

EMERGENCY 6: *Skin Like Leather*

Natasha's grandmother swears by Crisco as a body moisturizer. Natasha herself keeps a bottle of imported Tuscan olive oil under the bathroom sink and pours it on her body straight from the bottle. (Warning: Don't spill on bathroom floor. Natasha is forever sliding across her tiles.) You can scent it with sprigs of fresh herbs like rosemary.

EMERGENCY 7: *The Shining*

This is why ladies walk around with those powdered compacts—that darn oily T-zone. Soak a cotton ball with witch hazel

---

WISE WOMAN

Naomi Wolf, author of *The Beauty Myth: How Images of Beauty Are Used Against Women*

What's Happening Beyond the Beauty Myth?

Ten years later, what has changed? Where is the beauty myth today? It has mutated a bit: it bears looking at with fresh eyes. Today you would be hard-pressed to find a twelve-year-old girl who is not familiar with the idea that "ideals" are too tough on girls, that they are unnatural, and that following them too slavishly is neither healthy nor even cool. Junior high schools bring in eating disorder lecturers and post collages of destructive beauty ideals in the hallways. I would say that when what started as an outsider's slightly threatening argument becomes the conventional wisdom of a Girl Scout troop, it is a sign that the times were right, and that girls and women were ready to say no to something they found oppressive. This is progress.

and wipe off the grease. For major oil leaks, dab on a half a lemon, directly and lightly.

Q & A with Bobbi Brown, friend, celebrity makeup artist, beauty industry icon, and author of many Bobbi Brown beauty books

Q: *You work with so many beautiful women. What makes a woman beautiful to you?*

Bobbi: A woman who is comfortable in her own skin, a woman who is herself.

Q: *What's the most common makeup mistake young women make?*

Bobbi: Most young women don't wear concealer—or if they do, they wear the wrong shade. A good concealer is the secret of the universe and can magically make undereye circles disappear. Look for a creamy formula that's yellow based and is one shade lighter than your foundation. Steer clear of concealer that's too light, or has a pink or white tone to it. You'll just end up looking like you have a smear of something under your eyes. And never use concealer to cover blemishes. Concealer is designed to be one or two shades lighter than your skin tone, so this will only draw attention to your blemish.

Q: *Uh-oh. I always use concealer on zits. So what do I do instead?*

Bobbi: To cover a blemish, opt for a foundation stick or blemish cover stick that matches your skin tone exactly. You can use the pads of your fingers to apply it directly on the spot and blend in by gently patting. Finish off by setting it with powder.

Q: *How can we go from office to cocktail party in the bathroom mirror in one minute?*

Bobbi: For the most modern look, add snow Shimmer Wash Eyeshadow with a charcoal liner, apply more blush, and spritz on some perfume.

Q: *I've put on way too much blush. I look like an overripe apple. What should I do?*
Bobbi: Take a velour puff and blend it in.

Q: *At the office, I want to look polished—but not too "done."*
Bobbi: All you need is concealer, foundation, blush, eyeliner, mascara, and lipstick.

Q: *What's the one tool you never go to a job without? Or two.*
Bobbi: Concealer and blush.

Q: *I was up all night writing. I'm exhausted. Can I fake a good night's sleep?*
Bobbi: Use concealer with a concealer brush, eyeliner, pink blush, yellow powder, and a blemish cover stick.

Q: *And my favorite question: If you were stranded on a deserted island, what one beauty item would you take for yourself?*
Bobbi: SPF 25 face cream!

Q: *Thanks, Bobbi! We think you're beautiful!*

FINAL THOUGHT

Like the proverb says, beauty is in the eye of the beholder. You can paint and primp and wear the latest fashions, but what's most important is that you feel beautiful on the inside. At the same time, it feels gratifying when we try to be the best we can be and look the best we can look. Not for others but for ourselves. We don't have to measure up to any ideal. We just have to be ourselves—beautiful, naturally.

body
emergency!

If you ever need proof that God is a woman, just take a look at Her greatest accomplishment—the female form.

Tall or short, strong and muscular, round and curvy, to me there is nothing in this world more wonderful to behold than a woman who is confident, gutsy, and healthy. And what other creature on this planet can do so much, so well? Run a corporation *and* a marathon; balance a family budget *and* a baby on her hip; win an Oscar, visit space, perform open-heart surgery, and give birth to the entire human race, not to mention every leader in it.

Women ROCK this planet! So I ask you, when we have soooo much going for us, why do so many of us get so down on how we look?

It's a perplexing question, but it's one we have to tackle—for ourselves and our sisters and our daughters-to-be.

Body Happy

Believe me, one thing I know about is the damage a negative body image can do to a young, impressionable girl. It happened to me and it happens to millions of other young women every day. I spent the early part of my adolescence trying to diet away my healthy, strong body to fit society's version of what is beautiful.

The self-loathing women feel starts ever so subtly when they are young. It creeps up and sinks in until it becomes an inner, automatic response.

Think about it—do you remember when you were a teen and you picked up your first fashion magazine? Didn't all those cover girls look so very glamorous and successful and happy and flawless and supersexy? Didn't you want to look just like them? Only . . . you *didn't* look just like them.

Ahh—that's where the problem begins.

It's a documented fact that 98 percent of all American women are naturally larger framed or curvier than traditional, reed-thin fashion models. So when all of us who were normal, healthy girls began comparing ourselves to the atypical images we were shown in fashion magazines, two things happened: (1) we made ourselves emotionally sick with envy, and (2) we made ourselves physically sick from starving.

I had to ask Dr. David Herzog of the Harvard Eating Disorder Center if he could shed some light on this obsession. "Culturally, the issues have to do with extremes," he said. "We seem to have extraordinary difficulty operating in moderation. We are either stuffing ourselves with fast food and sitting in front of the television for countless hours, or exercising like crazy. We are also remarkably vulnerable to exaggerating negative thoughts about ourselves, so that if we have a negative self-image, we distort it to the extreme, and if we put on five pounds, we become very upset. Emotions and activities are all in extremes, and there isn't the perspective of being able to laugh at oneself in the process."

I receive hundreds of e-mails per day on my website (www.emmesupermodel.com) from impassioned young women who torture their beautiful bodies because they see unrealistic or unhealthy female body types portrayed in magazines, TV, and films. Some of them are also getting pressure from parents, siblings, and boyfriends to conform to society's standard of beauty. For a small percentage of women, being skinny and willowy is genetic. This is their natural body type. But most of us, at our healthiest and most vibrant, don't fit this mold. There are three basic body shapes and a variety of skeletal structures to consider, so why should only *one* body type be celebrated when there are so many of us? Vive la difference!

There are many other flowers in the bouquet. I'm here to tell you it is time to take back our bodies and take a stand for who and what we are—Women: beautiful, strong, and proud!

Even the traditional models and fashion designers are stepping back and reevaluating the images they are putting out there and what a "healthy" and "beautiful" body means. Model Kate Moss, once known for her birdlike frame, reentered the modeling world in early 2001 with a few pounds on her. And we now have a burgeoning full-figured modeling industry that is infiltrating the mass media with glamorous and self-accepting photos of women of all sizes.

The first way to start boosting your body self-image is to think of your body as your friend, not your enemy. Think about it: your body is the vehicle that takes you dancing all night and gets to be hugged first thing in the morning and takes you for long walks along a tranquil stretch of beach. You and your body make one heck of a great team. You are life partners.

I honestly believe our bodies really *are* our temples. We come

Cindi Leive, Editor in Chief, *Glamour*

Changes Are Here

Today, more than ever, women are demanding more realistic images in the media. They are sick of being force-fed size zero models. Even women who aren't plus size feel this way. There is a true hunger for reality. In the past, we'd run stories about body image, anorexia, or loving your body—and then we'd get letters from women saying, "That's all very well and good, but then I turn the page and see pictures of skinny-minnies!" We thought, "You know what? They're right!" and we realized we can have a greater impact by showing bodies that look like real women instead of just preaching about body love and acceptance. There is an enormous range of body types and it's important to see them.

Ten years ago, we thought about these issues. But when the then-editor showed pictures to a focus group of gorgeous, plus-size women, the readers rejected the images. They thought the women looked too much like themselves . . . and they weren't ready for that—"that's not why we buy *Glamour*," they said.

Boy, have things changed. We used several full-figured models in our May/02 issue without calling attention to their size. If we are doing

in such gloriously different shapes and sizes and every single one of us deserves to be worshiped.

But I can promise you no one is going to be kneeling at your altar if you're not already rejoicing in your own unique beauty. And that doesn't mean squeezing into a size-six party dress, girl-friend! It means being strong and healthy no matter what shape or frame you were born with. The only way to achieve this is by treating your body with respect—treat it right! Eat healthy, move your derriere, and tell yourself everyday that you are creative, intelligent, thoughtful, and beautiful inside and out.

WISE WOMAN

a story on shampoo, why can't we use a size 14 model? If we're doing a story on relationships and love and we need a picture of a couple in love, why not make her a size 12? We did a fitness story, and we showed three women working out . . . and one of them was a healthy size 16. In that issue, we have a beautiful picture of a full-figured model, Mia Tyler, in her bikini with a little bit of roll around her tummy. And you know what? She looks incredibly sexy and confident and voluptuous!

Showing these images is more powerful than just telling women to love their bodies. We had an unbelievable response from readers. Ten days after the issue hit the newsstands, we received over one thousand letters. One said, "There is a God, and she works at *Glamour!*" Other women wrote that they cried when reading the issue. One wrote: "You made me want to cry tears of joy . . . you freed me!" And not all the responses were from full-figured women. Others wrote that they really appreciated seeing all body types represented on our pages.

This is so different from ten years ago. Things are changing. This is the moment. Something very important is happening. Women are becoming more confident; they are saying, "Look, I'm a beautiful woman and I'm proud of my body."

We at the magazine pledge to reinforce, on an ongoing basis, that women of all sizes are beautiful.

10 Ways to Love Your Body
(From the National Eating Disorders Association—
www.nationaleatingdisorders.org)

Think of your body as the vehicle to your dreams. Honor it. Respect it. Fuel it.

1. Become aware of what your body can do each day. Remember, it is the instrument of your life, not just an ornament.

2. Create a list of people you admire—people who have

contributed to your life, your community, or the world. Consider whether their appearance was important to their success and accomplishments.

3. Don't let your weight or shape keep you from activities you enjoy.

4. Wear comfortable clothes that you like and feel good to your body.

5. Count your blessings, not your blemishes.

6. Every evening when you go to bed, tell your body how much you appreciate what it has allowed you to do throughout the day.

7. Find a method of exercise that you enjoy and do it regularly. Don't exercise to lose weight or to fight your body shape. Do it to make your body healthy and strong and because it makes you feel good.

8. Think back to a time in your life when you felt good about your body. Tell yourself you can feel like that again, even in this body at this age.

9. Start saying to yourself, "Life is too short to waste my time hating my body this way."

10. Eat when you are hungry. Rest when you are tired. Surround yourself with people who remind you of your inner strength and beauty.

Get Moving!

Now that you've decided to love your body, let's take care of it. That means feed it right and give it exercise and fresh air and water. Like a plant . . . or a pet!

Think of yourself as your own pet: If you had a dog, would you keep it cooped up inside for months at a time and never take it for a walk? If you did, the Humane Society would be banging at your door and putting you in jail for cruelty to animals. So many of us should be charged with cruelty to humans (ourselves)! So often, we don't treat our bodies with the same respect we'd give a dog.

To feel alive, to feel good, you need to *move*.

And I don't mean you should exercise to burn calories or lose a dress size or look a certain way. Let the fact that it feels good inspire you. Let the fact that it cuts down your stress and helps you feel confident and self-assured inspire you.

The physical changes that come with exercise (losing weight, building muscle) are just by-products. If you focus *only* on the numbers on your scale or the definition in your abs, it's possible you are setting yourself an unrealistic goal and will give up after one month of kick-butt working out if your results don't keep pace with your high expectations.

Focus instead on the sensation. Exercise feels great!

B eing an athlete has been one of the most important constants in my life. It's fueled my self-confidence when other areas of my life were shaky. When I had nothing else to fall back on, I could rely on my powerful strides, jumps, and throws to lift me up and take me—and others—forward. By the time I was seven years old, I was a strong girl, a strong swimmer. That summer I remember using those strong arms and shoulders of mine to save a young boy from drowning in a lake where my family visited one weekend.

When I was approaching the end of high school, the prospect of college was uncertain. My mother had died, my college fund had dwindled, and my future looked bleak. But my athletic ability pulled me through—I attended Syracuse University after winning an athletic scholarship for rowing.

If I hadn't been a big, sturdy, disciplined rower, I would never have been able to pursue a thrilling career as a highly paid and extremely busy model in the budding industry of full-figure fash-

ion. Just because we weren't stick-thin didn't mean we could "let ourselves go." We had to be tight, firm, and shapely—a level of fitness I had attained thanks to all my grueling 5:00 A.M. rowing sessions.

Today, I am a busy mom who has to keep up with my baby daughter Toby's sunrise schedule. Believe me, this is the biggest physical challenge of them all compared to running a clothing line, writing a book, creating a doll business, writing a column, and God knows what else.

Toby demands a lot of energy and so does everything else. But I find the energy I need because I worked hard on being fit, both mentally and physically, for so many years.

My body took care of me and hung in there when I had my share of disordered eating and overexercising during my postcollege years. Now it's up to me to protect it, maintain it, and bless it from time to time. Yes, sometimes a busy week goes by and I don't get a workout. But I finally have learned not to beat myself up about it. I just get myself back on track without the guilt.

For those of you who think that working out seven days a week, twelve months a year is what you need to do for a healthy routine, think again. Your body needs time to repair between workouts. Balance it out and give yourself time off.

It's true, sports and exercise have come easily and naturally to me (wearing makeup and smiling for the camera, now, that was something I had to learn!). But just because you might not be born to pole-vault or perform a triple axel doesn't mean you can't have a healthy, strong, and beautiful body. All it takes is practice, patience, and, more than anything else—CONSISTENCY. It doesn't have to be a painful, grueling, drill-sergeant type of workout. Just move. Get up and start doing *something* now!

Once you commit to starting, start small. Don't beat yourself up if you miss a day here and there.

Walk to the store instead of driving, take the stairs instead of the elevator, shoot hoops with the kid next door instead of flicking on the tube. You don't have to climb a mountain your first time out . . . but you could try getting halfway up the foothill.

"If you've never worked out before or you are really out of shape, you have to start with the basics," says Nicole Weedon, A.C.E certified personal trainer. "Walking is the most basic and natural thing you can do. Find a good pair of cross-training shoes, bring plenty of water, and get yourself outdoors. Try to find a dirt path or soft surface to walk on. This minimizes the impact on your knees. And if you can't get outside, a treadmill will work great too.

"Start with a brisk walk for fifteen minutes, 3 to 5 times a week. If after fifteen minutes you feel like you can go further, add on another five minutes to your walk. Keep tacking on five minutes until you feel comfortable doing 45-minute brisk walks. Every week you should see progression. When you are doing hour-long walks with relative ease, you'll be ready to move to the next level.

"Keep it simple," says Nicole, "and stay positive. A lot of people give up when they start an exercise program because they aren't sure what to do and fear failure. If you give it a shot and stay consistent, you will see results and start feeling great. As Emme says, the key is to build a base."

Sometimes it's a challenge to put on those running shoes and get moving—especially if you're feeling rusty. At moments like that, I use the buddy system. Call a friend and meet at a designated corner for an energetic walk. Why not form an exercise group and try a variety of physical activities during the change of seasons. Tennis in the spring and summer, aqua aerobics or swimming in the summer (or even all year-round if you can find an indoor pool), cross-country skiing in the winter, and so on. If you meet in the afternoons, a rotating person in the group needs to be on duty to watch the others' children for an hour or so. If you choose to meet in the early morning, a rotating person once again should take turns performing the morning wake-up call. It's great to have that extra push when you need it and get your butt out the door. There is power and motivation in numbers! Or, if you can afford it, set up a few sessions with a trainer to get you started, then take what you've learned and do it yourself. You are not the only one who needs a little motivation once in a while.

Emme

WISEGUY

Chris Noth, actor, (*Sex and the City*) and
Antonio Sini, his faithful trainer

The Buddy System!

Antonio Sini, head trainer at Crunch in Manhattan, has kept *Sex and the City* actor Chris Noth in fine form for steamy on-camera scenes since 1998—and for good reason: "If he looks good, I get the credit; if he looks bad, I get the blame!"

Noth credits Antonio for keeping him motivated. "I find working out the most boring thing in the world," says the actor, "but Antonio makes sure I do it, he makes sure I do it right, and we have fun. If I do it alone, every second I'm thinking, 'I hate this! I'm bored with this, I won't do it!' "

They mix things up to keep it interesting: "We do different exercises like stair-climbing and outdoor strength training," says Antonio. "I'll set up obstacle courses for him where he's constantly moving from one obstacle to the next—like what you'd do in a playground. I keep him moving. And if he works hard enough, I give him a water break!"

The sweat pays off. "Exercise changes your whole outlook on life," says Noth. "I work out as much for what's going on in my head as I do for my body. Working out makes you clearer of mind and more positive in spirit."

Okay, you're doing great. Now that you're warmed up, you need a routine.

Here's my routine: forty-five minutes of weight resistance training twice a week for my overall body tone using low weights and a lot of repetitions. Then I'll either do a cardio workout on the treadmill, a spinning class, or box. Outside of the gym, walking is a part of my daily life. Whether I park at the far end of a parking lot or take Toby out for a stroll, I walk. No matter what. When I need an adjustment in my routine (or a major kick in the rear end), I schedule a couple of workouts with my trainer, Dave Paladino, at Northern Valley Sports Academy. As Dave says, "Life accomplishments can only be attained through great health." Well, if that isn't true enough! It's just juggling the various roles of mom, wife, and businesswoman that's difficult when I want to get my personal needs met. Whether you're a mom or not, here is a slice of advice from Dave that we all can use:

"Being strong and fit will make your day easier just like a good education will make your children's futures easier. Let's face it, moms, if you're not healthy, who will do all these GREAT things for your children and family? Without your health, the road to all great things becomes much more challenging. So I say this: carve some time out for yourself to get a fifteen-minute, half-hour, or, even better, an hour-long workout. Remember a healthy and strong mom pays great dividends to all those around her. There is ALWAYS time for your health."

I figured with my newest little addition in my life, I needed to make some lifestyle adjustments. First of all I had to ask Phil to feed Toby for me two mornings a week and give her her bath one night; this way I was able to carve out the time I needed to be physical. Then I had to get into an early-to-bed and early-to-rise schedule so I could have the energy to get out and go. When I don't get my exercise in or get enough sleep, I feel sluggish, and if I let more than a week go by without so much as a push-up, I start making excuses—and you know where that takes you: nowhere.

You need to find what works for you. Here's a suggested starting point to help you take your first step on the road to fitness (or to get you motivated again):

911 TIP Don't forget, before starting any exercise program, you should see your doctor and get a complete check-up.

Four Weeks to a Stronger You

EQUIPMENT
Sneakers
Visor
Sunscreen and SPF lip balm
Comfy workout clothes: shorts, leggings, onesies (all-in-one leotards) T-shirts, sweatshirts, superabsorbent socks
Waterproof watch with a heart monitor

THE WORKOUT
(Beginner-Beginner Level!)

Week 1
15-minute stretch and
15-minute walk each day.

Week 2
Add 5 minutes to stretch and walk
The slower you do these exercises, the better:
4 sets of 10 sit-ups, accordion crunches, extended leg lifts with hands under your butt to protect lower back, left crunches, and right crunches.

Week 3

Add another 5 minutes to stretch and walk. Speed up the
pace of your walk.

4 sets of 15 sit-ups, crunches, leg lifts, and left and right
crunches.

Week 4

Add another 5 minutes to your walk, making it a 30-minute
brisk walk.

4 sets of 20 crunches, sit-ups, leg lifts, and left and right
crunches.

> **TAKE NOTE:** *Substitute walking with biking,
> skating, gliding, shooting hoops, cross-country ski-
> ing, running, or playing tennis. Whatever rocks your
> boat and gets your heart rate up. If you've always want-
> ed to try yoga, get a beginner's yoga tape. My pick is the
> Yoga Journal's Beginner's Tape. I love it! Check out
> www.yogajournal.com or call 1 800-I-DO-YOGA, or
> 203-699-4494 outside the United States. You can get the
> Essential Beginner's Kit for $44.00. This includes: 1
> nonslip 68" mat, 1 reinforced cotton strap, 2 durable
> foam bricks, and 1 thirty-minute instructional video.*

If you are presently inactive and decide to take on my Four
Weeks to a Stronger You routine, you will definitely feel the difference. This is just building a base and it's not too strenuous. But
you will have created a new lifestyle for yourself. One that will
keep giving back from what you put into it. Now that's the best
investment around! Imagine your body is a house and you are its
architect, busily laying down the framework. You are building a
strong, sturdy base that will last a long time.

Emme

As you build, it's important not to fall into the trap of "routine rut." You need a routine, yes, but you also need to keep your body interested. Thirty minutes on the treadmill every day, day in and day out, can get boring.

Exercise is for life and if you are going to do something that long it had better be fun. Maybe you're like some of my friends who find exercising the perfect time to catch up on their reading—one pal never sets foot on her Stairmaster without a Walkman loaded with the latest bestselling book on tape. She's listened to more books in the past three years than I've read in a decade. Talk about a literary workout!

Personally, I like to concentrate on my breath and movements. At a gym I don't like to chitchat. I want to go in and hit it hard and listen to good ol' classic rock 'n' roll. When I'm out for a jog on a country road, nature is my music. I love to hear the birds sing, or a brook babble . . . and the soothing rhythm of my own breathing.

The point is—mix it up. Find different activities that not only get your motor going but turn your crank, too. Ladies, choose your weapons! Be it cross-country skiing, hiking, biking, rowing, walking, dancing, rollerblading, snowshoeing—whatever it takes, as long it gets your engine running.

Don't feel you have to stick with traditional sports—be bold in your workout, experiment!

I "found" yoga in my midthirties. Boy, am I happy that I ventured into the Yoga Zone in New York City because I really needed a lift from my exercise boredom. Walking into that beginner class literally changed my life. I feel soooo good during the poses (asanas) while the sweat is pouring out of my body. Now, if only I could do those darn headstands.

But it's the by-product, after the fact, that is so incredible. For the rest of the day, my rib cage seems to open wide and suddenly

I'm breathing deeply, freely, and easily. Not only do I feel I've had an incredible workout, but I bathe in a serene peace that stays with me for hours.

The bonus with yoga is that there is no pressure to compete with other people who can twist themselves into pretzel shapes. It's understood that in any class there will be students who are more experienced and less experienced than you are. Just have fun and get what you want from it. No pressure. Just show up as you are. I love that attitude!

> **TAKE NOTE:** *My yoga teacher,* **Mauri Pioppo**, *talks about Yoga. "Yoga gives me balance. I have the tendency toward too much range and energy and yoga gives form to my flow so I can channel that energy and be productive. For me, yoga expands time and gives me the gift of feeling awake and present. It helps to define my truth. As a teacher yoga provides me with the opportunity to connect with people in the most profound way. Helping my students practice is an intimate partnering and involves a great deal of trust for teacher and student. It requires me to remain humble and grateful for all the abundance in my life."*

Whether you pick something transcendental like yoga or go with something more rough 'n' tumble like road hockey—throw yourself into it with a passion. Like I said before, start slowly, work up gradually, and remember to congratulate yourself for every stretch and step, no matter how small.

With exercise, as with most things in life, the key to success is *consistency*. I can't say it often enough: CONSISTENCY. Find a time in your day that is best for you and stick to it—30 minutes a day will do the trick. Again, if you skip a day, fine, don't beat yourself up. Just try to get out and get going tomorrow.

USE YOUR VOICE:

Keeping healthy is the most important thing you can do for yourself, but did you know that 44 million Americans today are without health insurance, and the number is growing by 100,000 per month? (Source: www.freedom.house.gov.) Despite the many reasons for this (including cost), we all need to demand health insurance coverage whether we are waitresses or CEOs. Our government needs to take a better look at how to prevent this horrible situation from getting any worse—for instance, by offering better incentives to businesses to provide coverage—especially for children, the elderly, and the unemployed.

Write your state representatives: (www.house.gov/writerep/).

There's nothing that will make you sicker quicker than looking at an exorbitant doctor bill. So while you're exercising and eating right, make sure you have some kind of health insurance for general checkups as well as major emergencies.

Nourishing Body and Soul

Now that you're well on your way to the world of deep breathing, sweating, and groaning, I have to make one thing perfectly clear: *Without proper nutrition, you'll never be healthy or strong no matter how much you exercise.*

Proper nutrition does not mean liquid diets or pills that make you jittery or injections of cow urine (I had a friend who did something like that. The thought of it makes me so queasy, I'd lose weight just visualizing it) or any other get-thin-quick schemes you see on late-night infomercials.

The goal here is not to lose weight. Put away your fat calipers and measuring tapes and computerized calorie counters and radical diet books and bathroom scale. Toss them all in a ditch and torch 'em! Burn, baby, burn . . . and be free.

The goal here is to let your body be as healthy as it can and find its natural weight and shape. The shape you were born with, at its best. There is no effective way to do this other than to listen to your body and have a good balance of moderate exercise and vitamin-rich food. It's that simple. After many years of trying to figure out the whole mystery around weight loss and how I could control my body, I realized:

1. You can never "control" your body. Mother Nature is way too smart for that and she will eventually kick your butt if you mess too much with the plan of things.
2. If you make a genuine effort toward your exercise regime and eat nutrient-dense foods, your body will naturally be what it should be.

The key word here is *balance*. You need healthy portions of food from all the major food groups several times a day. I'll let an expert explain:

How Should You Eat? Keep it simple, says **Evelyn Tribole**, **M.S., R.D.**, author of *Intuitive Eating*

I like what they say in the Listen to Your Body campaign by the National Eating Disorders Association: "Eat what you want, when you are truly hungry. Stop when you're full. And eat exactly what appeals to you. Do this instead of any diet, and you are unlikely to ever have a weight problem, let alone an eating disorder." This makes sense!

For more information on eating-related issues:
www.nationaleatingdisorders.org
www.4woman.gov
www.anorexiasurvivalguide.com

Call a truce with food!

Food is neither your enemy nor your best friend. It won't mend your broken heart and it won't send you to hell.

You've got to listen to your body and honor your hunger. That means eating like a normal person. In this society, we've gotten so whacked out about food that we don't know anymore when we're hungry, when we're full, or what we're "allowed" to eat. Food portions have gotten out of control in restaurants these days with owners trying to lure customers to get the most for their buck. But our metabolism hasn't increased to keep up with these gigantic meals.

Somewhere along the way, feeding our bodies got too complicated. Someone declared a war against our food and our bodies, with our heads and our hearts as the battleground.

According to *Psychology Today* (February 1997), in 1987 Americans spent $33 billion on the diet-related industry. In 1997, we spent approximately $50 billion.

And the irony of ironies?

The entire diet-related industry is based on a 98-percent failure rate. Someone out there has been making a hell of a lot of money preying on the insecurities of women—and now men and boys, too. And it's not getting anyone any thinner or healthier like it promises.

The bottom line is this: You must make healthy, long-lasting, positive changes in your lifestyle to change your body and your health. Period.

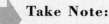

Take Note:

Did you know that . . .

*42% of 1st–3rd-grade girls want to be thinner (Collins, 1991).

*46% of 9–11-year-olds are "sometimes" or "very often" on diets. (Gustafson, Larson, and Terry, 1992)

*In the United States, conservative estimates indicate that after puberty, **5–10 million** girls and **1 million** boys and men are struggling with eating disorders including anorexia, bulimia, binge-eating disorder, or borderline conditions. (Crowther et al., 1992; Fairburn et al., 1993; Gordon, 1990; Hoek, 1995; Shisslak et al., 1995)

Instead, try this.

Try to eat like a kid again. Children run around outside and then come home when they're hungry. They eat what their bodies want and they leave food on the plate when they are full, or if still hungry, ask for seconds without hesitation. We have to relearn this as adults. To see food as fuel and not to fool ourselves with it.

We have to let ourselves off the shame/guilt track when we indulge in a piece of chocolate or smack our lips around a Krispy Kreme doughnut. This does not make you a bad person. If your main diet is filled with the nutrients you need, a little splurge isn't going to kill you.

Remember: BALANCE IS THE KEY.

It's natural for many of us to have an emotional link to food. So often we eat when we are sad or angry or depressed. Or sometimes we just want to have a treat because it feels good to treat ourselves. Within reason, indulging in foods like cakes and potato chips and fast foods is not a crime to your body. WITHIN REASON.

If your entire diet consists of these foods, your body isn't nearly as healthy as it can be.

At home, I stock my fridge with succulent pears and beautiful leafy vegetables, garlic bulbs, red and yellow onions, leeks, raw and roasted nuts and dried fruits, corn, sweet and new potatoes, and other produce from the organic market. Spelt and whole-grain breads, almond and cashew butters, lots of honey, cheeses, the list can go on and on. In my freezer, I load flash frozen (frozen right after being picked, washed, or cooked) squash, collard greens, okra, spinach, kale, strawberries, blueberries, papaya, and mango. This way, I can enjoy the fruit and veggies I like all year-round.

But I also have a shelf in my kitchen and a drawer in my freezer dedicated to my collection of chocolate kisses, Snickers bars, carob-coated giant rice cakes, chocolate-covered cherries, and Tropical Source Dairy Free organic chocolate. I am free to choose what I want. You'd be surprised how liberating this is, and my visits to the chocolate drawer are not as frequent as you'd think. It's because I know it's always there if I want it so there's no power struggle involved. When I feel the urge, I have some—it's as simple as that. I eat a variety of foods and this keeps me sane and healthy.

Speak Out! (You Say You Wanna Revolution . . .)

In the beginning of this chapter, I talked about taking back your body and your health and feeling proud about it. This, I feel, is a main step to changing your life.

Now . . . *to change the world!*

Like our *Glamour* editor in chief, Cindi Leive, you can take action to change how society perceives a woman's body. If you want to make changes, you must be part of the process. If you just wait around and hope things will change of their own accord, you'll be waiting a loooong time.

"Every time I see a billboard, every time I see a commercial, every time I walk into a boutique that doesn't carry a size bigger than a 10, I speak up," says actress Camryn Manheim. "Advertisers invest in girls hating themselves."

The world *is* changing. But there is still a lot of work to do.

"The way our culture deals with physical appearance is a recipe for disaster," says Kelly D. Brownell, Ph.D., Professor of Psychology and Director of the Center for Eating and Weight Disorders at Yale University.

Men and women are under tremendous pressure to have a certain look. Sadly, when people do not reach the ideal, they accept society's message that an imperfect body reflects an imperfect person. Preoccupation with weight, relentless dieting, and battered self-esteem are often the consequences.

The pressure is so extreme that nobody has the right body. Even the models you see on magazine covers have had the picture changed with a computer. If the models aren't good enough, how is a normal, regular person to feel?

There is a "disconnect" between biological reality and social ideals. For instance, women are supposed to be thin and busty at the same time. Women diet to lose weight, sometimes making their bust smaller. The weight loss may not be enough and the breasts need to be larger. Bring on the scalpel! The plastic surgeons then get rich because people want breast enhancement to get bigger and liposuction to trim down in other places.

It is a terrible, terrible culture when people feel they must deform their natural bodies with surgery in order to reach an ideal. The ideals are completely arbitrary and are not based on what is needed for good health or happiness. Think of the messages we give our children when every adult is unhappy

with the way they look. We raise generation after generation of young people who dislike their bodies.

At the same time as the ideal becomes harder to attain, the population is gaining weight. This is due to what I call a toxic environment. High-calorie food is everywhere. In places where people never dreamed of eating fifteen years ago, we now expect food (gas stations, shopping malls, drugstores). Soft drink companies pay schools lots of money to position their products and thousands of schools bring in fast-food companies to sell foods in the cafeterias. Fast food is a way of life.

These two powerful, opposing forces—one seducing people to eat and the other telling them they are failures if they do—create heartache everywhere. It is important to resist both pressures and to have a healthy relationship with food. If food is seen as a means of making the body healthy, then people are buffered from eating too much or too little.

B e a part of the revolution, not a part of the problem. Here are two ways the National Eating Disorders Association suggests you can speak up:

1. Write a letter of congratulations to an advertiser for sending positive, inspiring messages that recognize and celebrate the natural diversity of human body shapes and sizes. Compliment their courage to send positive, affirming messages.

2. Make a list of companies who consistently send negative body image messages and make a conscious effort to avoid buying their products. Write them a letter explaining why you are using your "buying power" to protest their messages. Tear out the pages of your magazines that contain advertisements or articles that glori-

fy thinness or degrade people of larger sizes. Enjoy your magazine without negative media messages about your body.

Q & A with Evelyn Tribole

Q: *What are the signs of a potential eating disorder?*

Evelyn: Worrying way too much about what you eat. Constantly feeling guilty about what you eat or always worrying about the last meal or the next meal, that's a clue. If you have too many rules about your eating, that signals a problem. You can't eat past six o'clock. You can't have carbs. Rigid, nonflexible rules that keep you obsessed about food and thinking about it all the time.

Q: *What are the effects of yo-yo dieting?*

Evelyn: When you starve, your body thinks it's in a famine and your metabolism starts to slow down. But then, you get so sick of the deprivation and you get so hungry, you overeat. And the cycle continues. It erodes the trust between you and your body.

Q: *What do you think of the current fad diets?*

Evelyn: They are serious trouble—especially the ones on the bestseller list. You might have a friend who has completely cut out carbs and is losing tons of weight. Well, check in with her six months down the road and she probably can't stop eating the carbs now.

Q: *How can we help a friend with an eating disorder?*

Evelyn: It's important to say something. The last thing we want to be is someone's food police, but we're talking about something life threatening here. If someone is in profound denial, make it clear to them how much you love them and what your con-

cerns are. State what you've observed—that the person is not eating, their mood has changed, they are less energetic. State the facts. So even if they want to deny it, they can't.

Q: *What can we do to help ourselves love our bodies?*

Evelyn: I like to give simple exercises to do. Mainly, you need to get comfortable in your "here and now" body. That means, wear sizes that fit you here and now, not if you're going to lose twenty pounds. People have trouble spending money on nice clothes because they're waiting. You have to focus on today and say nice things to yourself. People who are overcoming an eating disorder are in the habit of saying nasty things to themselves. "I'm fat. I'm ugly." Would you say that to your best friend? To your sister? To your mother? Get in the habit of apologizing to yourself. Respect your body. Nourish it, feed it regular meals, and listen to it. Is it hungry, is it tired, does it need a hug?

FINAL THOUGHT

Your body is a beautiful, strong creation that can take you wherever you want to go if you take care of it first. Society and mass media have gotten us all muddled up about our physical selves and how we should look and eat and move. I hope one day all women will rejoice in their shapes and the amazing things their bodies can achieve.

fashion emergency!

I used to be a walking Fashion Emergency. Me? Yes, me—a fashion model and a fashion designer who hosts a show about fashion!

But before I ever set foot in Manhattan's Fashion District I spent the first twenty-five years of my life in old, beaten-up sweat-pants. What did I know about fashion? *Nada.* What did I care? *Nada* again.

Slowly, after many a polyester-stretch-pants-and-gold-chain-belt fiasco, I developed a good fashion "sense" and found my style: comfortable, flattering, functional, feminine, colorful (after I got over my all-black stage), and fun. Meaning: classically trend-forward but not trendy, and body-enhancing. And somewhere along the way, I'm not sure how, I became a fashion "expert." Since I began hosting E! Entertainment's *Fashion Emergency* five years ago, hundreds of men and women have approached me—in the street, at the gym, at the dentist's office, at the airport—with their various fashion dilemmas. They come bearing bad choices in need of a good closet clean-up.

The problems may vary, but the origin is often the same: *not knowing what suits your personality, your lifestyle, and your body type* before blowing your entire paycheck at the mall on clothes that are wrong for you.

Once you understand these basics, your personal style will emerge and fashion dilemmas will be like hemlines of years gone by—old news! Out of style!

So open up your closet door; let's find the fashion maven within . . .

From Flagstaff to Fashionista!

Stepping off the plane from Flagstaff, Arizona, at age twenty-five onto Manhattan soil, I proudly wore all the colors of the rainbow on my cable-knit, crew-neck sweater.

I looked around to see what everyone else was wearing.

Black, black, black.

What, did somebody die?

They wore black in the restaurants, at the dry cleaner's, and while drinking cocktails. All I saw was blackness. In every shade, every texture, every form—black. If it was possible, you might even say I was blinded by the blackness. (Have I made myself clear, yet?) Who knew there were fifty shades of it? Not I. Black was and is the coolest noncolor to wear in New York City and I arrived with not a stitch of it.

Not only was I the wrong color, I was the wrong decade. My suitcases were stuffed with corduroy pants, preppy sweaters, white stockings, and tacky gold chain belts. My wardrobe reeked of college and Brat Pack movies.

It was time for a total overhaul.

But . . . I was totally broke.

I owned two decent blouses and two decent skirts and I wore them in every combination possible (four) to my job as a receptionist. I splurged on a $69 dress made of nylon that singed in the dryer one day.

And then I got serious and focused on the mission at hand: I needed a good wardrobe and I needed it *now*.

I went to discount stores and rummaged through sale racks at major department stores, and after days of searching I found some awesome clothes at half price! Who knew? Anne Taylor, Liz Claiborne, and Talbots were my salvation. Slowly, one at a time, I bought good quality, classic items on sale: a black cashmere sweater; gabardine wool flat-front pants with cuffs on the bottom; a beautiful, sheer, black, button-up blouse to wear over a sexy lingerie piece. Lots of black.

To mix with these few cherished items, I collected tried and true basics: black Lycra tank tops, black side-zipped cotton pants, good black T-shirts. I filtered this sea of black in with my existing wardrobe and within a few months, I was looking like a real, honest-to-goodness New Yorker.

Then I had to walk the walk.

Another big makeover was my shoe selection. I needed to find well-heeled, comfortable shoes that would serve two purposes: (1) get me to work, and (2) look good once I got there.

This meant I had to get to know a good, dependable, shoe repair guy—pronto. A shoe repair guy in New York is a girl's best friend. What with all that running up and down those busy streets

911 TIP   **It's a shoe-in.** If you're running out the door and you notice your shoes need shining badly but you're out of polish, grab a polishing cloth or a piece of white bread or your hand lotion and rub gently.

and racing through subways and dodging traffic, I was going to need a lot of spit shining and scuff smoothing.

So there I was, shoes shined and head to toe in black. It was 1988 and I was ready for the Manhattan secretarial pool.

What Every Girl Should Have in Her Closet

Emme's Essentials

☑ Long pants.

☑ Short skirt (just above the knee).

☑ Long skirt (grazing the shin).

☑ Camisoles (with adjustable straps for finer dressing and Lycra layering pieces).

☑ Shirts (that are a variety of lengths, cropped at the top of your abdomen, cropped below your belly button, and tunic).

☑ Cardigan (sets with camisoles).

☑ Sweaters (different textures and qualities).

☑ A couple of LBDs (see section on Little Black Dress).

☑ A trench coat (tan or black).

☑ A sheath dress (black or red).

☑ A couple of dusters (short for petite and long for tall women; double knit, crochet, tape yarn, burn-out velvet).

☑ A great black shoulder bag.

☑ Comfortable, well-soled shoes.

☑ Shawls (always dresses up a casual outfit on cool or cold nights).

☑ Reliable undergarments (panty-line free).

OLDER & WISER

If I knew then what I know now, I would have saved my money and bought four quality pieces of clothing per year instead of running out and reacting to every 10 percent off or 40 percent going-out-of-business sale. I bought so many things I didn't need. On-sale items are usually out of season two times over. Why wear something that is yesterday's news? My sale items used to hang in my closets with price tags still on them for years.

Tips for Everyday Dressing

Wouldn't it be flattering if someone stopped you on the street and paid you a terrific compliment, describing your fashion style as **bold, modern, sexy, flirty, fresh, strong, sophisticated, alive, spirited, sultry, smart, polished, confident, and feminine?**

Well if it hasn't happened already, it will once I get through with you!

Anyone can learn how to dress well, and the first step is to conquer your fear of fashion. It's like a fear of flying, but with pleats instead of planes.

If I can do it, so can you. I was the one who paired pink and green together in high school and lived in coffee-stained sweatshirts throughout college. Most of my wardrobe consisted of job uniforms: waitress (Sonic drive-in fast food); an NBC page; lifeguard; TV reporter (the studio gave us clothes to wear); model (I wore what they gave me); and host of *Fashion Emergency* (again, the studio provided clothes). I never had to give clothes a second thought—it was all done for me.

That was all well and good until I became known in a public

way. Suddenly, photographers appeared at the funniest places— at the movies, getting off a plane, on vacation—to take my picture. And the camera doesn't have the compassion of your cute mailman or that tall FedEx guy or your favorite omelet maker at the local diner who always tells you "jooou look fab-u-lous!"

When I step out my front door, I keep those cameras in mind. And yet, I try not to let them run my life. There are days when I still run to the coffee shop in my old sweats and a ragged T-shirt. From the very beginning I vowed not to take all this fashion stuff *too* seriously!

Everyday Tips That Only a Model with a Clothing Line Could Tell You

1. Make sure the clothes you wear fit you properly. There is nothing worse than ill-fitting garments. If first impressions are made in the first ten seconds, make an effort to have your clothes represent you properly. If you've lost weight, take jackets and skirts and pants to a good tailor. If you buy a suit and you need to shorten pants, skirts, and jacket sleeves, ask the establishment to do it for you. Forgo your ego, or the ten-pounds-from-now mentality. Do not buy clothes that are too small or way too big. If you have a difficult-to-fit body shape, buy a size larger and do a few minor alterations to give you the shape that highlights your assets.

2. Know what colors work or don't work with your skin color. To know this you have to experiment. You want your outfits to "pop" when you walk into a room, not wash you out or clash with your skin tone. Experiment as much as you can with the colors that come out each season. Once you find a hit, buy a sweater, blouse, or shawl in that color and get ready for the compliments. An automatic hit would be matching the color of your eyes to a garment.

3. Purchase both a personal steamer for traveling and a commercial one for home. A steamer is quick and simple, makes wrinkles disappear faster than with an iron, and it makes your clothes look fresh and neat. I am speaking from experience here—irons and I are not friends!

4. Please purchase a black bra. Every woman needs a black bra to wear under blouses, T-shirts, tank tops, and dresses that are not white or beige. If a black bra slips out, it's okay—even interesting and sexy! But if a white one can be seen underneath a black top or a white strap peaks out on your shoulder, it's distracting to the line of your smooth, slimming silhouette.

5. Do yourself a favor and get fitted for a bra in a department store. Sometimes bra experts are hired to do fittings and give consultations. Your "sisters" (and I don't mean blood relatives) will thank you! I learned a few years ago, from being a Playtex spokesperson, that 75 percent of us are wearing the wrong size bra! (I always wondered, how do they conduct a test like this?) Your entire wardrobe will fit better and look fresher.

6. Give yourself a weekly manicure. I wear a very sheer pink on my fingernails and go for all the reds and plum colors for my toes. Even clear makes a nice clean statement. Make sure your nails are all one length, shaped, clean, and have smooth cuticles that aren't hanging and torn. If you think your clothes tell who you are, your nails *spill the beans* on you! Face it, your nail condition says tons about how you handle stress and how much control you have in your life. I come from a family of nail biters and it's one habit I've worked hard to break. If I get a manicure or do my own manicure every week, I don't pick at my nails and they look great.

Emme

7. Get your hair cut and styled, and if you color it, make sure you stick to your color schedule. My hair salon (Salon AKS, NYC) throws a fit from time to time when I go on national TV and haven't made it in for my highlight touch-up in three months. What can I say; sometimes I'm a bit tardy. But after I see photos or TV shows of myself with those dark roots . . . Ugh! I promise, Franco, I'll come in sooner next time!

8. Layering. Never use a bulky fabric as your layering tool under clothes. Instead, remember, Lycra is your friend. You always want to create an elongated, slim, smooth silhouette no matter what size you are. There are a few ways you can achieve this:

- **Your undergarments:** Find seamless bras and underwear (higher on the hip . . . *Barely There*, by Bali, has a great line) or a thong, which is my panty-line-free savior. Seamless equals no bulk and who needs additional bulk? I find my thongs at Mimi Maternity (yes, maternity—however, there is a one-size-fits-all that works wonders for all women . . . I love them and buy them in bunches).

- **Shapewear:** I'm not talking an armor of girdles, here. I mean something nice and comfortable and smooth on your skin that hugs your body curves. If you can find an all-in-one tank top/biker short combination with an ease (slit) cotton crotch, you might not have to wear underwear or a bra if you're supported enough. I need to wear my seamless push-up bra underneath for more support. Invest in a few of these shapewear suits. Buy two black and one nude. You will feel great when you wear these under sheath dresses, long skirts, and pants. Hand wash and line dry to keep them in good form. (One of my faves? Bodyslimmers by Nancy Ganz or Victoria's Secret.)

- **Sportswear tank tops:** In my clothing collection I created the "power cami," which is a stretch camisole that comes in all the colors of the rainbow and offers support and coverage under wrap dresses, wrap tops, and sheer blouses. Great for work and first dates. Camisoles help clothes drape beautifully without clinging, and they hide bra lines.

9. Accessories.

- To store earrings, necklaces, pins, and most other accessories, go to JCPenney or any fish tackle store and buy a clear organizer box. Then, when you look for an item you'll find it easier than by searching in a regular jewelry box.

- According to where you are and what time it is, accessories should vary in color, value, and size. For work, wear the pearls or simple gold or silver pieces. Keep the baubles and glitter for night!

- Don't wear too many accessories all at once. No more than three of the following pieces should be on your body at one time: hair accessories (not including ponytail ties or basic black headbands), bracelets (other than a grouping on an arm), necklaces, earrings, rings, watch, anklet, brooches, or pins.

- If your fingers are plump, stay away from too many rings.

- If you have a short neck, stay away from the long and dangly and the chandelier trend in earrings.

- If you are petite, keep your accessories simple or they will overwhelm you. If you have a large frame, you can handle large cuffs and an abundant layer of cascading semiprecious-stone necklaces.

- Don't call attention to a large bust with brooches and pins.

- Less is best. Let one major piece of jewelry stand out. My father, mother, and two great-aunts each gave me substantial "cocktail" rings. It makes my dressing so much easier when I go out to a cocktail party or nice dinner when I wear one of them because that's all I need. I can't wear a bracelet or

Emme

another ring (other than my wedding ring) because the cocktail ring makes too big a statement to share the limelight! I throw a simple stud necklace (diamond or cubic zirconia) to give me a little sparkle around my face, but other than that, I'm set with a great conversation piece.

- I have one pet peeve that irritates me like a fingernail running down a blackboard: Don't mix your metals. Wear gold with gold and silver with silver/platinum/white gold. Wear like with like. If you decide to wear silver for the evening, then do it all the way down to the hardware on your purse. Don't wear a silver charm bracelet with silver rings with a gold watch and a gold chain shoulder-strap purse. A versatile investment regarding purses is to find bags without hardware at all so they will better match whatever jewelry you choose to wear. This way you can use one bag with many different accessories. If you want to mix it up, buy a two-toned watch so whatever jewelry you wear works with the watch.

My fashion stylist friend **Jennifer Crawford** is an accessory enthusiast. When she needs to add pizzazz to an outfit, she's been known to improvise with various household items as she's running out the door to a party.

"I was going to a party in the summer and wanted a cool purse at the last minute," she says, "and I had these great vintage swim caps with flowers all over them. I turned one upside down and punched holes near the top edge. I had some bright-colored rubber tubing so I pulled it through the holes and knotted it. It made for great shoulder straps and a cute bag.

"Another time, a friend of mine was going to a funky New York party so we cut up a T-shirt and rhinestoned it. I had a pair of red fishnets that we cut the legs off of and we sewed them to the T-shirt for the sleeves. It looked very cool!

"And then there was the time that my girlfriend and I were

WISE WOMAN

Jennifer Crawford, stylist

Accessorize!

Jewelry: Vintage jewelry can be fun. You can get rhinestone pins (which you can also wear in your hair) and pearls at vintage and thrift shops. Chunky and funky can look great, like big gems, which sometimes you can also make yourself.

Belts: These are good for pants and skirts. They can be thin to wide and made of fabric, leather, or suede, and can be anything from a buckle to a crochet or a macrame belt with fringe. You can get white cotton twine and macrame your own wide tie belt.

Scarves: I suggest fun, bright, colorful patterns for your neck and hair. You can also tie them to the strap of your handbag or fold a large square scarf in half (triangle shape) and tie it on the side of your waist (so the point comes down one side) over a skirt or pants. You can tie a crocheted shawl in the same way—it looks great.

Wraps: Sheer or lace wraps (or fabric by the yard) can look great over a cami for evening time.

Hats: Wear funky to sexy, cowboy to cocktail hats. You can accessorize the hats with pins, scarves, and flowers.

Bags: Use other colorful (can be patterned) handbags and shoulder bags. A lot of stores have great shopping bags that you can use in addition to your handbag to carry extra items.

Ties: Throw a man's necktie on with your suit to give it a whole different look.

Emme

going to a Sunday afternoon garden party and we wanted to look really festive, so we took a couple of vinyl, fruit-patterned table-cloths and cut them in a big circle. Then we cut holes in the middle for waistbands. We sewed elastic in the waists and glued pom-pom braiding to the bottom edges and had two very cute skirts. We were a hit!"

The Little Black Dress

A woman's dress should be like a barbed-wire fence: serving its purpose without obstructing the view. —SOPHIA LOREN

The little black dress deserves a section all its own, it has such power, such class. It's an institution.

Remember that scene in *Jerry Maguire* when Renee Zellweger shows up in the kitchen in her little black dress (henceforth known as the LBD) for her first date with Tom Cruise?

"That's not a dress," he says to her, drooling, "it's an Audrey Hepburn movie."

Right on! Every young woman needs to have at least one marvelous LBD that hangs in her closet and fits and is dry-cleaned and ready to slip on *right now*. If you fluctuate in weight, find a style you like and buy two of them. I love those Diane von Furstenburg style solid black (or with a little black print) wrap dresses. They fit most body types and look great with a trench coat.

You might be inspired by famous LBDs of other eras.

Rita Hayworth wore that velvety strapless one in *Gilda*. Sophia Loren had that V-necked halter. Do we even need to mention Audrey Hepburn again? She had so many LBDs—but we should especially note her LBD in *Breakfast at Tiffany's*. Even Julia Roberts, smart girl, wore vintage black Valentino when she won her Oscar.

Every beautiful leading lady has an LBD in her repertoire. Why don't you be a copycat? After you pick out which stellar style is best for you, you can get a copy of it via ABS, the Allen Schwartz knock-off line (www.absstyle.com). Schwartz makes reproductions of famous LBDs and not-so-little black dresses for the mass market, but at one-eighth the price of the originals.

Is It Me?

It takes trial and error to find your own Look. I remember when Brooke Shields wore those tight Calvin Klein jeans in the eighties. It was a good look for her, and I wanted it to be a good look for me, too. I'd lie on the floor, suck in my stomach, and zip those size 10's up until I couldn't breathe.

But just because someone else is wearing it doesn't mean it's your cup o' tea.

I'm still haunted by memories of a black and white, polka-dot, baby-doll dress I once wore to a wedding. As the dress billowed out in front of me, a woman approached, smiling: "When are you *due*, dear?" On Princess Diana, the dots were fab. On me? I looked like a loaf of Wonderbread.

I cringe at photos taken the night I met Phil's parents. It was 1988 (a bad year for fashion, true, but that doesn't let me off the hook). There I am, wearing an ear-to-ear grin, red corduroys tucked into my calf-high L.L.Bean boots, a gold chain belt with tassels on the end, and an old cashmere sweater with two moth holes on the shoulder.

Poor Phil was love struck and therefore fashion-blind: "I looked at you in those red corduroys and little belt," he said, "and I thought, 'I'm so in love!' " He must have been.

I am still, to this day, always on the verge of a Fashion Emergency.

I was a guest on *The Today Show* two years ago when the HBO series *Sex and the City* sprung the big flower fashion trend. So I wore this giant, and I mean *giant*, silk flower on my dress thinking I was being so cutting edge and hip. Meanwhile, my gut was telling me it was just too enormous. But I didn't listen to the little voice of my inner stylist trying to get my attention.

The next day the TV station was flooded with phone calls from perplexed viewers wanting to know "what the heck was that *thing* on her shoulder?" Yes, I am guilty of following a trend gone south, but despite having the photos to prove it, I am still going to give things a try. I don't ever want to take fashion or myself too seriously.

Kendall Farr, fashion stylist and author of *The Pocket Stylist* (due out Spring 2004, Gotham) gave me so many helpful ideas about dressing, especially during my spokesmodel days at Revlon. For my press appearances, there were few sexy, womanly, or current clothes available in size 14 so Kendall had them made for me. This woman has style written all over her, so I naturally had to ask her how to find it:

"A woman 'finds' her style when she is absolutely true to herself. We all know intuitively what works best for our bodies, but we are bombarded with so much information and a trends axis that spins faster and faster. It's easy to get caught up in looks that really don't work for our individual shapes all because we want to feel current, fashionable, and as if we are 'in the game.' Choose great fit, flattering shapes, and great fabric first, and worry about trends and what's HOT second. Personal style, after all, transcends fashion every time!"

Famous fashion faux pas:

- ☒ Following trends that don't suit you. (OK, OK, sometimes we're blind.)
- ☒ Too many accessories, too many mismatched prints.
- ☒ Caught in a time warp: Jennifer Aniston's shag hair.
- ☒ Shoes beyond their prime. (Charity drop-offs.)
- ☒ Nothing dressy to wear (i.e., going out at night in jeans and a T-shirt because it's all you had).
- ☒ Suits that were either way too small or way too big.
- ☒ Brown sheer hose with black shoes.
- ☒ Pantyhose with runs in them.
- ☒ Fuchsia-pink nails, Lee Press-On Nails.
- ☒ Plunging necklines at the office.
- ☒ Skirts that hike up north (inappropriate skirt lengths for the office or occasion).
- ☒ Closets that made you crazy after years of accumulation (more about this later).

So just because the magazines say so, don't follow trends just because they are trendy. The flip side of this guideline is: If you find a trend that works for you—buy ten and wear it to the ground.

Who cares if, two years later, it's not cutting edge anymore. If they look good on you and you feel good, those two pros cancel out the latest, hottest trend.

I have a friend who lives in the same white shirt every summer. She absolutely loves this specific brand so she buys them like eggs—by the dozen—and wears them with jeans, with leggings, with skirts. If you find something perfect for you, buy more. Wear one until it's worn through, then pull out a fresh new one.

I have one heavenly pair of St. John knit pants that I wore to death two winters in a row. I called up the manufacturer and begged them to make more: "Please, where are these pants? I need them! You've got to make more of them!"

They didn't. So I took drastic measures—*literally*. I pulled out my measuring tape and designed my own version of them for my clothing line. A girl's gotta do what a girl's gotta do.

I didn't stop there. I grabbed my favorite, flare-legged, velour dance pants that I wore everywhere—to formal events with a tunic top or casually with a big, bulky sweater and clogs—and I cloned them, too.

Your Body Specifics: Body-Shape Dressing Quick and Simple

The key to dressing well is to create a balance between top and bottom. And, FYI, most people's tops and bottoms were not created equal. Take a good look at your shape in a mirror while you read about the shapes described here and try to figure out which one fits you best. Also, if you can, get your colors done by a specialist. Knowing which colors work with your skin tone will save you tons of money by keeping you from buying those magenta sweaters (it's not easy to look great in magenta).

APPLE SHAPE

Generous bust
Thick waist
Narrow hips
Usually strong shapely legs like my girlfriend Jacci's. Her legs are to die for.

TIPS
- ► Keep focus away from middle.
- ► Wear tailored pants.
- ► Have fun with capris and cigarette pants . . . prints too!
- ► Leggings are great with a long top.
- ► Find draping tops instead of structured, fitted tops.
- ► If you wear a short top with leggings you will look boxy, so think again!
- ► Straight skirts (go for prints, if you like) with a long top like a man's button-up . . . stand the collar up!
- ► Keep lapels narrow and small on straight jackets.
- ► Pick shoulder bags that hit right at or below hip.

Apple Shape

HOURGLASS SHAPE

Shapely breasts
Defined waist
Shapely hips
Rounded rear
Nice legs

TIPS
- ► Call attention to your lovely waist.
- ► Stay away from jackets, blouses, and sweaters that are too tight. Go for shawl-collared jackets with an embellished camisole and an above-the-knee skirt—this creates proportion in the look you've created.

Hourglass Shape

- Work with monochromatic blouses and pants. With skirts, you can wear prints if they are on the small scale.
- Don't cover up your curviness—that will make you look bigger than you are.
- Don't wear stiff fabrics (linens). Instead, choose draping, stretchy fluid knits (fluid jersey, washed silk, velvet, wool crepes).
- Wrap dresses and wrap skirts will show off your shape . . . bias cut is what you need to allow enough room for your shape.
- If you're concerned about bosom fall-out with cross-front tops and dresses, wear a body-hugging camisole underneath for optional coverage when leaning over.
- If you feel self-conscious about your curviness, wear a layering piece in Lycra, tucked in, and a button-up tab-sleeve tunic to go on top.
- Stay away from chunky jewelry near your bust or neckline.
- Simple boat scoop necks or deep V sheaths look beautiful on you—they drape around curves without pulling at them.

ATHLETIC INVERTED TRIANGLE SHAPE
Broad shoulders
Average bust
Average waist
Narrow hips
Shapely legs

TIPS
- Run from shoulder pads. Don't walk—run! Take them out of all your blouses, jackets, and outerwear pieces. You already have wonderful shoulders—no need to make them bigger!

Athletic Inverted
Triangle Shape

▸ Pants, all of them, are great. Bell, flare, narrow, capri, cuffs—
go for it!

▸ For soft structure in suit dressing and jackets, find gabardine,
natural silk, denim, linen, double-knit fabrics.

▸ Keep colors and prints on the bottom and more neutral tones on
top to create balance between a broad shoulder and narrower
bottom.

▸ To create a more feminine feel to your wardrobe, choose draping, more fluid tops and dresses that wrap your body instead of
those that stand stiff away from your shape.

▸ Button-up, small-collared dresses with chain belts are great for
you.

▸ Boat neck tops and dresses will accentuate your shoulders (if
you like that, go there like I do; if not, go for
more of a deep V).

STRAIGHT/SQUARE SHAPE

*Upper body, waist, and lower body average
    and/or equal to one another*
Flat tush
Thin legs
Short-waisted

TIPS

▸ Draw attention down to legs with fitted pants,
capris, or leggings.

▸ Elongate your upper body by staying away from
belted dresses, jackets, and shirts . . . these
draw attention to a thick waist.

▸ Simple and loose dresses are your best friend.
A nice, simple, light tweed, button-up, beltless
dress above the knee would be balanced and
complementary.

Straight/Square
Shape

- ► Narrow skirts and narrow straight pants elongate. A-line, no way!
- ► Keep jackets fluid and loosely fitted—not stiff and structured. This hides a thick waist.
- ► If you are short, stay away from trimmings on the bottom of your pants.
- ► Work on creating depth to your upper body by wearing a printed or textured jacket or cardigan over a monochromatic shirt/blouse, pant/skirt combination.
- ► If you have a short neck, take out any shoulder pads or your neck will disappear. Wear clustered earrings rather than long dangly ones. Lean toward more notch collars . . . helps lengthen your neckline.
- ► Choose soft, medium-weight tops that are nonclingy to drape well over an elasticized waistband (soft flannels, knits, sheers, jerseys).
- ► Overblouse tops look good tucked in.
- ► Wear hose that is your skin tone . . . this will help you elongate your look.

TRIANGLE/PEAR SHAPE
Vital: Know a good tailor

Wide hips
Small bust
Thick legs
Slender stomach
Really nice waist (you have to buy all of your pants and skirts one or two sizes larger and take them in, right?)

TIPS

- ▶ Draw attention to your shoulders to balance your lower body.
- ▶ You are the one type that I would tell to find very simple but nicely fitted shoulder pads and put them in all your shirts, blouses, even T-shirts. NEVER use huge thick shoulder pads no matter how narrow your shoulders may be.
- ▶ Wear a halter dress, blouse, bathing suit . . . anything asymmetrical would be modern and the lines are very complimentary for you.
- ▶ If you like skirts, try both A-line and flowing styles. Buy straight skirts 1–2 sizes larger and take in the waist. The more flowing the skirt, the better, because it will not overstate your hips.
- ▶ Flat front pants in a never clingy material.
- ▶ Wrapped skirts or sarongs have a nice fit across the hips.
- ▶ Empire dresses fit snug under your bust will probably flow around your hips.
- ▶ Wrap-front blouses that show off your waistline; bare your tummy if you want. Don't be afraid of showing some skin.

Triangle/Pear Shape

Where to Get Stuff Cheap

I once hit pay dirt at the Salvation Army in Beverly Hills (this is where very wealthy people unload expensive clothes when they get bored with them). I was rifling through the racks and found a totally amazing black leather jacket for five dollars. FIVE DOLLARS. In a real store, it might have been five hundred.

Emme

I grabbed it, took it to a seamstress and had it fixed up (it was slightly battered and needed buttons), and wore it for the next six years. Paired with my black wool pants, my five-dollar jacket looked like a million bucks (and so did I).

As well as looking through secondhand clothing stores, try the following:

SALES AND DISCARDED ITEMS ONLINE

www.bluefly.com
www.girlshop.com
www.netaporter.com
www.styleshopdirect.com

BEST OFF-PRICE STORES

Filene's Basement
888-843-8474

Marshall's
www.marshallsonline.com

Nordstrom Rack
www.nordstromrack.com

Doss Shoes
800-945-7677

Loehmann's
www.loehmanns.com

Daffy's
www.daffys.com

Burlington Coat Factory
www.coat.com

Frugal Farmers
888-Frugals

T.J. Maxx
www.tjmaxx.com

Jeremy's
415-882-4929
510-849-0701

WISE WOMAN

Kim France, Editor in Chief, Lucky Magazine

Shopping Rules

Kim is an expert at buying great stuff cheap. "I found a wonderful Helmut Lang pea coat on sale five years ago," she tells the story. "It was navy wool with one stripe around the bottom—a classic piece from a classic season. It was also twice as much money as I'd normally spend, but I'm still wearing it. It was one of those great moments in shopping—a real triumph!" Here are Kim's shopping suggestions:

1. *Don't buy something just because it's on sale.*

I have this rack in my closet that fell down the other day and all the clothes fell and I realized it was all sale items I had never worn. When you buy an item on sale, don't just think of the money you're saving, think of the money you're spending. Don't say, "But it only costs $300 and it's normally $600." If you didn't want it retail, chances are you're not going to want it or wear it if you buy it on sale, either.

2. *Take advantage of early season sales.*

Stores do a lot of promotional events and midseason sales where you'll see, say, a rack of cashmere sweaters on sale for just a few days and then they go back to the same price after that. To keep tabs on these sales, you really have to be a girl who scopes the mall. Or if you have a saleslady pal who will call you up and tell you when they happen, that's great. Hey, these people often spend most of their days folding and refolding, so if a customer is sweet to them, they'll usually be helpful in return.

3. *Assert yourself.*

I was in L.A. with a friend and she saw this crazy, flat pump made to look like the heel fell off of it and she just *had* to have them. They had her size, but they only had one of the shoes! The other of the pair was at another store. We never did figure out why this was so. Anyway, she asked the saleslady to order it and for the rest of the day, *all day*, as we

Emme

WISE WOMAN

drove around L.A., she kept calling the saleslady every fifteen minutes to check in, telling her, "I'll be back, I'll be back," until she did go back and fetch those shoes. If a store has something on sale and they don't have your size, ask a salesperson to call up other locations, or you call yourself. Usually, if they know that's the only thing keeping you from making that sale, they'll do it. If you see something you really, really want—you've got to PUSH.

4. *Get your timing right.*

The best time to go shopping at a sale is a Friday night. Most stores are empty then and they usually stay open late, too. All the other shoppers are probably crashed on the couch and you'll be the one having the real fun.

5. *Leave no store unturned.*

At a sale, everything is everywhere. The store is a mess because salespeople don't bother to stack everything carefully like usual. You have to search through the piles. You never know what you can find where. You can find a pair of cute undies tossed into the sweater pile. Things get put back in wrong size areas, too. I think people do that on purpose so they can hide something they're not sure of and come back later and get it.

6. *Bring a friend.*

This is a controversial one. But I know I need to have a friend with me because I can't deal with salespeople giving me their opinion—you can't always trust them. A friend is a good adviser because she's not all caught up in the frenzy of the sale.

7. *Read the fine print and try them on.*

Find out what the return policy is. My grandmother who lives in Texas brings back bras she bought from Saks Fifth Avenue *three years later* to return! Some stores are great this way, others give you a week to return.

WISE WOMAN

Try things on—don't just assume something will fit or look right. I've seen a lot of sale items that were really cute, and then I try them on and, of course, the buttons are in the wrong place or something else is wrong.

8. *Sign up for special deals.*

You can do this either at the stores or online. It's a pain if you don't like getting junk mail, but if you don't mind that, it's helpful because the stores hold private sales before the public knows about them.

9. *Don't overlook rejects or factory seconds.*

If the lining is slightly ripped and you can see there's no terminal damage done, or a small thing, like a button is gone, hook and eye is missing, these are easy and inexpensive to fix. Stains are difficult . . . I wouldn't walk out of the store with a stained item. If it's not terminal, go for it!

10. *Be patient.*

Wait for sales! For example, winter coats often go on sale in November. Depending on where you live, you might not even need to wear one until then! So why not wait? Especially if you are buying a trendy item that you will only wear one season, you shouldn't pay retail. You're allowed to buy a few trendy, crazy items each season if they're on sale.

11. *If you miss a sale, ask for a discount.*

You can walk into the Gap, buy a shirt, and if it goes on sale three days later you can go in and say, "I bought this retail and now it's on sale," and they will refund you the difference. This doesn't happen at all stores, but at a lot of them. But doing this means you have to be a vigilant shopper. If you have the time to do this, go ahead. I don't. And the same sometimes holds true if a sale is just about to happen. I was trying on some designer shoes recently and the salesgirl said, "You know what . . . these shoes are going on sale on Tuesday. I'll give you the sale price now. . . ."

12. *Save receipts.*

They are important if you need to return something.

What to Wear on a Job Interview

Clothes define you.

Clothes define where you work, what part of town you live in, what your interests are, what kind of temperament you have, if you're neat or messy, and if you have good self-esteem. There was a time when I didn't have any dressy things or real businesslike attire—everything I owned was casual: khakis, jeans, cords, and lots of sweat tops and pants and athletic wear.

Then I entered the nine-to-five world, with its business dinners and cocktail parties . . . what to do? Well, I had to bury my pink sweaters and green shirts because my days at boarding school were over. Oh, and don't forget . . . my last pair of Top-Siders wrapped with duct tape. (Don't even ask!) Nope, won't be seeing those again. This was one closet cleaning I'll never forget.

If you're in the working world, you must dress appropriately.

When I had to interview candidates for the position of vice president of sales at The Emme Collection, I remember one person in particular who came highly recommended. She was bright, talented, vivacious, experienced, but she was a mess that day.

Her clothes were stained. She wore white shoes with ripped dark stockings. Her hair was in a lacquered bee's nest, circa 1962, and it was coming undone.

My first impression? "What will the buyers think when they see *her*?"

I didn't hear the brilliant things she was saying. I was too busy staring at her pink frosted lipstick usually reserved for a Las Vegas lounge act. I couldn't hire her. We needed someone with outer savvy as well as inner passion.

In every professional business environment, people expect

certain dress codes to be met. It's like a key fitting nicely into its assigned lock. Once you catch on and know which key fits which lock, it's really easy. As you move along your career path, you must expect changes in all areas including your wardrobe.

Let me give you a few helpful rescue-wardrobe themes that can get you on track in time for your big interview . . . or on the road to success at the job you have now.

TYPE 1: *Buttoned Up*

Lawyers, bankers, accountants, corporate businesswomen, and investment brokers. Basically, you don't want to stick out like a sore thumb by not following the dress code with this crowd. The more conservative the job, less is best regarding makeup, hair style, and color.

WHAT TO WEAR:

Well groomed is key. A crisp white button-up shirt (French cuffs are beautiful on a woman, especially when you take your suit jacket off).

A tailored navy, heather gray, or black, plain or pinstriped suit with either pants or a 23–25-inch skirt (falls right above or at knee).

Black, dark navy, or sheer hose. (I hate wearing hose! To make my legs look like they have hose on, I give myself a close shave with my razor and then lather the gams up with some fabulous cream with liquid eye shadow shimmer in it . . . this always does the trick.)

Hair: trimmed regularly and simply styled.

Manicured nails are a must.

TYPE 2: *Creatives*

Creative careers allow you to choose clothes that are more expressive, more free-flowing (fashion industry, magazines, tele-

vision, advertising, decorators, musicians, makeup artists, actors, dancers, artists, and so on). Go there and be yourself with your personal, cutting edge, trend-forward style—the more designer vintage, the better.

My design team is a testament to this advice. Lenard Matias, my former head designer and a totally creative dresser, looks so chic in such a simple yet thoughtfully put-together way. I love his dirty jeans ensemble with his satin shirt and cool cuff links. Erin, one of our loyal designers, knows how to push a few yards of disregarded matte jersey into a complete sweater-dress/wrap ensemble in a way I've never seen before. Oh, these creative types!

WHAT TO WEAR:

I almost feel stupid telling creative people what to wear so I'll let Lenard put in his two cents here:

Dress appropriate to the interview with a dash of fabulousness. For example: I have a very long Donna Karan tuxedo jacket and pants (no satin trim). I would wear that with simple loafers with no socks or chic sandals, a simple French-cuff white shirt (starched) with fabulous cuff links. Then I'd unbutton the neck and have some fabulous ethnic jewelry around my neck. I don't like to wear a tie unless I have been requested to. If so, then I'd add a solid or neutral-color tie. I'd wear this outfit to meet the president or CEO of a company. In other instances, I'd dress a lot more relaxed: great French-cuff shirt with no cuff links and groovy slim sateen or wide-leg pants in a super wool-blended fabric, or a great outerwear piece, a cool fine-gauge sweater tee and great pants (could be tinted in a color) with a great leg shape and some great shoes. The key is to look smart but also not to lose the individuality, always have one piece of fabulousness.

TYPE 3: *Face to Face*

Salespeople, managers, real estate agents, teachers, travel agents, and so on. You are always trying to warm people up to buy/hear/listen to what you are trying to sell/tell/share with them. You can push them away if you dress too above or below their income level. You want to match wardrobe choices as much as possible with those of the customer (not the student!) you are trying to attract. Teachers should wear easy-care, comfortable clothes. Do not match what students wear—this is inappropriate.

Comfort is key. If you're comfortable, then your client/customer/student will be comfortable around you.

WHAT TO WEAR:

Here you can wear elastic waistbands in skirts and pants if
   you choose.

Double-knit tunics and pants or skirts.

Fluid jersey cardigans and sheath dresses.

Washable silks.

Linen jackets, pants, and dresses.

Trench coats.

In case of a sudden Fashion Emergency, stay cool.

For one modeling-job interview, I put on a pair of thigh-high fishnet stockings (sexy!) under my knee-length skirt. You know, the kind that magically stay up all by themselves? Right. When I walked into the reception area, I heard snickering. I looked down. One of my stockings had fallen down to my ankle and the other was making its way there fast.

   *&$#@!!!!!

I backed up into the hallway, took them off, shoved them in my purse, and walked back in again as if nothing had happened (and hoped my beet-red face didn't give me away). It happens to us all . . .

Emme

I was on my way to a job interview for a job I was desperate to land. I was wearing a suit with a white blouse, and the jacket didn't close all the way. I was very early to the interview and stopped to have some coffee to wait out the time. As I was getting out of the car, I caught a tree branch to the chest, which snapped my bra strap and broke it.

I had seven dollars in the bank, four dollars in my purse (in change!) and my credit cards were totally maxed. I was an hour from home and the interview was in forty-five minutes. You could totally see everything through my shirt, I started to panic. I figured if only my suit jacket would close so that you wouldn't see my shirt, I would be okay, but it was too late to diet now! I went into Starbucks feeling like I was going to die. I had a brainstorm when I walked in. I borrowed an apron from the manager (she saved my life!!!!!) and tied it on like a halter-type shirt. I turned it inside out and I taped it with duct tape in the back so it wouldn't fall off my body. It actually looked really nice.

The staff at Starbucks told me that was their new "night out" look. I went to the interview and I am sure they didn't notice. It didn't matter, anyway; the president of the company interviewed me in cut-off jean shorts and a surfer T-shirt with holes in it.

—"Suzanne"

Underneath It All

There's no use wearing your perfect LBD or a great interview outfit when underneath it all you're wearing ratty underwear from three years ago with the elastic all stretched out. I don't care if *Bridget Jones's Diary* brought back in vogue the big white underwear your granny used to wear. Maybe only you will know what's under there, but you deserve something pretty.

And there's a chance maybe you *won't* be the only one who

sees what's underneath: There I was, walking across Fifty-seventh Street one day last spring and all the men I passed were hootin' and hollerin'. I remember thinking to myself, "I must look *hot!*" A second later, I saw it. My fake snakeskin skirt had rolled right up to my waist in the back and had stayed up over my undies and pantyhose during my entire midtown stroll. I was mortified! (But at least I knew that under my blushing cheeks, I was one foxy lady.)

Underneath It All, Every Girl Needs:

- ☑ An off-white or flesh-colored seamless bra.
- ☑ A black bra.
- ☑ A flesh-colored and a black one-piece shaper with Lycra.
- ☑ A full Lycra slip in black and in flesh tone.
- ☑ A strapless halter-top bra, French-cut briefs, thongs, and full panties.
- ☑ A flesh-tone and black bustier (wear it with your tuxedo pants).

You don't have to go to Victoria's Secret to get dainty stuff. JCPenney and other department stores have these basics, too. You don't have to be rich to be sexy.

Draw Me a Picture

Understanding fashion terms can be downright confusing. When I get baffled, I turn to my design director, Lenard, for enlightenment. He's sketched up a few diagrams for you to enrich your fashion vocabulary and intrigue your visuals. (He's done this for me plenty of times. . . .)

Necklines

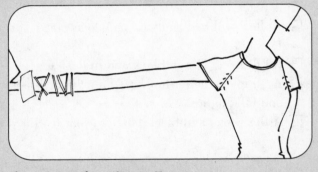

Crew Neck Cap Sleeve Top

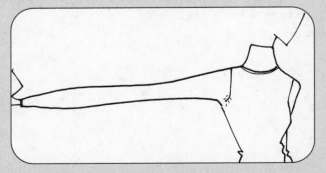

Mock Turtleneck

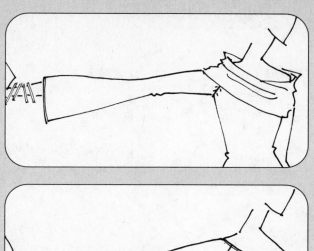

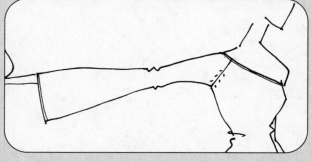

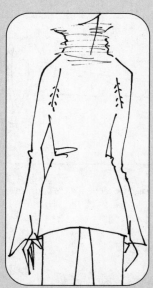

top: Cowl Neck

middle: Asymmetric Neckline with
Bell Sleeves

left: Crush Neck

Necklines continued

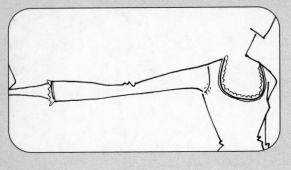

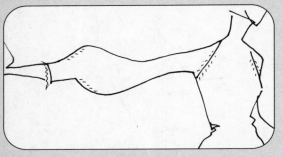

Scoop Neck with
Three-quarter Sleeve

Turtleneck

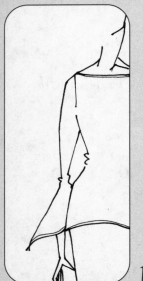

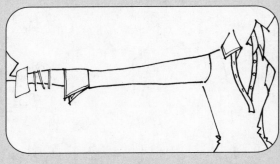

Johnny Collar with Three-quarter Sleeve

Boat Neck

Tops

Tunic with Mandarin Collar

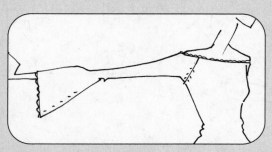

Bell Sleeve

Tank Top

Tops continued

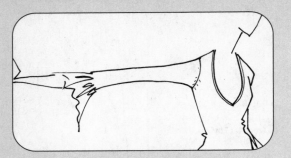

Flutter Sleeve with V Neckline

Peasant Top

Camisole

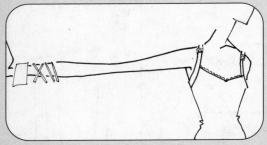

Beaded Halter Top with Shawl

Wrap Top

Balloon Sleeve

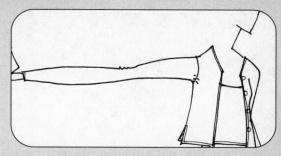

Twinset (Cardigan and Camisole)

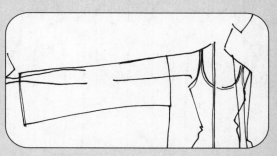

Kimono Sleeve

Corset

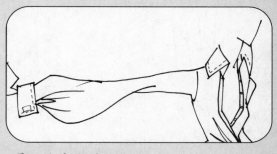

French Cuff Menswear
Wrap Shirt

Pants

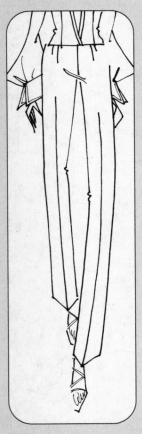 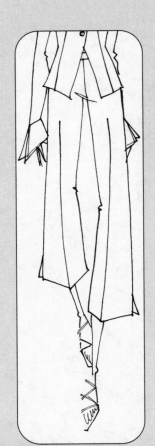 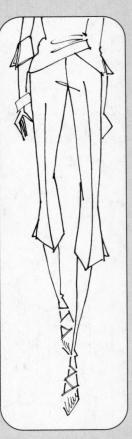

Cigarette Pant   Crop Pant   Capri Pant

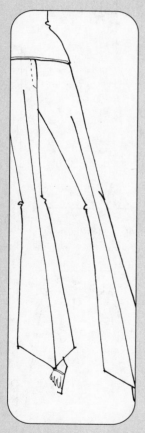

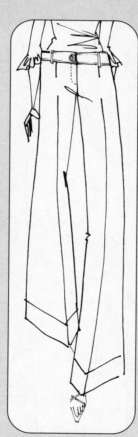

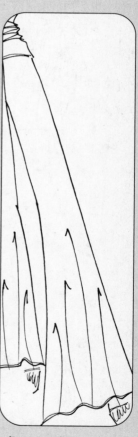

Boot Cut Pant

Hepburn Trouser
with Cuffs

Palazzo Pant

Skirts

Flounce Skirt

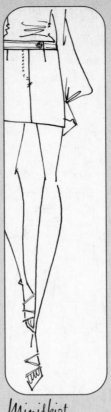

Miniskirt

Long Skirt

bottom left:

Short Slim Skirt
with Slit

bottom right:

A-line Skirt

Dresses

Slip Dress Wrap Dress Bustier Dress

Dresses continued

Side-gathererd Dress

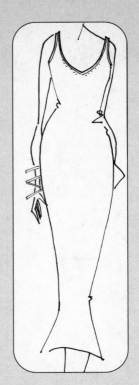

Sleeveless Sheath

Shoes

Sling Back

Strappy

Stiletto Heel

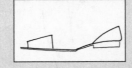

Slip-on

Mule

Flat

Pump

Coats

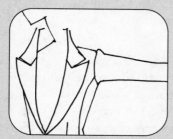

Peak Lapel Jacket

Duster with
Ankle Pant

Trench Coat

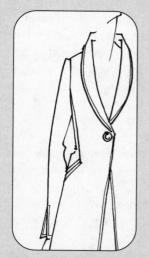

Shawl Collar Jacket

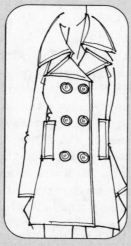

Pea Coat

Notch Collar Jacket

Out of the Closet

Granted, having my own clothing line is a beautiful thing. But sometimes, it's overwhelming. I have so much in my closet it's like a dam ready to burst. My state of mind mirrors my closets: If they are jumbled, so is my brain. My buddy Aida Turturro feels the same way.

WISE WOMAN

Aida Turturro, actress, *The Sopranos*

Organizing Your House

Organizing is immediately rewarding. That's why I not only do it for myself, I do it for my friends, too. Organizing your house can be a very emotional thing. When you finally tackle it, you feel lifted.

Your space around you affects how you feel. Some people have messy closets. Some people have paperwork everywhere. You feel overwhelmed. But when you sort it all out, you get the feeling of, "Ahhh, let's move on."

I've organized friends' filing systems for them. I've gone to my friends' homes and we stay up until 4:00 a.m. organizing their house and rearranging the closets. It's about loving the space you are in.

Some people don't realize what it does for you to clean out that closet, throw out stuff, paint that closet, decide what you really want, and give the rest to charities. That clutter can kill you.

I've been doing this for sixteen years and I love it. Tackle one thing at a time. Go through the clothes. Go through one drawer. Do one room. If you're doing your clothes closet, do categories. Put things in piles. Then see which ones you really, really wear.

It's about getting rid of the excess. Six good skirts are better than ten so-so ones. People feel a hundred times better and move forward in their lives because your space has a lot to do with yourself.

After I've helped friends organize their homes, they've said to me: "Thank you, you changed my life." They say, "Why didn't I do it sooner!"

Organizing your closets gives you clarity.

911 TIP Keep an emergency "toolbox" in your purse or at the office. Hair spray, hand wipes, deodorant, dental floss, double-stick tape, clear nail polish, emery board, brush, safety pins, eye drops, breath mints, powder compact, mini perfume, toothbrush, wrinkle-free spray.

Here's how I do it: I take out all my clothes from the closet and go over them, piece by piece, asking myself: "Does this fit me today? Do I wear it?" Not, "Will it fit me when I lose twenty pounds?" These are moments of truth and I am ruthless.

I make five piles:

To give away.
To keep.
To store.
To mend.
To dry-clean.

I get out the Windex and paper towels and wipe down the closet and vacuum the floor. I take out my plastic boxes that I bought from JCPenney.

One box is for belts.
One box is for sweaters.
One box is for scarves.

Then I put my "keepers" back in the closet.
All blacks together.
All whites together.
All browns together, etc.

My nine-year-old friend Amanda even keeps her closet by color!

Emme

911 TIP For all you sweater girls out there: Fold your fine sweaters and knits; don't hang them or you will have hanger marks on your shoulders.

Clothes to give away to friends or to charity go in plastic bags. Clothes to store go under your bed in plastic boxes with cedar balls. Then I move to the lingerie drawer, where I group:

All bras together.
All body shapers together.
Full-length slips with Lycra together.
Nylons together.
Sexy lingerie: garters, etc.

I line the drawer with lavender paper and throw in a lavender sachet for good measure. Then I do the whole thing over again with my *shoes.*

When it's over, I feel like I've lost fifty pounds. The whole process, which takes a few days, is such a boost to my self-esteem. No more opening up the closet door and hearing last year's pair of jeans scream out at me: "You don't FIT me, you don't FIT me! *HA, HA ha . . . !!!*"

Q & A **with Jennifer Crawford,** fashion stylist

Q: *What are today's "fashion rules"?*

Jennifer: The old, strict fashion rules like "don't wear white after Labor Day" don't really apply anymore. I love the fact that almost "anything goes" now as long as it's done in a tasteful way. But I have some of my own personal rules I can share with you:

NEVER cut yourself up horizontally with too many colors. For example, don't wear a shirt, skirt, hose, or tights, and shoes all in different colors. It's a much cleaner look to match the hose to the skirt or the hose to the shoes or keep the same color from the waist down.

NEVER overdo the designer-logo-print look. I would just wear one accessory with a logo; never more than one at a time, whether they match or not.

ALWAYS go for it, have fun, and try new things. I think people get set in one look and always look the same and are afraid to try something new. Just check with a friend who has good taste on your way out the door.

DON'T wear the same designer (high end) head to toe all the time. Mix it up with other labels. I don't think it looks like you dressed yourself; it gives you the same look a kid has when dressed by the parent. You need to put your personality into your outfit.

NEVER overaccessorize, it makes me crazy. Too many people wear too many accessories at one time. I always say, LESS IS BEST!

DON'T wear shoes with an ankle strap if you have large ankles. It draws all the attention down there.

ALWAYS pay attention to your undergarments—they are as important as your outfit. Especially pay attention to lines showing and your choice of color. Sometimes you'll want color to show through.

FINAL THOUGHT

The door opens, the crowd turns, you hear a collective gasp in the room: "She looks fab-u-lous!" or "Where did she find that dress, in the bottom of a garbage heap?" *Just kidding.* Look, everyone is too busy feeling insecure about how they look in public to notice the color of your hose or how you've accessorized. On an interview or a first date, yes, there is a lot of checking out going on. But generally you don't have to sweat it as much as you might think. As long as you're comfortable, others will be comfortable with you. As long as your clothes are laundered and clean, you will make the right impression. So whether or not you get your colors done or stick to matching your eye color for blouses and wraps—you'll be fine. Fashion is here to play with—not to make you stark raving mad trying to find the latest of the latest. Believe me, I have acquaintances who go mad trying to do this!

Let fashion and dressing free you to express your uniqueness. Go ahead and be your own Miss Thaang!

money
emergency!

L ike that old J. Fred Helf tune laments: "If money talks . . . it ain't on speaking terms with me!"

There was a time in my life when money and I had a serious communication gap. Our relationship was like a rebellious teenager and a frustrated parent. We lived in the same house but we spoke completely different languages.

But over the years my relationship with money has matured—it had to! But it's been a long and sometimes painful process. I remember a time when I was starting out on my own, and I literally didn't have a dime to my name, so I lived on hard-boiled eggs, potatoes, broccoli, and butter for an entire week. There were times, years later, when I was making good money as a model but kept maxing out my credit cards because I couldn't pass my favorite shoe stores without buying a little something that fit my dainty size-11 tootsies. When it comes to finances, it matters less how much money you make and more how you spend it.

Today I'm a mother and at the helm of my own business, so

money and I have a new and uncomplicated understanding. I treat it with respect, and it's there when I need it.

Money can't buy you love, true. But it *can* buy travel, comfort, a home, fabulous shoes, and an exquisite dinner at Le Petit Zinq on the Left Bank. It ain't love—but sometimes it sure can make you feel mmm-mmm gooooood.

But if you abuse it, money can turn your life into a *living hell.* It can destroy your credit, damage your health, ruin your relationships with friends, and even wreck your marriage.

Sound like an exaggeration? It isn't. A lot of marriages that end in divorce do so because of money problems. You've got to learn, and learn early, how to take care of your money because there isn't anyone you can depend on to do it for you.

(And don't even *think* you're just gonna marry some rich guy who'll take care of you for the rest of your life so you won't ever have to worry your pretty head about such stuff. That's old news.)

What's it gonna be, girl? For richer or for poorer? The choice is yours.

Gimme Some Credit!

Credit card: friend or foe?

Let's just say it's an attractive, mysterious stranger whose acquaintance you want to make—but with whom you must be wary. Why? Because having a card establishes good credit, and good credit is a tool to get what you need in the world. But a few wrong moves and you are in danger (more on the perils of bad credit later).

The first hurdle is *getting* the card. It's one of those catch-22 situations where you need a card to get credit, but you can't get one if you don't already have credit. (Which came first, the chicken or the egg?) If you're in college, there are probably credit card

WISE WOMAN

Linda Ellerbee, TV producer

Independence

It's so important to be financially independent. For a woman, it's the most important thing there is, along with feeding the soul. You can't be dependent on someone else for your money because it will leave you feeling awful. Even if you are married, I recommend separate bank accounts. I found myself alone with two children when a man left me for a younger woman. I vowed at that time I would never be dependent on anyone else ever again for the support of my kids or myself. Have your own money. Period.

companies pounding on your dorm door trying to seduce you with the pleasures of their pristine plastic cards.

Students are usually offered first-time cards with low limits and low interest rates—a great way to establish good credit (again—only if you're careful). I was offered one in college but I panicked: "Oh my God, this can only spell T-R-O-U-B-L-E!" I convinced myself, and I didn't sign on.

When I left college and went boldly out into the world, my cautious decision backfired. I tried to buy a car and was rejected because my accumulated credit added up to a big fat zilch. Being turned down for a car loan was the least of my worries—my lack of credit had all kinds of serious repercussions. There were apartments to rent, phones to connect, cable to hook up, etc., etc., etc., all of which demanded a good credit report! I kicked myself in the butt for not nabbing that card when I had the chance.

911 TIP Get a credit card as early as possible to begin establishing credit.

If you don't get a card in college, you can do what I did—get a parent or friend with good credit to co-sign for you.

As soon as you get your impatient and hungry paws on that shiny, unadulterated card bearing your name in embossed gold letters, heed this ancient commandment:

If You Buy It—The Bills Will Come.
And sooner or later you gotta pay.

Sooner is better. The longer you wait, the more you have to pay because you're paying interest. Interest is how the credit card people make their money! They are not fools. They want you to take a long time to pay off what you owe because every month they take their cut.

They also hope to brainwash you a bit. They hope that when you use their card instead of cash, you don't even feel like you're *spending money*, so you charge up a storm. I have operated under this delusion.

Let me make a confession: I am a shoe junkie. From leopard-print stilettos to comfy canvas mules to flowered hippie platforms to sleek leather slides . . . my feet get all tingly just thinking about the options.

Ten years after using my credit card in good faith, I turned bad.

Flushed with my new modeling pay, I'd walk into a Gucci store (or a Nine West, or a Sigerson Morrison, or a Via Spiga) and if they had something beautiful in a size 11, I had to try it on. And if the shoe fit . . . well, you know . . . I was like Cinderella.

I was reckless, spending two hundred to three hundred dollars a pop every time I was in the neighborhood. Problem was I was *always* in the neighborhood—my office was down the block! Also in the 'hood was Henri Bendel. I'd stroll down Fifth Avenue and—*whoosh*—it was like a powerful wind yanked me off the sidewalk and forced me to the cosmetics counter.

I ask you—what's a girl with a card suppose to do? Next to shoes, lubricants, lotions, and liniments are my moral and mortal downfall. This cream lifts. This cream tucks. This cream separates. This cream performs acrobatics with your exfoliating epidermis! No cash? *No problem! Ka-ching!*

I could hear Betty and Wilma from *The Flintstones*: "CHARRRRRRGE IT!"

Soon, I hit my limit, and there was hell to pay.

And so I learned the second credit card commandment:

> **Only buy what you can pay for right away:**
> **Minimum payments are for suckers.**

If you're Julia Roberts and you earn $20 million per movie, go ahead—knock yourself out and buy another pair of Jimmy Choo shoes. Julia knows she can cover it. Do you?

If not, the interest that credit card companies charge ranges from 9 percent to 25 percent. If you spend like a drunken millionaire but pay only the minimum each month, your forty-dollar bottle of exotic African bath gel will end up costing you a hundred or even more in the long run. And you'll still be paying for the darn thing long after you've gotten out of the tub and toweled off.

When I got married, I was making minimum payments on two cards. My hubby, Phil, very money-smart, asked me: "Are you CRAZY?!" (He asks me this question a lot, as you will soon see.)

As an engagement present, he paid off my debts with his bar mitzvah money ("What a sweetheart!" coos Natasha), then watched as I cut up the new batch of cards I had just received in the mail. He stopped me just on the brink of doing more damage.

911 TIP You need only one card to establish your credit. Don't give in to the dozens of offers that arrive in the mail.

Heed my friend "Tamara"'s tale of woe: She sunk so deep in credit card debt she couldn't keep up minimum monthly payments on her five cards. Her credit plummeted; she couldn't rent an apartment or even get her phone connected.

She took drastic action: cut up all her credit cards and had her bank "consolidate" her debts. They paid off what she owed, then she owed the bank one big lump sum. It took two years to pay it all off, and five more years before her name was cleared and her credit pure and good again.

My buddy Natasha was nearing the credit danger zone when she moved from Toronto to New York five years ago. You can imagine her giddiness when she learned that her credit rating in the United States was as pure as driven snow. She started off with a clean slate, thanked her lucky financial stars she could start anew (it was like being given a chance to live life over again), and vowed never to make a late payment again. She's kept her promise.

But let's hope you don't have to move to another country or enter some kind of witness protection program to escape anxious creditors. Take charge of your charge card.

911 TIP Are you in credit card trouble? Here are three wonderful online credit-counseling resources to check out:

http://www.DEBITADVICE.ORG
http://www.CONSUMERCREDIT.COM (1-800-769-3571)
http://www.NFCC.ORG (National Foundation for Credit Counseling)

Also, if you have no idea what your credit rating is and want to find out, go to your bank and arrange to have it mailed to you (for a small fee, of course). Knowledge is better than ignorance.

Today, I am a consumer in control.

I walk by Henri Bendel. I take a look at the goodies. I ask myself: Do I *really* need it?

Once in a while, I weaken when faced with a jar of exotic mango facial scrub brimming with solid milk cleansing grains made from yogurt cultured by a hundred-year-old Bulgarian farmer in the mountains of the Old Country. Who wouldn't?

But mostly, I just walk on by. It's liberating to just say No.

Piggy Bank
(When to Start Saving? Yesterday.)

I wish I'd started saving the day I drew my first breath.

My financial whiz consultant, Gregory Prato, never tires of reminding me that if I saved $8.20 per day—the amount of one Krispy Kreme doughnut and one café latte per day—put the money in a high quality 10 percent earning mutual fund, I'd have approximately $1.3 million saved by age sixty.

MAMMA MIA! NOW THAT'S A BIG, SPICY MEATBALL.

"This is a story to tell younger people who say they can't save right now," says Greg, "that they 'don't have enough money,' or 'don't make enough.' This proves that you can do this easily on a waitress's salary!"

Start saving today. Here's how.

Put 10 percent of every paycheck you get into a savings account. It doesn't matter if it's a dollar or a thousand dollars.

"You have expenses, you invest in your career, and that's important. But you have to take a little bit out each month for yourself that will work *for* you," Gregory says.

My first experience with putting money into savings was a disaster. When I was nine years old, I inherited a sum of money from

WISE WOMAN

Trisha Yearwood, singer

Accounted For

I'm a banker's daughter, so I've had to balance my checkbook since I was five years old. My sister and I had savings accounts when we were little to teach us about saving money and being able to financially take care of ourselves. I never felt like I needed to depend on anybody. I had a checking account by the time I was a teenager to teach me slowly how to manage my own money. Sometimes I'd put money in the piggy bank—sometimes I went to the mall with it. That was okay, too.

I work in a very unpredictable industry. Some years are great financially and there are also lean years. The banker's daughter in me made me a very conservative spender. I always ask my accountant and my business manager when I want to buy something. It's good. I'm thirty-seven years old. I'm probably not going to be on a tour bus at eighty years old singing, "She's in Love with the Boy," so I save for my future.

A woman learning how to take care of her money is not a feminist idea; it's just a practical idea. So what if you meet Prince Charming and he takes care of everything.

I know some women whose husbands took care of everything and then when their husbsands passed away, they didn't know how to write a check! In my sister's family, all the credit cards are in her husband's name and she learned a few years ago that she didn't have any credit! What if she needed it? Here she was, a grown woman with good money and no debt, and she had to work really hard to get a credit card!

my grandmother and my parents invested it using a well-known financial consulting company.

One morning over breakfast, many years later, we see an article on the front page of *The New York Times* saying the company is being investigated for wrongdoing and my broker was among the dubious bunch.

911 TIP Think about tomorrow. What you save today will grow.

After major, major hassles, I finally got a little bit of the money back—money that was immediately put toward my college tuition fees. But that inheritance was supposed to be the rock-solid foundation upon which my life-long financial future was to be built, and it was mostly gone, never to be seen again.

My second experience with saving money was much more rewarding and far more romantic. As soon as Phil and I got engaged, he proposed another merger: "Let's open a joint savings account. Let's start building our future right now."

I saw his bet and raised it. He had diligently saved thousands of dollars for my engagement ring, but I told him, "Honey, forget the rock!"

We needed to start saving for our new apartment and for new furniture.

"We can't cozy up in front of a piece of jewelry. But we can use that money to find a place with a fireplace we can snuggle in front of together. The ring can wait."

We put the dough into our new savings account. Diamonds may be a girl's best friend, but a joint savings account and an overstuffed love seat are more romantic—and more practical.

Budgets (Drawing the Lines)

Emme's Budget, age 21
Incoming Money: $15,000 annually as a reporter in Flagstaff, Arizona.
Rent: $320/month
Food: $100/month

Emma

Gas: $25 to go to friend's gas tank

Fun: $150 (movies, drinks, occasional pizza)

The other day I was watching a rerun of Oprah. Onstage sat a woman, her husband, and their two preteen kids. The family was staging an intervention: Mom had a spending problem. Whenever she walked into a shopping mall she got a huge adrenaline rush and spent uncontrollably.

Not only was she living the fantasy that using credit cards "didn't count as spending," but she refused to believe the family was headed for financial ruin. She was in denial even though creditors were calling their home nonstop. The kids' college money was used up and they were on the verge of losing their home.

In front of the audience (and millions of viewers), the husband let her have it straight.

"I am getting a lawyer, and if you don't get in control, we are getting a divorce!"

Oprah's relationship expert, Dr. Phil, pointed to her and said: "Lady, you better *wake up and smell the coffee*!" The audience stood up and cheered.

This is an extreme example of someone who had absolutely no idea how much she had, how much she spent, how much she owed, or how much damage she had done to her family and herself.

I'm grateful that, out of necessity, I learned how to keep a budget as soon as I got out of college. Budgets are simple and they can save your hide.

Here's the general, simple way to do it:

Get a notebook or a ledger. Look at your paycheck and write down the net amount you earn on one side of the page and a list of your expenses on the other side. Make sure your top five expenses include those all-important essentials that keep you fed, housed, and healthy. (A lot of young people skip health insurance because it's so expensive, but my suggestion is to find some plan, *anything*, than can fit in your budget to help you in case of emergency.)

After you pay the essentials, you pay yourself—remember the 10 percent rule!!!!! When you take charge of your finances and organize your money this way, you're sending a powerful message to your subconscious: I AM IN CONTROL!

Damn straight. Don't let anyone knock you off budget, screw up your financial planning, or separate you from your hard earned dough.

If you really want to get serious, roll up your sleeves and get ready to number crunch. Be honest and ruthless with yourself and you will learn where your money is going. You can also use a personal finance computer program like Quicken or Microsoft Money to help organize yourself.

With a bit of discipline, a budget can lead you to financial freedom.

SAMPLE BUDGET LIST

INCOME

Salary and wages

Tips

Investment Income

Interest from savings

Interest from other accounts

Royalties

Dividends

Other

TOTAL GROSS INCOME _____

Deductions from Gross Income

State income tax

Federal income tax

Health insurance

State disability insurance

Social Security or self-employment tax

Other (specify)

TOTAL DEDUCTIONS _____

NET SPENDABLE INCOME _____

(Subtract deductions from gross income)

FIXED MONTHLY EXPENSES
(expenses that will keep a roof over your head)

Household:

Rent/mortgage

Property tax

Telephone

Utilities

Cable TV

Subtotal _____

Insurance:

Life

Health

Homeowner's or renter's

Personal Property

Subtotal _____

Debt Payments:

Household items

Credit cards

Bank loans

Personal loans

Other

Subtotal _____

Education:

Tuition

Room and board

Books

Other

Subtotal _____

Transportation:

Car payments

Car insurance

Parking

Commuting

Other

Subtotal _____

Memberships:

Clubs/Gym

Other

Subtotal _____

TOTAL FIXED EXPENSES _____

FLEXIBLE EXPENSES

Groceries

Restaurants

Cleaning products

Yard care/Gardener

Cleaning person

House repairs (windows, fixing the faucet, etc.)

New appliances

New furniture

Home improvements (new patio, additions, painting)

Clothing

Laundry

Dry cleaning

Auto repair & upkeep

Gas & Oil

Personal bus or train fares

Health (not covered by insurance)

Other

Personal:

Hair, face, and body products

Hair salon

Movies

Hobbies

Vacation/Travel

Newspapers

Alcohol/Tobacco

Other

Gifts:

Birthdays

Weddings

Religious celebrations

Anniversaries
Other

Contributions:
Charitable
Religious
Schools/colleges
Other

Now, subtract your fixed expenses from the figure you get from gross income minus deductions. The numbers won't lie and the truth will be told. Here you will see if you are in the red (bad) or in the black (good), which expenses are too high, and how much money is available for investments.

---

911 TIP From www.cnnmoney.com

- Expect the unexpected. Build a cash cushion worth three to six months' living expenses in case you lose your job, get sick, or have other emergencies that would cut your income drastically. National Fraud Information Center hotline and advice: 1-800-876-7060.
- For information on getting a card and rebuilding your credit? Log on to **www.myvesta.org.**
- If you believe you've been the victim of ID theft, contact the credit bureaus **Equifax**, **Experian**, and **Trans Union**, and ask that a fraud alert be placed on your account. These are the three major credit unions. If you want to get a credit report, they cost $8.50 each or you can order three at once for $29.95 from **myvesta.org.** (The FTC is the first place to report ID theft— they direct you from there. If the theft is not on file with the FTC little else can be done to prosecute offenders.)
- If you've got more debt than you can manage, get help now. Try the Consumer Credit Counseling Services or **myvesta.org.**

I remember a college girlfriend who came from a wealthy family. My budget constraints exasperated her.

"What's the big deal? It's just ten bucks to go to the pizza joint! Come on!"

I was too self-conscious to tell her *that ten bucks was my food for the whole week!* My brain was like a road map on how to eat and live cheap with well-marked routes. I knew which fast-food joints sold cheap tacos along with a free soda. I knew how to get to work using one bus instead of two—saving a token.

As a young reporter in Flagstaff, I was expected to look stylish for the camera—trouble was my measly income of fifteen thousand a year. Thank God for a local clothing store that supplied all of our on-air clothes in exchange for a credit at the end of the news. And it was at this store that I discovered the beauty of layaway.

I had spotted a suede, hunter-green coat with leather trim in their shop window and, man, I wanted that jacket. I put twenty-five bucks down and added "leather coat" to my budget list. Every payday I put ten dollars toward it. When it was finally paid for I wore it into the ground.

I tried hard to spend according to the financial plan I'd drawn up, but Murphy's Law was at work: There was always the threat that some catastrophe would throw me off my budget—like my little car that *couldn't* or the time I got whiplash courtesy of a colleague's fancy driving. I was in so much pain I had to go to the chiropractor, which left me scraping the bottom of the barrel money-wise. I remember having tears in my eyes as I wondered how I was going to afford to eat. My roommate Kim said, "Don't worry, I've been there. Buy a potato, put some butter on it, and then put a dollar of gas in your car. You'll be able to eat and get to work. You can do this until the next paycheck. You'll be okay."

I did just that and survived a really tough time. You can, too.

Bills, Bills, Bills

It looks really cool in the movies when the down-on-her-luck heroine living some kind of artsy, bohemian lifestyle lets her bills stack up in a dusty pile under her bed and she doesn't answer the phone because it's probably the landlord shouting about her bounced rent check and so what if the power is off andjustwhocaresanyway.

Some rich, cute guy like Richard Gere in *Pretty Woman* always finds her lack of discipline "amusing" and comes to her rescue.

In real life, it's not so cool. In real life, Richard Gere isn't going to pick you up with his very white stallion or limousine and take you to his castle. Even Sarah, the Duchess of York—who married a prince and lived in a palace *in real life*—is now paying off debt. So do what you know you need to do.

Organize

1. Make a place to keep your bills (a shoebox, a folder, a shelf) and lots of stamps.
2. When the bills come in the mail, open them immediately—and then put them away immediately. Try not to have a piece of paper touch your hands more than once (meaning: Deal with it, then move on!).
3. Make out your checks, seal your envelopes, and write the due date on the outside of the envelope in pencil. If you need to wait for paychecks to clear or other bills to be paid, you know how long you have until you must drop it in the mailbox.
4. Send bills at least five days before they're due.
5. Buy a ledger book to write down what is owed, what has been paid, and dates payments were sent.

6. Check if you can make payments by phone or online. If so, mark deadlines on your daily calendar and make the phone call (or log on) by the due date.

I had a friend who paid her bills only when she got "final notices." She had no idea late payments were recorded and went against her credit rating. "No one ever told me!"

Well, I'm telling you. Ignorance won't win your case in court.

Taxing Out

Natasha's dad always says, "There are only two things in life you absolutely must do: pay taxes and die."

I learned this lesson the hard way. A year into our marriage, Phil and I were in the middle of cocktails with friends in the living room before treating them to an anniversary dinner at a really elegant restaurant. The phone rang. A minute later, Phil was as pale as a ghost.

"It was our accountant," he said, pulling me into the kitchen. "Big trouble." Apparently, I hadn't paid any taxes that year for my new, sideline career as a model and now we owed the Internal Revenue Service (cough, choke) . . . seven thousand dollars!

Dinner that night turned out to be at the local pizzeria. The next day, we handed over all our wedding-gift money to Uncle Sam, who didn't even say thanks!

It was really, really scary. I had been clueless. I thought because I had two jobs going at the same time—I was still a real estate marketing executive when I started modeling—the tax I was paying on my marketing money was enough. To me, the twenty thousand I had made from modeling was "yippee" money!!!

Woohoo! Unfortunately, the good folks at the IRS were a tad miffed I hadn't invited them to the party.

Since then, I tell every model or freelancer starting out to save 35 percent of every paycheck she gets and put it away for taxes—whether it's two hundred dollars or ten thousand. When the government comes to collect, you'll probably owe more like 25–32 percent. Then you can put the rest into your savings account. If you don't prepare for taxes, the fines of paying late and the compounded interest on what you owe can set you back for a very, very long time. Trust me. If the IRS knocks on your door, you better be ready to fork over the dough.

Taxes are confusing. When does anybody teach us this stuff anyway?

On my first visit to a tax office I said, "Give me the easiest darn form you have."

They did. It's even spelled "E-Z"—how much simpler can you get? It basically instructs, "Put your income here, the year here, and sign here." That worked for me. Just tell me how much I owe and show me where to sign. You can go to any major tax place, like Schwab, and pick up these forms. Or you can go to a tax preparation office and for a few hundred bucks hire someone to do your returns for you.

 Take Note: *For more tax information go online at* ***www.irs.gov*** *and* ***www.taxes.yahoo.com.***

I used to shove receipts into my pockets and then get home and shove them into a big green garbage bag and not look at them again for as long as possible.

Every April, spring and tax time arrived. I'd spend three frenzied days with no sleep and too much coffee (it was like being back in college, cramming for exams), dumping out all my

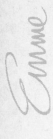

receipts on the floor, trying desperately to read my faded little taxi printouts at six o'clock as the sun rose.

After a decade of banging my head against the wall, I developed a saner system.

I now have an envelope for each month where I write different categories: food, hair, makeup, nails, taxis, etc. At the end of each month, I sit down *like a normal human being* and add up the envelope's contents and write it on the front. At the end of the year, I have twelve neat envelopes that my assistant sends to my tax guy.

Done.

Clean bookkeeping, clear head.

Make a Statement

Every month your bank sends you a statement of what's going on in your bank account—withdrawals, deposits, and minor charges. Check over your statements with a keen eye because, yes, even the bank and other worldly institutions make mistakes or take advantage of a girl like you.

I never used to check. Then one day I was glancing at a statement and saw all sorts of charges for ten dollars and twenty dollars and had no idea what they were. I called the bank and found out that I was paying charges and fees every time I used an ATM or wrote a check. I'd had no idea. It added up to at least two hundred dollars per year.

If I'm going to throw away two hundred dollars, I'd rather it be on something I *want*. I switched to an account that didn't charge me for every move I made.

Keep track of how much is going into and out of your account so you don't make any slip-ups yourself. Bounced checks at the dry-cleaner and manicurist just are not cool. Even a ten-dollar bounce wreaks havoc with your credit (and doesn't make you popular where you do business).

Bounce, Bounce

Same advice goes for credit card reports: check them!

Looking over my VISA bill, I noticed my gym had accidently charged me twice in one year for my membership. I called them and the manager was apologetic and remedied the situation. I bet a lot of people lose money this way.

Once I called up my credit card company to check a charge I didn't recognize and found it was for an Italian restaurant I had never even been to. Listen, if I've enjoyed grilled calamari and garlic bread somewhere, I'm gonna remember it.

When you hand over your credit card, you never know who's going to make note of your number. You never know if some waiter might get creative with a pen and change your forty-dollar light lunch into a four-hundred-dollar banquet. I arranged with my credit card company to telephone me if there are big expenditures that are "out of character" for my usual spending routine.

> ▶ **TAKE NOTE: Hey, I don't remember buying a Suzanne Somers Thigh Master!**
>
> *If you see a charge on your credit card that's not yours, call your creditors immediately and call up the establishment and investigate. If the purchase is not yours, the credit card company should delete the charge and give you a new card with a new number.*

Rainy Days and Mondays

I never leave home without a bus/subway token, a credit card, an ATM card, a quarter, and ten bucks in small bills. This is in case of an actual (little) emergency like my car breaks down and my cell phone conks out. Thelma and Louise could have made it to Mexico *no problemo* with this stash.

And then there are emergencies of the soul.

There are times when you need to treat yourself to a little something or you will go batty. Everybody needs that feeling of "Oooh, that feels good!"

It doesn't have to cost a lot: You can get that "Ooooh" feeling by slowly sipping a four-dollar Saturday-afternoon double mocha cappuccino grande at Starbucks as you try to figure out *The New York Times* crossword (five dollars). A foot massage in Chinatown (fifteen dollars). Or go to a double-bill matinee and have pop-corn—*with* butter (thirteen dollars). Light a candle, get in the tub, and slather yourself with one of those sweet, gooey skin scrubs that smell good enough to eat and soak for an hour as the steam rises (six dollars).

Rainy days are days when you've had a bad day at the office, need to stay in on a Friday night, order takeout Chinese, and not feel guilty about it.

Rainy days are when you wanna buy yourself a bottle of wine to take home and share with a friend . . . just because.

Rainy days are when you need to buy a new ten-dollar lipstick that makes you feel like a million bucks.

Rainy days are when your friend needs cheering up, so you take her out for tea and scones with clotted cream and straw-berry jam!

I used to save rainy-day money by hiding it.

I would leave five-dollar bills inside pockets and between pages of books and I loved finding them weeks or months later. (Just watch you don't throw it in the laundry.)

> **TAKE NOTE:** *The Beatles sang, "The best things in life are free . . ." With all this money talk I want to remind you that money isn't the be-all, end-all. When I lecture at colleges and ask students what they want to do with their careers, some say, "I want to be a millionaire!" I tell them, "Don't let money be your goal. It's just a by-product. Do what makes you happy in the process or else you'll end up lonely with no one to share your fortune with."*

Q & A with Gregory Prato, financial consultant, vice president at Merrill Lynch

Q: *What is your best saving advice?*
Gregory: Think small and pay yourself first. If you are twenty-one years old and saved just $3,000 a year (2002's IRA contribution limit) in a high-quality stock mutual fund *averaging* 10 percent per year, you would amass nearly $1,325,000 by the time you were age sixty.

Q: *How does a girl find a good financial adviser?*
Gregory: If you don't know anyone, call two or three major firms and two or three independent advisers. The problem is when you call them you are going to be given the "broker of the day," meaning the individual assigned phone duty to handle folks like you who randomly call in. This obviously makes it hit or miss. Ask the following questions: How long have you been in the business? How many clients do you have?

Emme

How do you get paid? How often can I expect to hear from you? Do you provide financial planning services and is there a fee for this?

Also ask friends whom they use. Narrow it down to three that you feel you can trust and then "follow your gut."

Q: *What's the best way to invest?*

Gregory: The key to investing is not putting all your eggs (that would be your hard-earned dollars) in one basket (that is any *one* investment). Initially, the most important objective is to develop your *own* (not your best friend's) risk tolerance (this is where that financial adviser will come in handy). Once you find out how risk tolerant (or risk adverse) you are, you will divide up, or *allocate*, your investment dollars among stocks, bonds, and cash. The fancy term for this is *asset allocation*. How much you plan to invest will usually be the deciding factor as to whether you allocate your dollars into mutual funds or individual securities. Once again, your newly acquired trusted adviser will be able to help you out here.

Q: *What should I do if I'm late paying a bill?*

Gregory: We have all at one time or another been late paying a bill. The credit card companies, however, show no mercy. First they whack you in the head with a late payment charge, then they start hitting you with double-digit interest for the time the balance is overdue. Talk about a bad hair day. If this happens, give them a call. My experience is if you're nice to them they will almost always let the first one slide. If the person on the phone is unforgiving, ask to speak to their supervisor. If they put you off, hang up and try again with a different representative. As a last resort, threaten to close the account out and then follow through if they still don't accept your groveling.

Q: *How do I keep from getting to my credit card limit?*

Gregory: By all means use your credit card; just pay off your balance *each* month. Credit cards are the greatest investment in the world . . . for the credit card companies that is. Where on earth can you get a guaranteed 18 percent (or more) return on your investments? The credit card companies know and it's on the balance that thousands upon thousands of people carry each month on their charge cards. Carrying a balance on these high-interest credit cards is the equivalent of financial suicide. STOP IT NOW!

Q: *Any other tips?*

Gregory: Get the point(s)! With so many cards competing for your business, don't stand for a credit card that is not tied in to some sort of rewards program, be it airline frequent flier miles, points toward merchandise at stores, or, as many now have, both.

FINAL THOUGHT

Money is both a means and a means to an end. It can make you or break you, get you from here to there, buy you this or that, build your status or ruin you. The green stuff is perplexing but one thing's for sure: having some is better than not having any at all.

Money can't buy me love—that is certainly clear, so don't let anyone tell you different. Love isn't in a thing you hang on a wall or something you wear on your arm. Money can be deceiving. It pretends to show who is powerful and who is not by what they own. Have you ever wanted to sell all of your possessions, sit back, and see what happened? You hear about people downsizing their lives (selling everything) and feeling like a ton of bricks was lifted from their shoulders. Why? They chose to be free from the

possessions they bought. They had filled their lives with things that represented power, status, and identity. They no longer needed the possessions because they figured out that deep within themselves they were already powerful on their own.

Money can help heal the sick, feed the poor, and rebuild New York City.

Yes, money makes the world go 'round, but the question I want to leave you with is: Will you be its master or its slave?

career
emergency!

D o you bound out of bed every morning eager to start your day in a career that invigorates and challenges you? Or do you drag yourself listlessly out of slumber and sleep-walk your way to a job you despise and slave over just to pay the bills?

I know too many people who have spent a lifetime in trades that mean nothing to them. For whatever reason—money, family, fear—they never explored or expanded their unique talents into careers. To these people, their jobs have little to do with who they really are or what they once dreamed for themselves. I think some people aren't even *aware* that you can actually have a dream and then make it a reality. Many of us are conditioned just to go for the money part of a job, not the heart part.

I know a woman who was an incredible—and I mean *stupen-dous*—musician as a teenager. She was the lead in a local band that drew devoted audiences wherever they performed. After col-lege, she went to law school because that's what her family of

lawyers expected and encouraged her to do. "Music is just a hobby," they told her, "it's not something serious."

She is miserable today. She hates law. But it still has never occurred to her that she might have followed her talents into the music business and been a success. Late at night sometimes when her husband and children are asleep, she takes out her guitar and strums a few tunes and gets sad and doesn't really know why. I think, if you ignore your passion . . . a bit of you dies with it.

But it is *never* too late! Whether you start at age five or fifty-five—doing what you love to do will lift your spirit and bring you fulfillment.

Natasha's father, Basil, is at work on his first novel at age seventy-five. He always had the dream to write but got side-tracked along the way by his disapproving parents, money, family obligations, and time constraints. As soon as he retired from teaching high school, he dusted off his old manual typewriter with the jagged ribbon and got to work.

"I wrote two pages today!" he often calls Natasha to report. He is as giddy as a kid who has discovered finger painting for the first time.

Whether you discover your career passion early or late in life, it is important to pay attention to it and let it unfold. Your inner passion is *you*.

Finding Your Passion

In college, I took a philosophy course as a fluke. But by the end of my first lecture I was enthralled. I dreamed of Descartes. I slobbered over Sartre. I pontificated about Plato. I was convinced I was going to be a highly paid professional philosopher after graduation. (I obviously hadn't been checking out the want ads.)

And then I had a philosophical crisis of epic proportion. I

told my stepfather I planned to major in philosophy and he freaked out.

"No WAY!" he yelled.

I cried, I moped, I fell apart. Then I pulled myself together and wondered: Okay, what else can I do? Well, I always loved talking. I loved exchanging information and I *loved* telling stories. And the first time I walked into a campus radio and TV station I got goose bumps on my goose bumps because I had found all those, the three things I loved, in one place. Hello, showbiz!!!

Lights, camera, action!

Finding your passion is like finding your career soul mate. You "date around" a bit, trying various jobs, but one day you find something you love so much you wanna marry it and see it every morning before your first cup of coffee.

Some people are born knowing their passions.

Mozart was writing symphonies by the time he was five years old. As a teenager Arnold Schwarzenegger was flexing in front of a mirror and envisioning himself as Mr. Universe.

Mozart and Arnie? Who knew they had so much in common! But they both had a passion for what they loved—and they followed their dreams and their dreams came true.

When I was in high school I'd imagine myself in front of the camera talking to interesting people about their interesting lives. It's mind-blowing the moment your vision intersects with reality. After I had done my first major TV assignment in college—an on-camera interview with basketball player Pearl Washington—I lay in bed all night as my heart went boom, boom, BOOM! I felt like I was doing exactly what I was supposed to do in this world.

Destiny. Or as the Italians say it: *Destino!*

It's the feeling an athlete gets when she's in a great groove. I had that same thrilling feeling the first time I stepped on the set of *The Tonight Show* as a studio page. After watching Johnny Carson for years and yearning to meet him and do what he does,

there I was—five feet away from him. I could imagine myself in that chair, hearing Ed's voice . . . *Heeeeeere's* Emme!

I'm a big believer in creating your own destiny. Big breaks do come along, but they don't mean a lot unless you've prepared for them. Like many people, the journey to my dream job followed a long and winding road with a lot of twists and turns and unexpected detours along the way.

WISE WOMAN

Camryn Manheim, actress, (TV's *The Practice*)

Everything Connects . . .

Life is like a connect-the-dots puzzle. Before you see a picture emerge, you must lay down five thousand dots. Each dot seems meaningless at the time. But as the years go by, the dots start to connect. But to make the dots, you have to take action. Nobody knocks on your door. It's a myth you will walk down the street and be "discovered."

Life is like a pension plan and the universe is your employer. It will match what you put into it. If you put in 20 percent effort, you will operate at 40 percent. But if you put in 100 percent, the universe will match you and you'll be operating at 200 percent.

Don't be afraid to try something new. Steven Spielberg started with a "first." Stephen King started with a "first." Even William Shakespeare started with a "first." Everybody has to stumble on his or her "firsts." Everyone started off questioning whether he or she can do it or not. You don't know the answer until you take that leap of faith. But we all have the power to transform our lives at any given point.

You can reevaluate your goals daily and you shouldn't be afraid to change course midstream. At the end of every day, I ask myself, "Do I have any regrets?" I never regret things I *did* do. I only regret things I *didn't* do. That proves to me that chasing your dream, standing on the mountaintop, and yelling out loud what you want, is better than *not* doing it.

Brainstorm

Not everybody is like Arnie and Mozart—lucky enough to discover their passion at a young age. Sometimes it can be confusing trying to decide where to focus your energy and which dreams to chase. It can help to write down all your dreams and, if you have to, go after them one at a time until one of them clicks.

When I was starting out, my aspirations were pretty darn vague. All I knew was I wanted to meet exciting people and do exciting things. I wanted to have an impact on people's lives. I wanted a flexible schedule. And if I had to be in an office at a desk, at the very least I wanted good lighting. Those blue-tinged overhead fluorescent tubes zapped my chi. Yuck! Our buddy Liza calls it "hag lighting."

Here was my dream list:

Marine biologist (I loved dolphins)
Archaeologist (I loved history and artifacts)
Athlete (I loved rowing)
Sports reporter (I loved sports)
Talk show host (I loved Johnny Carson)
Philosopher (I shopped, therefore I was)

When you think about what you want to do, let your imagination run wild. What would you do if *anything* were possible? Don't be shy. Write down ALL your dreams no matter how ridiculous you think they are.

Dream Big 🌟 POW 🌟 Dream Vast ⚡ZAP⚡ Dream Silly

Remember when I said you could watch movies all day as a career? A journalist I know, Leah Rozen, actually gets paid to watch movies. Talk about a dream job—Leah's the movie critic for *People* magazine.

"I fell in love with movies when I was twelve years old," says Rozen, "and I spent more than a dozen years as a reporter and editor before I finally started getting paid to tell people my opinions about what I saw on the big screen. Being a movie critic is the best job I'll ever have . . . and it beats actually working!"

I have another friend whose teachers would have bet he'd never amount to much. He was constantly getting in trouble and being sent down to detention for doodling cartoons in class. Well, he doodled himself all the way to the bank. Today's he's a millionaire, creating computer-animated special effects for blockbuster films.

Create Your Career from Something You Love to Do

Don't just make a list of your dreams and goals—make that list a reality by reading it every day!

Stick the list on your bathroom mirror and stare at it each morning while you brush your teeth. Put a copy on the fridge door so you'll see it every time you grab a snack. Make that list sink in. It's got to become part of your psyche. Don't keep it in your sock drawer. Put your dreams *in your face*. Don't ignore your passion!

I had a friend who was so good with animals, we used to call her Dr. Dolittle. And when I say Dr. Dolittle I'm not kidding—if you ever saw her with animals you would swear she was talking to them. Critters just loved her and would do whatever she asked them to—and the feeling was mutual.

"That was my dream!" Wendy recalls today. "To be Dr. Dolittle! I knew what I wanted to do from age four."

But she didn't know how to make it happen and the last thing she wanted was to go into the family tie-manufacturing business. Understandably, she wasn't happy. She moved on to other jobs and began a career in advertising, but still the fulfillment people get from having a passion for their work was missing.

"I was miserable. I finally realized I *had* to work with animals," she says.

She started training dogs and riding horses in her spare time. That inflamed her passion for pets so much that she quit advertising, began volunteering at a vet hospital, and headed back to NYU to study sciences.

"I want to be a dog behaviorist," she announced to me one day.

"A *what*?" I'd never heard of an animal behaviorist, but I knew if anyone could get into an animal's head, she could. She had a gift and I cheered her on for being brave enough to embrace it.

Other people saw her talents, too. One day when she was in the park with her dog, Clouseau, several people asked her where she had found such a well-behaved canine.

"Who trained your dog?" they all asked. That was exactly the kind of inspiration she needed to start her own dog-training business—no matter what anyone else thought.

"My parents were horrified," she said. But eight years later, she's like the character in the film *The Horse Whisperer*. She's the Edgar Cayce of the animal kingdom. She literally gets paid to talk to animals! Her workdays are never, ever boring.

For one job she was phoned by a woman who asked her to figure out why her dog kept peeing every time he trotted into the kitchen.

Wendy communicated with the dog telepathically over the phone.

"Your kitchen was a different color before your husband

died, wasn't it?" she asked the woman, who was recently wid-owed.

"Yes, it was," the woman replied in amazement.

"Well, every time your dog goes into the kitchen, the change in color reminds him of the loss of his master and he gets upset, and pees. You have to change it back!"

The woman took Wendy's advice and changed the color back to the original.

Voilà! The dog stopped peeing in the kitchen.

In another case, a cat owner called her in a panic because the pet was missing.

"Did you look in the dumbwaiter?" Wendy asked, over the phone.

"Yes, we already looked there."

"Well, look again, and this time take a flashlight. She's down there."

And so she was! Talk about having a specialized talent.

"You have truly found your niche," I told my friend. "You are doing exactly what you are *supposed* to be doing."

I believe all of us have these God-given talents. Some of us just have to work harder than others to find them.

Take Action

I took my first baby step toward a dream job by applying for a summer intern position in the sports department at WTVH, a small CBS affiliate in Syracuse, New York.

Right off the bat, the sports editor told me to forget it.

"Nothing here for you, kid," he said.

But I knew what I wanted and paid no attention to his dismissive words. I was like a determined pit bull—I had sunk my teeth into the idea of working in the sports department and I wasn't

WISE WOMAN

Julie Payette, Canadian astronaut

Dream Big!

I remember when I was ten years old—I didn't speak English and was living in Montreal. I was a little girl who wanted to fly. Everyone just patted me on the head and said, "Sure, sure. You'll grow out of it."

Then I remember watching TV and seeing the Apollo astronauts walk on the moon and drive the lunar rover. I thought, "That's great! I want to do that!" The idea that you could wear a space suit and go in a rocket to the moon? That was for me. I was so inspired. Everybody thought I was just this crazy kid with these crazy dreams. But many years later, to my amazement, the dream became reality. After years of training, I became a member of a Space Shuttle crew, took off from Earth, and was granted the extraordinary privilege of working in space, floating in weightlessness and looking down onto our beautiful planet. I couldn't believe how far away I was and how far I had come since those years in Montreal. It was a fantastic adventure, from beginning to end.

I believe that with effort, anything is possible. If you have the will, the confidence, and acquire the skills—you can do anything. But you must pursue your dreams and Go For It! You can do anything you want in this world. You have your destiny in your own hands. You can accomplish great things. It's just a question of choosing what you love and putting the effort into it. Shakespeare once wrote: "Knowledge is the wing wherewith we fly to heaven."

So please, dare to dream!

going to let go. I sent a note to the sports editor at the end of that month—and another every month after that.

"Hello again, it's me, Emme, looking forward to taking a break from my rowing blisters this summer to do some sports reporting. If anything comes up, you know where to reach me. . . ."

Poor guy. I kept bothering him and he kept telling me, "Look,

there's nothing available, and even if there was, we've never had a female sports intern before."

That just made me even more determined.

"I don't care!" I kept answering him. "It's about time you DID hire a woman—and that woman is going to be me!"

After nine months, he finally broke down (I should say I *wore* him down) and he gave me a break. I had no illusions that I was going to start at the top.

"Look, kid," he said when he told me I could start work. "It's a thankless job, tedious work, lousy hours, and you aren't going to get paid a cent."

Yeeee Haaaa. Sign me up!

I started out as a glorified gopher, logging in baseball scores and fetching coffee for the *real* reporters. I hated logging those baseball scores and every tiny tedious detail of every inning.

But that's how the ladder to success works—one rung at a time. The first rung is often a really crappy place at first, but it is a huge step—maybe the biggest you'll ever take in your career. I mean look at it: One day I was being told I'd never work at a television station because I'm a woman—the next day there I am. Getting coffee and running errands, sure, but I was there . . . and just waiting to take that next step.

It didn't take long. Soon, I was editing sound bites and in a few months I actually did my first on-camera stand-up. Watch. Learn. Ask lots of questions. And when there's a need, be there and be prepared. I asked a thousand questions and made just as many mistakes, but I learned.

And it proved invaluable.

Three years later, when I was a full-fledged, general assignment reporter in Flagstaff, the main sports guy suddenly quit and they needed someone to cover Major League spring training.

Hellooooo! (Opportunity was ringing the buzzer.) I was the

only one at the station who'd done duty in the trenches—er, dugout.

I was immediately christened the temporary sports anchor/ reporter and sent off to spring training, where I interviewed some great sluggers—Mark McGwire and Jose Canseco to name a couple. It was a total big deal, and I got it because I had pushed my way into that "thankless" intern job and had been doing my "homework" ever since.

Action Begets Action

When I talk to college students, I hear a lot of attitude concerning their starting salaries. They say, "There's no way I'm going to take an entry level job! I want to start at fifty thousand . . . a hundred thousand. . . ." Well, once again, wake up and smell the coffee (and I don't mean an expensive double latte mochachino).

You need exposure and experience. You want to be an actor? Fetch coffee on a movie set and watch the actors work. You want to be an astronaut? Go to a space camp (yes, they do exist). You want to be a novelist? Find a local writer and ask if you can do some typing for him or her. The money might be peanuts, but the training will be invaluable.

And if you find that you don't like a job while interning, that's invaluable, too.

When I was a sports intern, I realized I loved talking to athletes but hated doing the day-to-day minutiae the job demanded. I found out right then and there that being a sports anchor—one of the jobs on my dream list—wasn't for me. It was a relief—I discovered I was a doer, not a watcher, and could move on to chase other dreams with all the more passion.

WISE WOMAN

Sue Hendrickson, paleontologist/marine biologist

Sue discovered the T-rex skeleton "Sue" in 1990—it is the most complete skeletal structure of a T-rex dinosaur ever found. It's now exhibited at the Field Museum in Chicago, IL.

Detours

I grew up in a suburb of Chicago and I ran away at age seventeen. I was bored in school and I wanted to go out and see and do and learn everything. Serendipity led me to where I am today. I traveled around the country, I lived on a sailboat in Marin County, and I always wanted to have the freedom to choose what I wanted to do. There was an aquarium shop nearby and I used to go and look at the tropical fish. I decided to go to the Florida Keys and become a professional diver for tropical fish.

Two years later, I started doing modern salvage work, and then historical salvage work. I supported myself by diving for lobster and selling it. I would work three months out of the year and make enough money to travel the other nine months.

I got hooked on fossils when someone showed me an insect in a piece of amber that was 23 million years old. I became a self-taught fossil expert and began supplying them to museum collections.

I am totally addicted to the thrill of discovery. It is truly a thrill—physically, mentally, and emotionally—when you make a discovery. It's this huge WOW. That "wow" keeps me going. It sure isn't the money, because this is not a lucrative business.

Finding Sue, the T-rex, in 1990 made all the history books. I feel like she "waited" for me. Another favorite moment was in Chile, up in the high plateaus with volcanoes all around me, looking for meteorites. There weren't any animals, insects, airplanes . . . no noise at all.

I like to look for little things. When I was on the wreckage of a ship that sank in 1600, I found some gold dust lying at the bottom of the hull. When I find a human ring I always put it on for a moment. You immediately connect with whoever was wearing it when they died and imagine what was happening at the time of their death. I'm in total AWE of that kind of thing.

If I were to give advice to young women, I'd say to follow your dreams. You can do anything you want if you try hard enough. When I was younger, I was the only woman on the boats and barges. I had to prove myself all the time and do 150 percent all the time.

Never give up. I would have regretted it if I never took that first step. Be really stubborn about it! Have persistence, curiosity, and don't listen to the naysayers.

JUST DO IT!

Never Ever Give Up

On my first day on the job as a "real" reporter in Flagstaff, I handed my news director my script and watched her rip it up. She did the same thing every day for two weeks. I'd hand her a script and she'd rip it into little pieces right before my eyes.

If she didn't rip it up she'd mark it from top to bottom with her angry red grease pencil—crossing out whole sections, circling words, scribbling, "This doesn't make sense!" in huge, block letters you could read across the newsroom.

"Oh my God! What did they teach you in school?" she'd yell at me. "How can you expect to be a reporter?"

In desperation I called my friend Frank, who was a vice president at NBC. When he picked up the phone I was near tears. "I can't do this! They don't like me here! I'm totally humiliated! I'm leaving!"

Absolutely not, said Frank, who'd seen more than a few rookie reporters humbled into quitting.

"Hang in there! Don't give it up and you'll make it. You'll be fine, you'll see."

He was right. My news director's "tough love" approach shook me up, but it was for my own good. I was quickly whipped into shape and within a few months I handed her a clever story lead that had everybody rolling on the floor.

In a nearby highway accident, a truckload of Idaho potatoes had been tossed all over the freeway. That night in the news, I reported: "There was a SPUDACULAR event on the highway today . . . no casualties except for mashed potatoes *everywhere. . . .*"

I was henceforth known at the station by my new nickname— "Spud"!

I've come a long way since my reporting days in Flagstaff. I have accomplished many of the things I set out to do and many more I had never planned. Even though I've had my share of successes I constantly set new goals and find dreams for myself. And I still write them down, no matter how silly they may seem to me or anyone else.

Here's this year's batch.

Emme's career goals/2003–future

1. Produce/direct a film and have it debut at the Sundance film festival.
2. Go on an archaeology dig off the coast of Italy or near Pompeii and find pieces of a civilization from the second to fourth century B.C. or earlier.
3. Sing back-up vocals live with a classic rock band like Aerosmith.
4. Produce a children's TV show.
5. Write a series of mystery novels and have them adapted for the big screen or TV.
6. Train for and enter a triathlon.

7. Be invited to the White House for dinner, bowling, and a movie.

8. Continue expanding my network of empowering, enlightening, encouraging, and outstanding women in both my professional and personal life. To initiate change in the world with these relationships would be most rewarding.

9. Meet and interiew Doris Day, James Lipton (host of *Inside the Actor's Studio*), Larry King, Charlie Rose, Bill Moyers, and Johnny Carson. This list is huge so I've saved space by naming only a few. I would have loved to interview Dinah Shore.

10. I want my clothing to be available to women of a variety of income levels so that all women can have the opportunity to feel and look good every day.

11. See my friends' children playing with an Emme Doll one day!

12. Own a Yoga/healing center studio.

13. Have a working organic farm in upstate New York where I'd grow fruits and vegetables and make fresh cheeses and raise animals.

Remember, whatever you don't accomplish this year, add onto the next year's list. Eventually you will get to it, even if it takes a lifetime.

Go with the Flow

My very first job was taking clumps out of the holes on a golf green. Today my job is president of Emme Associates, Inc., creative director of The Emme Collection, model, spokesperson, author, worldwide lecturer, and, last but not least, mom. It took twenty-three years and twenty-nine jobs to get from there to here and it's been a long winding road with lots of detours. Take a look at my career path:

Golf green clumper, age 14
Grocery checkout girl, age 17
Lifeguard, age 17
Roller-skating waitress, age 18
Aerobics instructor, age 18
Physical trainer, age 18
Cocktail waitress, age 19
Deckhand, age 20
Production roadie, age 20
CBS affiliate intern, age 20
Waitress, age 22
Shoe saleswoman, age 22
Benetton salesgirl, age 22
NBC page, age 23
TV reporter, age 24
Receptionist, age 26
Wife, age 26
Marketing director, age 28
Model, age 28
Massage therapist, age 29
Author, *True Beauty*, age 32
TV host, E! Entertainment Television's *Fashion
    Emergency*, age 34
Revlon spokesperson, age 34
Magazine columnist, age 34
Creative director, The Emme Collection, age 35
Mother, age 37
Clairol model, age 37

Doll creator, age 37
Author, age 38

And I hope there's plenty more to come!

Like mine, your goals may change along the way. You too may take detours that turn out to be dead ends or avenues to exciting opportunities you never dreamed were possible.

I thought being a reporter was what I wanted to do, but life has a funny way of shaking your dreams loose. In Flagstaff, I was a television reporter, which made me a minor celebrity—even so, I had a measly salary, a broken-down car, and found that my job was actually starting to bring me down.

I covered the most depressing stories you can imagine: disasters, fires, murders . . . you name it. There came a day when I knew I just couldn't knock on one more door and ask grieving parents how it felt to lose their child. Ugh . . . I felt trapped and drained and wanted out. But still, what drew me to reporting was my love of telling stories and talking to people. I just had to find a more fulfilling way to do that.

I needed a change so I moved to New York and took a job as a receptionist at an investment firm.

I needed the money, but this job was definitely *not* on my wish list. I was totally off course and I knew it. But like I said about detours, sometimes a wrong turn sets you in the right direction.

That job led me to a job as a marketing director (again, *not* on the list). But one day I was on a business trip for my marketing company and flipping through the in-flight magazine I saw an article about full-figured models.

ZING!

I felt the hairs on the back of my neck stand up. My heart started thumping and I felt electricity surging through my body as I read the article. I called up the modeling agency as soon as I got off the plane and before I knew it I was modeling part-time on my days off and on lunch hours. Soon I was so busy modeling I left marketing altogether. A new dream and a new career had been born just by taking a detour. . . .

But even modeling wasn't enough after a while. I was starting to learn that one thing *always* leads to another if you keep your heart and your options open. Just when I was getting restless with only posing for the camera and feeling a need to use my voice, I was signed by Revlon to be their first full-figured spokesperson. That job gave me even greater exposure and led to my TV show *Fashion Emergency*.

> **Take Note: Say "thanks."** *As you climb up the ladder of success, give thanks to those who helped you along the way. Send an e-mail, flowers, or make a phone call. And especially send a thank-you note after a job interview. If you don't get that job, they'll remember you for the future. The phrase* thank you *is one of the best in the English language. Pass it around!*

The Interrogation
(Job Interviews)

I went on a job interview once for an opening at a department store. It ended up being like an audition for a permanent role on The Twilight Zone. *The manager was a fussy little fellow who sat behind a big desk in a second-floor office with a window that looked down on the sales floor. He kept an eye on his staff as he asked me questions . . . or I should say, asked me* half *questions because it seemed he wanted me to finish his sentences.*

I didn't quite get this at first. So, he'd say, "The most exciting opportunity in this field at the moment is . . . " And then he'd trail off.

There was a very uncomfortable moment of silence and then he'd head out to left field and start again.

"Department stores are to consumers as water is to . . ."

I just smiled, kept my mouth shut, and thought, "Okey, dokey . . . is someone going to drop a net on this guy?" This went on for about ten minutes until I finally started to catch on. When he started up again I was ready.

"If a customer walked into the store," he asked, "and asked about our most valuable merchandise . . ."

"Oh . . . an umbrella," I yelled like a schoolgirl, giddy that I had finally opened my mouth and said something, anything. Besides, it did look like rain.

Unfortunately, I'd actually cut him off before he'd finished his half sentence because he just blinked at me in disgust and turned back to his window and the goings-on in his store below. It seemed the interview was over.

It would have been funny if I weren't broke at the time and really needed this man to hire me. It was my first lesson in how powerless we can be when we don't have money and lack direction. Needless to say, I didn't get that job, but I vowed to brush up my work skills so I wouldn't find myself trying to finish some fusspot's sentences ever again.—"Amy"

One of the most important mottoes you can have for job interviews is one we learned in Girl Scouts: BE PREPARED!

When I was twenty-four, I was invited to interview for one of my dream jobs: an on-air sports reporter for ESPN. They actually sent me a ticket and flew me all the way from Flagstaff to Connecticut. Yeah—the big time, I thought. Talk about exciting.

But as fate would have it, I woke up that morning with a splitting headache. I swallowed a few expired aspirins and stumbled across the street to the local greasy spoon, hoping that a bit of food would help clear my head.

Big mistake. The pancakes and sausages made matters much worse and I spent the next half-hour gagging in the bathroom. By the time I got to my interview, I had completely forgotten to do the single most important task before any news-related job interview: *Read the morning newspaper!* In my specific case, that would have been the sports section of *USA Today*. Especially that specific day! The night before, my alma mater football team, the Syracuse Orangemen, had ended a game in a controversial tie that sparked a major furor between the coaches and the lead quarterback. There it was, on the front page, for everyone in the world to see. Everyone except me.

Of course that was the first subject to come up in the interview.

"So, what do you think about what the extraordinary quarterback Don McPherson and SU football coach Dick McPherson said yesterday?" asked my interviewer, eager to debate the hot topic of the day.

I hemmed and hawed and started to sweat bullets on his slick leather couch. I looked up to the photo of Mark McGwire hanging on the wall and prayed for divine intervention.

What is he talking about? I screamed in my still-aching head.

I tried to change the subject and prattled on about something else. He just looked at me with a bewildered expression on his face as I sank deeper into the wet leather couch. I had fumbled the ball and I didn't get the job.

It may have been just as well because, as I've said, I love sports and I love talking to athletes, but I don't really give two hoots about reporting scores. That would have been a big part of that job, so although at the time I was crushed at how badly things went, what was meant to be took place.

But that's not the point. Even if in hindsight the job wasn't meant for me, I still should have been prepared—it's good practice and shows that you're a professional gal who cares about what she does and respects other people's time. On top of that, it's always nicer to turn down a job offer than be told no thanks.

Do Your Homework

I sometimes *still* drop the ball even when I think I'm prepared.

I recently headed off to an important meeting with film producers who were checking me out for a plum role in a major Hollywood movie. I was sure I'd done my homework. I had "googled" the company over the Internet search engine google.com. (You can find out an unbelievable amount of information about a company on the Web—from how much money it's making to how much toilet paper it buys for the executive washroom.)

I googled their production company so thoroughly I could have written an article about them for *The Hollywood Reporter*. I was pretty confident until I got to the meeting.

Unfortunately, I had investigated the *wrong* company. I strode into that meeting thinking it was Merchant Ivory, which brought us the beautifully romantic *A Room with a View* and *Remains of the Day*. I had imagined myself in period costume sipping tea with Anthony Hopkins in a rainy English garden.

So I was a tad confused when the script the producers showed me was about a power-hungry ad executive who lives in a Malibu beach house and tramples on her colleagues with stilettos.

"You do such beautiful work," I praised them, rattling off my memorized list of artsy-fartsy films I thought were theirs.

They froze in their seats. Eyebrows lifted.

"You must be mistaken . . . ," one of them finally said, looking a little dismayed.

Uh-oh. Suddenly I saw my mistake all too clearly.

The name of the company I'd googled was definitely similar, but the movies they made definitely were not! These guys produced beat-'em-up, shoot-'em-up, blow-'em-up, car-chasing, ultra-action guy flicks.

I wanted to fold myself up into my smart-looking little brief-

Emme

case and disappear. The rest of the meeting was awkward, and, needless to say, I didn't get the part.

But at least I tried to be prepared, and I learned a great lesson: *Sometimes you'd better do your homework on your homework.*

And I've learned to keep a sense of humor when things go wrong.

Last year, I went to a luncheon given by AOL Time Warner for their mentor program. I was seated next to a casually dressed, unassuming man—but I couldn't make out the name on his nametag.

"Hi, I'm Emme!" I introduced myself.

"Hi, I'm Gerry!" We shook hands.

"So, Gerry," I asked, making small talk in between food courses, "what do you do with the company?"

Pause.

"Well, I happen to be chairman of the board. . . ."

UUUUgggghhhh! I rolled my eyes and laughed.

He laughed, too.

"Don't feel bad," he assured me. "I can't keep track of who does what either!"

I didn't let my faux pas get the better of me. Without missing a beat, I looked him dead in the eye and asked, "So . . . do you love your job?"

We were right back on equal footing and we got along swimmingly for the rest of the function.

---

911 TIP **What to Wear for Your Job Interview:** To be a success you have to look like one. Check out chapter 3, Fashion Emergency! for tips on what to wear to impress the Big Cheese.

Elinor Morris, general business and career consultant to many Fortune 500 companies; president of Management Resources Consulting

On Job Networking

Know Yourself: See yourself as a product and send out your message. You are your own advertising campaign. Show it through your résumé, bio, professional letters, work, interests, and commitments. Organize these into a focused message. Know what you want to be known as and make sure others know it. Be sure it's something people care about.

Know Your Customer and Your Marketplace: Know whom you are trying to reach and why. What do they need? What is going on in their world? Where do they hang out? Read newspapers, magazines, trade papers. Continuously search the Internet for targeted information.

Network: Create lists of people and networks that are meaningful. Who are the people doing what you want to do? Who has the ability to deliver contacts or give you the right information? Participate in association meetings, seminars, network groups, and make contact with them. Tenaciously follow up on relevant sources.

Office Politics
(And Other Messy Stuff)

Get Outta My Personal Space

For a long time I commuted to New York while I worked on the editorial staff of a national magazine. On the train I met a very tall, very imposing man who often sat with me. We found out we worked for the same large corporation; his position, in another division, was much more elevated than mine. Soon it became clear he was interested in me, even though I'd told him I was newly married and very much in love. I took on some freelance work for his division, and he started taking me out to lunch. Uncomfortable with the way things were evolving, I asked my mother for advice.

"Be direct," she suggested. "Let him know you understand where he's headed and tell him you're not interested. Do this in a very public place."

I agreed to meet him for an expensive lunch; the linens were crisp, the flowers aromatic, and the food delicious. When we reached the point where he began suggesting I stay in the company suite one night, I made my mother's move.

"Are you asking me to sleep with you?" I asked in a loud voice. "Is that what you want?"

I can still, some twenty years later, remember the way his face looked, pink and flushed, his bulging eyes sweeping the room to locate any suits at surrounding tables that may have heard.

We finished the lunch hastily, he walked me back to the building, and he never bothered me again.

The moral? Listen to your mother. —"Lucia"

I've always been able to deal with unwanted male attention like a lady—a lady prizefighter! When I was a cocktail waitress at a local college pub when I was twenty-one years old, an unruly customer slipped his hand under my skirt after I took his order.

I calmly put down my tray, planted my feet firmly on the floor, took aim, and socked him so squarely and so hard in the gut that I knocked him off his chair. He was stunned (and sore). And I was cheered! There was no way I was going to let anyone—especially a drunken groper—manhandle me. My boss was so impressed he promoted me to honorary bouncer for the rest of the night!

When I worked as a page at NBC at age twenty-two, I was asked to drop off a tuxedo to the dressing room of a famous actor, noted for his macho, sex-symbol status in the 1970s. He was also known around the studio for cornering young female assistants. I knocked on his door.

"Mr.————, I have your wardrobe."

He opened the door with a smile, took the hanger, and beckoned me to come in. I turned to leave.

"Oh, *NO you don't.*" He stopped me with his hand on my shoulder. "You have to stay in the room as I *change*, my dear. . . ."

I was prepared.

"Oh, *I don't think* so, Mr.————." I smiled, backing toward the door.

"Ah, but *I* do," he insisted, blocking my way with his body.

With a deep breath, I drew my well-muscled rower's body up to my full five-eleven height and stared hard at him.

"I need to get by you, sir," I said with plenty of steely resolve in my voice. "If you don't let me, I'll have to call security!"

He let me by. He could see he wasn't going to get anywhere with this young thing.

Confrontation Is Empowering

Natasha, on the other hand, was not as prepared to handle guys like this.

Working as a student reporter one summer at a newspaper, she was invited for after-work drinks by one of her editors—"to discuss my bright future career at the paper," she recalls. Under the table, he put his hand on her knee for about one minute.

"I ignored it," she says, "even though I was incredibly uncomfortable. I told myself I was making a big deal out of nothing."

The next week, he asked if she could drop him off somewhere on her way home at the end of the day.

"When we got in the car, he grabbed me and started to kiss me. I was shocked. I had to push him off me. I felt totally confused. Was he lying all that time when he said my work was good?

Is this all he had wanted? Did I lead him on? I lost a lot of confidence." She didn't report him and left the paper soon after.

OLDER & WISER

That was ten years ago. "Today, if a superior put his hand on my knee," says Natasha, "I'd push it off me and tell him very clearly to never do it again." I would have acted from a place of power, not as a victim, which is how I felt at the time. I would have set the boundaries immediately. *Don't be nice, be insulted!"*

"You're Fired!"
"You Can't Fire Me—I Quit!"

Politics can be brutal whether they are in the White House or in your office—I learned that the hard way. I got fired once because of my office decor.

A mere receptionist in an NBC production office in Los Angeles, I was eager to create the right "vibe" in this hypertense environment. I turned off the harsh, overhead fluorescent lights and lit scented candles on the filing cabinets. I did a little feng shui reorganizing. If given a chance, I might have led the TV execs in a group chant and meditation session during lunch hour. . . .

Unfortunately I never got the chance. I hadn't been there very long before the executive producer called me into his office.

"You know, Emme, it's just not working out. You work hard, but you're not the kind of production assistant we're looking for. I appreciate your efforts to . . . um . . . *calm* the office. But the truth is, all this calming is distracting. Besides, we don't *want* to be calm around here. This is *television* for God's sake!"

Oh. I was there to answer phones and make photocopies—not to set a mood. This was not my home. If they wanted an interior decorator, they'd have hired one. Could it be . . . they thrived on tension and harsh lighting? Well, I realized, YES, they did! What a great lesson. I understood that being let go from that job wasn't personal. There was nothing wrong with me and nothing wrong with them—our visions of the world just didn't gel and I was better off looking elsewhere for work.

Recently I was at the other end of the gun. At the office, we had to let go a terrific, hardworking employee due to budget cutbacks. Even that awkward situation taught me a lesson about office politics. Despite being let go, the employee left with grace and style. She thanked us for the special time she had with us and for the experience she'd gained. She left with a smile and without a single unkind word. Because of that, I will definitely hire her back some day if the opportunity arises.

"This door may be closed right now but another one will open

OLDER & WISER

So maybe my attempts to calm the office didn't work
. . . then, but I never gave up in my quest to have a serene working environment. Over a decade later I was finally on my own at The Emme Collection. It became clearly apparent that my showroom team of at least a dozen, hardworking, passionate souls needed some help to relax big time between deadlines being met and living and working in New York City. It is stressful; so I asked my friend and yoga teacher, Mauri, to visit our showroom. We were hooked after the first time she sprayed her scented oils, lit a candle, and took us all through some relaxing poses right there on the floor. She's now a regular yoga teacher for us. Additionally, for my own working space, I have a lava lamp, low lighting, CD player, two large candles, and an incense tray to safely burn incense. With a little patience, there's a time and place for everything.

for you," I told her. "Go and stretch your wings! If you need a reference, don't hesitate to call."

So remember—it's easy to burn a bridge when you leave a job . . . but it's just as easy, and a whole lot smarter, to build one as you wave goodbye. You won't be doing yourself any favors if you shout, "Take this job and shove it!" as you're walking out the door.

The first time I ever quit a job was when I was a roller-skating waitress in Texas one summer during high school. I had to balance cheese dogs and slushies while gliding car to car on a set of wheels strapped to my feet. UGHHH—try it sometime if you need a shot of humiliation.

I was constantly crashing into the cars and praying I wouldn't spill anything. It was like that night after night until one evening when I tripped on a stone and dropped a huge, sticky, ice-cold, red slurpie into a southern gent's lap—all over his Wrangler jeans.

That was it for me—enough was enough. I hated the roller skates and was tired of coming home every night stinking of grease and burned onions. I handed in my uniform the next day. It felt liberating to leave a job I hated, and I knew if I was determined I'd soon find something better.

Sometimes you have to dump an employer like you dump a bad boyfriend.

When I started modeling, the small agency I signed with never sent me my checks on time. The checks were always (never!) in the mail and when I did finally get them, they bounced like a rubber ball.

I called the boss. I tried talking to the accountant. I even hired a lawyer to write a letter to the head of the agency. Nothing worked. I was going bonkers. They were earning money from me but never paying me my share.

After a few months of this, I picked up my portfolio and left. I wasn't going to let people take advantage of me like that, but I was determined to leave in a classy and professional manner. I sent my booker (the one who set up my client appointments) flowers and a nice note. My lawyer sent them a termination letter. I moved on. Don't let things get nasty, but don't ever feel you have to stay in an unfair and unhealthy situation.

> **TAKE NOTE** *Never burn your bridges; you may need to cross them in future travels. Leaving a job is not the time to tell the boss which employee is shagging which. Get a recommendation letter and leave well enough alone.*

Show Me da Money!

Women have blasted into space in rocket ships but here on earth they still get paid less than men.

"Nice" girls keep their mouths shut; strong, successful women demand what they deserve but are often branded as "difficult" for standing up for themselves. All is fair in the office and in the boardroom, so stop being nice and speak up. A pat on the back from the boss doesn't cut it.

The first time I felt bold enough to ask for a raise was at my yearly review at the real estate firm where I worked. I had worked hard and plenty of overtime, and helped triple their business that year. I decided to ask for a 25 percent raise. I'm not sure how I came up with that figure, I just knew I should start high.

"I'd like to discuss a raise," I told him.

I was nervous, but prepared.

"What do you have to show me to justify a raise?" my boss asked.

I named the list of my clients and provided data proving I'd been responsible for renting 75 percent of the empty office space we'd wanted to fill. I had printed the list out so I had it ready to show it to him right then and there.

He was impressed.

WISE GUY

Jay Leno, talk show host

Now here's a boss who cares. For the tenth anniversary of his stint on *The Tonight Show*, host Jay Leno gave each employee $1,000 per year of service. The only trouble is he has approximately 175 people, most of whom had been there for the whole ten years, so you do the math.

Don't waste your time in a job where the boss doesn't appreciate the work you do for them. Know there are other appreciative bosses out there, like Jay (maybe not *as* appreciative), and be open to change.

"Well, this is something I think I should consider," he said after hearing my case.

How'd it end? I got a 20 percent raise and a bonus! If you don't ask, you don't get.

Mentors and Role Models

My mom was my first mentor. She was a single mother who juggled two secretarial jobs to put food on the table and keep a roof over my head while it was just the two of us living in New York City. She never complained—she did what she had to do to take care of me for my first six years.

One job would have been enough to provide the basics—but Mom worked extra hard so I could have the little extras that make life so wonderful for a child—French lessons, weekly ice cream stops at Serendipity, or a pretty dress to wear to a birthday party.

My mom set an example for me as I grew up—I adopted her wonderful work ethic and it stays with me to this day. She never had to lecture me about it; she just set a good example and was there with good advice whenever I needed it. That is what being a true mentor is all about.

It was the late 1960s and Mom had these great friends from diverse backgrounds, careers, and income levels who'd come over and "rap" about life, politics, and the state of being a woman. Names like Martin Luther King and Gloria Steinem were dropped during these living room rap sessions. I admired these strong women sitting on our couch. I soaked it all in: their discussions, their passion, and their burning desire to change the world. I wanted to be like that.

Mom flipped on the TV and we all watched Dr. King give a speech: "For all people, for all little children . . ." I was mesmerized. My mom exposed me to so many positive role models and always encouraged me to follow my dreams.

After my mom passed away, I needed to find other people to believe in me, encourage me, and advise me. I discovered that if you keep your eyes and your heart open, you can find mentors and people who inspire you just about anywhere.

My junior high school phys-ed teacher, Lillian Papp, was one of them. Whenever she needed someone to get up in front of the class to demonstrate a tough athletic move, she'd say, "Emme, c'mon up!"

I remember the day we had to climb the ropes that hung from the ceiling. All the guys were strutting around, flexing their muscles and preparing to show up the girls.

"Emme!" yelled Ms. Papp.

I jumped up and showed the guys how it was done. They were pretty impressed with me. To tell you the truth, so was I. Why did Ms. Papp always call on me? At the time, I thought maybe she knew I needed the extra motivation. But I bumped into my dear teacher during a fashion show while she was visiting her daughter in Washington, D.C. last year and asked her why.

"Because I always knew you could do it," she told me. "You were always ready to get out there and show everybody else!"

Whether she knew it or not, she taught me that I didn't have to hang back while the boys rowed across finish lines or scored touchdowns—that being a girl didn't mean I was any less of an athlete . . . or less of a person! She was a mentor to me. Her encouragement and inspiration changed the course of my life.

When I first started out in showbiz (right at the bottom of the ladder as an NBC page), I quickly realized there were a lot of giant egos up there at the top of the ladder.

But I was incredibly lucky to meet a celebrity right off the bat who is one of the most down-to-earth and generous people I know.

I spent two hours with Doobie Brother Michael McDonald, who became a role model to me for how a famous person should act.

My job was to escort celebrities to and from their cars, make sure they arrived on the set on time, had enough to eat, and knew where the bathroom was. It wasn't always a pretty job. Sometimes, I'd meet my so-called idols as they were falling out of their limos dead drunk, bad-mouthing other celebrities, or trying to cop a feel in the dressing room. We were glorified baby-sitters to older, rich, famous infants!!!

But McDonald was different. He was in town to appear on *The Tonight Show* and as soon as we met he asked me about myself:

"Where did you come from? Where did you go to school? What do you want to do with your life?"

I'd say, "Hey, look, you really don't have to *talk* to me. . . . I'll just go sit in the back and be quiet."

But he would have none of that. I took him to the backstage area to get ready to go out to meet Johnny Carson. I got him to his spot and was preparing to leave (pages were not allowed to hang out backstage) when he said, "No way. You don't have to leave. You can stand next to me."

He then went on to introduce me to every person who approached him.

"Have you met my friend, Emme?" he'd ask.

Unlike the dressing-room lecher I mentioned earlier, this man wouldn't dream of trying to intimidate a young girl with his star power or strut around with celebrity ego syndrome. Fifteen years later I still remember how genuine and kind Michael McDonald was, and it affects how I am today when I meet new people. I check celebrity attitude at the door. I hope I run into him again one day so I can thank him for setting such a classy example.

If you don't come into direct contact with potential mentors, reach out and look for one. Many organizations and businesses have mentoring programs that will set you up with someone who's been there, done that, and wants to tell you all about it. Choose a person who is doing the job you'd like to do and write him or her a letter.

I did. Four years ago when I was in discussion with a major TV network to do my own talk show, I was perplexed at how to manage the network producers and corporate heads who wanted to turn my show idea into a circus. I needed guidance from someone who'd been there, so I went straight to the top. I wrote a letter to Oprah Winfrey (I had been a guest on her show a few times). A few weeks later, her assistant called as I was getting out of the shower.

"Miss Winfrey is on the line. . . ."

I had ten minutes to squeeze all the smarts I could out of her. Wrapped in a towel and dripping water onto the carpet, I asked:

"Oprah . . . how do I keep my vision intact and not fall into a rut of re-creating a formula show or being manipulated into doing something I don't want to do?"

She gave me advice that I repeat to myself today.

She said, "You have to stay true to who you are. You have great

Emme

energy and a lot going for you. People will try to manipulate you for their own means. *Work from your heart and you will always do well.*"

Now, that's worth repeating.

WISE WOMAN

Oprah Winfrey

Stay true to who you are. Work from your heart.

Q & A with Nora McAniff, executive vice president of Time Inc. and director of The Digital Heroes Campaign—a mentor program set up to connect teenagers with prominent people in online mentoring relationships. Mentors include Arnold Schwarzenegger, Camryn Manheim, Secretary of State Colin Powell, Judge Judy Sheindlin, Bryant Gumbel, Matt Damon, Glenn Close, Anne Currie, Anita Hill, Roma Downey, and me!

Q: *Why do we need mentors?*

Nora: When you're starting out and you don't have experience, you have so many questions. Sometimes you just need to be able to talk to somebody and be really frank and honest and say, "Hey, help me shape my career." Gerry Levin, the former CEO of AOL Time Warner, is one of our mentors. One of his mentees was amazed that the owner (at the time) of this big company was e-mailing him three times a week. The attention really helps kids flourish.

Q: *How?*

Nora: Here's an example. Last year, the mentee for actor Henry Simmons from *NYPD Blue* ran away from home. Six weeks later, when he came back, Henry shared his own life story with the mentee. He told him, "I'm just like you. I came from a poor black family. I ran away from home. I understand how you feel. Hang in there." The counselors couldn't *believe* the difference that talk made with this kid. He really responded.

Q: *Did you have a mentor?*
Nora: I didn't. It would have been great if I did. All of us in college would think, "Oh, this sounds like a great career," but who knows until you get into it? We've paired up a kid who wants to be a chef with a well-known Manhattan restaurant chef. How cool is that? To get to talk to somebody who's in the business you want to be in and tell you what it's really like? What a better way to learn and get inspired. Glenn Close joined this year. She has a mentee who wants to be an actress.

Q: *What is the best way to approach a possible mentor?*
Nora: Write them a letter, tell them about yourself, and send it to their office.

Q: *What's in it for the mentor?*
Nora: Sometimes the mentors get even more satisfaction than the mentee. Most people are willing to share, give advice, and give back. Young people should take that opportunity.

For more information on mentoring, log on to: *www.mentoring.org*.

FINAL THOUGHT

A career is not something that comes out of nothing and POOF, a fulfilling job is handed to you on a platter. It's a creation that comes from many jobs over time. Through trial and error, detours, raises, and firings, a career or many careers will develop around your interests. Your direction may surprise you. Ask any CEO

what his or her first job was and it will probably be far from what the person is doing today. Think about what really interests you, then write a letter to the personnel department at a place you'd love to work. Tell them why you want to work there and that you'll work your buns off if they'll give you the chance. If you continue to follow the direction of your dreams, you will work in a field that makes you happy. If you need to flip burgers, tend bar, or clean tables to pay the bills while you are looking for your dream job, then so be it. Just know that while you're salting those fries, all things are possible and you are on your way.

travel emergency!

I love to travel. I feel it was part of my destiny as a child and it continues to be a big part of my life as an adult. The thrill of discovering new cities and exotic people never leaves me—it's in my blood. My personal travel diary goes like this:

BORN: NYC

LIVED: NYC, Long Island, New Jersey, Dhahran, Saudi Arabia, Texas, Connecticut, New York State, Los Angeles, Arizona, New York City, and New Jersey (again).

VISITED: Florence, Tuscany, Rome, Italy; Sri Lanka, India; Athens, Greece; Beirut, Lebanon; London, England; Sweden; Finland; Estonia; Holland; Paris, France; Hamburg, Frankfurt, Germany; Sydney, Melbourne, Queensland, Australia; the Caribbean Island; French West Indies; Bermuda; Toronto, Canada; Puerto Rico; Mexico City, Mexico; and so on, and so on . . .

After so many jaunts across the ocean I should know a few things about stuffing a suitcase and sending a postcard, right? And if I don't have all the answers, my buddy Natasha certainly does. She's famous for her preflight dash to the terminal.

"Hold the plane!" is one phrase in which she is multi-multilingual.

"Attends! L'avion!" (at Charles De Gaulle in the City of Lights).

"Arresti l'aereo dell'aria!" (at Fiumicino, Aeroporti di Roma).

"Pare ese avion!" (at Madrid's Barajas Airport).

"I say, old chap—ring up the pilot and ask him to be a sport!" (at London's Heathrow).

Now, Natasha is a natural-born charmer, but I can attest to the fact that when she was really late trying to catch a return flight from Macedonia she was laughed out of the airport for suggesting they might be good enough to have the plane come back to get her after it had taken off. ("Was it so wrong of me to *ask?*" she says, in her defense.)

Getting to the airport, bus station, or train depot on time is a skill, an ordeal, and a necessity if you ever want to go anywhere.

But first there are the packing questions. Will you really require those frilly fuchsia undies on this trip? Do you want them to be seen by everyone in line at the random security check? Is your hair dryer necessary on that Himalayan climbing expedition? Then, who is going to drive you to your port of departure? Will there be traffic chaos? Bad weather? Do you have your passport? Are you headed to the right terminal? A thousand things can go wrong before you even get out of town—plan your initial escape carefully. And once you're on your way, you want to pray you're not riding in your plane, train, or automobile with a stocking-footed snorer who slobbers on your shoulder in his sleep.

Ideally, you want to travel in style and arrive in comfort—à la those 1950s movie starlets who always seemed to disembark their Pan Am flights with grand elegance, stepping gingerly onto the rolled-up stairway in their kitten heels clutching a little white poodle in their little white-gloved hands. First class all the way for dem dames . . .

Never mind that! Today we humble gals on the go are reduced to long lines at the terminal to get our tickets and even longer lines to get to the gate. So forget about looking like a dame—pull out your most comfortable waffle sneakers and wear them. You'll be so happy you did. At least your feet will be.

Suitcase Savvy

Some might brand me an overpacker. I like to think I'm just thorough.

There is always the very real possibility that my flight to Cancun will be rerouted to Juneau, Alaska . . . right? ("Honey, pack the mukluks, and have you seen my snowshoes?")

On my first business trip to Germany, I took two army duffel bags and overstuffed them with sweaters, shirts, coats, boots, and skirts. I went crazy. It didn't matter that this was a modeling job where I'd be wearing *someone else's clothes* all week long. One entire suitcase of mine was devoted to shoes!

Thank goodness Phil was to meet me in a week so we could take a train to Amsterdam for some playtime. *Great!* I figured he would carry all the bags. But when he arrived at my hotel he was walking funny. "I pinched a nerve in my neck." He pointed.

I pointed to my mountain of luggage.

"Are you *insane?*" he asked. (See? I told you he asks me that a lot.)

The hotel had no elevator so we kicked the baggage down the tiny, narrow staircase. We couldn't find a cab so we ran to the train station, dragging the load along the jagged cobblestones. Phil was in agony. And me? I felt awful—especially because I ended up wearing only a quarter of what I'd brought.

Packing for a much-needed vacation on Long Beach Island last year, I made the completely opposite mistake. Frazzled, I sped through a business meeting, zipped home, tossed I-don't-know-what into a duffel bag, and hopped into the car for the three-hour drive. Yeehaw! I had waves on the brain. I arrived and opened my bag to find I had packed:

A. Ten—count 'em, TEN—bottles of sunblock and four tubes of moisturizer.

B. Books. Books. And lots more books.

C. Two pairs of undies.

D. Five pairs of very swishy, totally beach-inappropriate, shoes.

E. Very little of anything I really needed. Oops.

I didn't have anything to wear to go out for dinner. I didn't have anything to swim in. I had no decent shoes to lounge in. I ended up borrowing Phil's shirts, flip-flops, razor—you name it, I stole it from him. When Phil saw my feeble stash, it was, *"Are you insane*??!!" all over again (it's kind of becoming our *thing*).

When it comes to weather, expect the unexpected.

I went to L.A. last May and arrived in 75 degrees of sunniness. I brought T-shirts, sandals, and light suits. A cold front moved in from Canada and the temperatures plummeted. I had to go to business meetings the next day in open-toe shoes while the rest of the city was bundled for arctic weather. Thank God for my pashmina scarf and my one cashmere sweater, which kept me warm the entire week.

Natasha has a girlfriend who was working in sun-kissed Greece one summer and was leaving to fly back to North America when she read about a blistering, unrelenting heat wave that was paralyzing her hometown area.

So when she hopped on her (student discount ticket) Air Bulgaria flight she was wearing only a T-shirt, shorts, and sandals. Well, the plane broke down (that's another travel emergency) and had to land in Amsterdam for repairs—for three days. Her luggage didn't make it and her wallet was—you guessed it—in her now absent backpack. Not only that, it was a Bulgarian national holiday and the Bulgarian travel desk was closed for the long weekend so no one could help her book a hotel. And to top it all off, a freak snowstorm hit Amsterdam that weekend, leaving her wandering the streets shivering in her shorts and sandals for a day and a half before she could get the Canadian embassy to lend her a few bucks for long pants and a cheap room. True story.

As for my dear Natash, she is rarely suitcase-challenged. She's been going to the Cannes Film Festival every May for nearly a decade and has the two-week trip pared down to one carry-on bag that she sticks under her seat. The contents: black jeans, one skirt, two tank tops, one dress, three T-shirts, one pair of sandals, one sweater, one pair of Keds, and a light raincoat she wears on the plane.

> **Moral of the Stories:** *As you pack, think about what you'll* need *on the trip and what you will* really *wear once you get to your destination.* And always buy luggage with rubber wheels *(plastic ones break easily). Check TV, newspaper, or websites (www.weather.com) to get weather information.*

"And my corkscrew," she adds, "for tasting the local rosé on the Carlton Beach at midnight." (And then she runs for the gate.)

After years of over- and underpacking, I've got my list of essentials pared down to the following for a one-week getaway:

Emme's Just-Right, Not-Too-Little-Not-Too-Much, Packing List:

- 1 fluid jersey johnny collar shirt
- 1 comfy pair of lounge pants in matte jersey
- 1 short cotton skirt
- 1 camisole for layering
- 1 black cardigan
- 1 colorful pashmina shawl (keep it out for the plane/train/ bus ride)
- 1 boatneck sheath dress, printed or solid
- 2 white crisp shirts
- 1 pair of comfortable walking/running shoes
- 1 pair of strappy sandals
- 1 rolled-up trench coat or windbreaker
- 1 collapsible umbrella
- 1 unitard and light sweatshirt
- 1 jogging bra
- 1 swimsuit
- 1 small black nylon purse/bag for day trips (Longchamp makes a variety of sizes that are perfect for travel and look simple yet chic. I buy these for a lot of my girl-friends.)

911 TIP Wear comfortable shoes you can slip on and off during travel. Taking off your shoes and stretching your feet keep the circulation moving in your legs so they won't cramp up or fall asleep.

Take on the plane or in the car:

1 qt. water bottle
facial moisturizer
1 good book
magazines
1 package of baby wipes
lip balm
sunglasses
ponytail bands
pen, paper
snack (like homemade gorp or trail mix)

> **TAKE NOTE:** *My favorite suitcase is the Louis Vuitton garment bag. Why? It fits twenty outfits, it's durable, and it has a lifetime warranty. Other favorites: Lands' End 22-inch Pullman case; Lands' End wheeled duffel; a Tumi rolling bag.*

The night before a morning flight, I set my alarm clock and check it twice. Sometimes I set *two* clocks.

I once overslept the morning I was to leave for a modeling job in Houston. I woke up forty-five minutes before the flight, glanced at the time, and yelled at Phil: "START THE CAR, START THE CAR!" and scrambled. We tore through the tolls— throwing change at the booth lady—and burned rubber, laughing and crying at the same time. We looked like bandits on the run.

So we get to the airport and I was running. My slide-on shoe slides off over the conveyor belt. I climb over to get it. Running, running, lungs on fire. I hip-check some poor old lady. *Sorry!* I throw my shoes off. Sweating. Got to the gate in my stocking feet,

911 TIP I don't fold my clothes, I roll 'em. It prevents wrinkles and saves space. Lay plastic wrap from the dry-cleaner's over a blouse and then roll it like a giant burrito. Roll up socks and stick them inside shoes. If clothes get wrinkled, give them a steam bath: hang in the bathroom, turn on hot water full blast, and shut the door for fifteen minutes. Or invest in a portable, hand-held steamer. Take Ziploc bags for dirty/wet clothes.

hair flying. Whew! I look around; the plane hasn't boarded. The flight was delayed two hours. Are you *kidding me*?!

Moral of the Story: *Wear shoes you can run in, set alarm(s), check for flight delays.*

Dog Tags
(And Other Documents)

I was packing for my first modeling assignment in Europe. The flight was in three hours. I looked at my passport; it was three months expired. *Help!* I called my boss, who sent me to one of those quick, turnaround passport places en route to the airport. Emergency averted. Always, ALWAYS, have your passport up-to-date and ready to take. Especially now with heightened airport security, don't leave home without it. Before your flight, make a list: passport, money, traveler's checks, credit cards, phone cards, phone numbers, hotel information, address book (to send post-cards).

Big Advice For Little Things:

- ☑ Carry important documents in your carry-on bag. Airlines lose luggage.
- ☑ Leave hotel info with friend/family in case of emergency.
- ☑ In your flight bag: water, moisturizer, vitamins, book or magazine, earplugs, eye mask, small pillow, water atomizer.
- ☑ In your toiletry bag: birth control, volt changer, international plug, traveler's checks.
- ☑ In your purse: passport, tickets, baggage claim, lipstick, change, credit cards.
- ☑ Pop a scented candle into your bag or a favorite CD to play once you get to your hotel room to make it homey.

The Air Up There

BREATHE . . .

As my airplane takes off, I prep for surgery. On goes my blue, surgical face mask—the kind doctors wear in hospitals. I can see the panic in the eyes of the other passengers ("Is she conta-

911 TIP Pack a portable pack of baby wipes. You can wipe your hands before eating, wipe up spills, or use in the bathroom if there's no toilet paper.

911 TIP **Taking the office with you:** I recently bought a Palm VII and have linked it to my Office Outlook program. It keeps me in order with schedules, appointments, addresses, phone numbers, and reminders while on the road and away from my desk.

gious?" they whisper). They don't know it's *their* germs I'm worried about. One time, I wrote on the mask with a felt-tip pen: JUST A COLD! and got a few laughs from the gang in the cockpit.

Let's face it. The air up there ain't so great. It's recirculated, so you're breathing in the cough from that kid who's hacking away twenty rows back. Sometimes I wear this funky air purifier unit around my neck that looks like a *Star Trek* prop and shoots out ions and purifies the air around you (you can get this at Brookstone or at Sharper Image).

I once asked a flight attendant how she keeps healthy when she's in planes all the time. She shook her head and pointed to an air filter above us. It was filled with black gunk. "I worry about that all the time. I'm not allowed to wear a mask, like you," she told me. "The airline says it would send out the wrong message to passengers."

COFFEE, TEA . . . OR WATER!

Some people drink alcohol on planes because it's free and they're nervous. But booze plus high altitude can do wacky things to your system. I took a flight to Australia for a job once—a long twenty-three hours in the air. I figured a brandy or two would ease me to sleep and I'd arrive all rested and ready to roll. Bad idea! All it did was make me groggy for the entire first day of my trip. Never again. Drink lots of water, stay hydrated, and limit your alcohol intake.

LOOKING FOR GOOD EATS . . .

If you don't like that prefab airplane food (and unless you're an astronaut, who would?) bring your own. I bring my homemade gorp with me on planes, trains, and automobiles: a mixture of granola, nuts, carob, and peanut butter chips.

Flying back from Italy last year, everyone around me ate the mushy macaroni from tin trays. I pulled out a colorful feast I'd bought at the Tuscan market an hour earlier: fresh bread, fresh basil, cheese, and the ripest, reddest tomatoes I had ever seen in my life. I broke the bread, cut up the cheese and tomatoes with the airplane knife, and sandwiched it all together. My fellow passengers were pea green with mouth-watering envy.

FELLOW TRAVELERS

It can get quite "cozy" squished in next to a stranger during a long voyage. Saying a quick and cordial hello to the stranger is very polite indeed. But no more is necessary unless you are in a chatty mood and your neighbor has something wildly interesting to say. So if you're seated next to a chatterbox who wants to tell you his life story and then sell you insurance, nip it in the bud. Read. Feign sleep. Or, when all else fails . . . be honest.

I sat next to a guy in a plane once and innocently asked him, "What kind of business are you in?" The dam gates opened. I had only myself to blame. After thirty minutes of his nonstop prattle (and we hadn't even taken off yet!), I had a bleak vision of the next five hours and prayed for a good in-flight movie.

Still, I kept nodding—giving him encouraging, eager-to-please responses like, "Oh, *how interesting!*" Inside my head I was yelling at myself, *"Stop being so nice!"*

I slowly reached over and pulled out the airline magazine. He kept talking. I opened to an article. He kept talking. I started to read. He still kept going. He was like a nightmare version of the Energizer Bunny. I knew it was time to be direct with him or else in another hour or two I would be forced to shove my trusty pashmina scarf down his throat to shut him up.

"Sir," I said sweetly, "I don't mean any disrespect, but I really need to take a bit of a nap now, I'm very tired."

It worked, sort of. He was quiet but I had to fake sleep for the rest of the flight. I could feel him watching me, waiting for me to "wake up" so he could pounce.

911 TIP **Jet Lag?** If you land during daylight, expose yourself to sun immediately. I heard it worked, so I tried it, and it has helped me. Most important, try to stay awake during the waking hours of the country you are in. If you're falling asleep in your soup, take a very short 1-hour nap . . . any more will mess with your acclimation to the new time zone. If that doesn't work, look into an herbal mixture either for a bath or a steam facial that helps jet lag. I use an herbal liquid specifically for jet lag from the Jurlique product line (manufactured in Australia and one of the purest most natural beauty lines made).

A plane ride is not a blind date. You don't need to entertain the person next to you. Be straightforward and say, "I really need to read/sleep/watch this movie now." If they don't quit talking, ask the flight attendant if you can change your seat.

Parlez-vous Francais?

YOUR ABCS

When I arrived in Paris my first time, I was surprised at how much French I had retained from conjugating verbs against my will in school for what seemed like forever. Standing at the hotel's front desk in the Latin Quarter—the smell of fresh-baked croissants wafting through the lobby—I hungrily asked for a room. At least, I thought I did. The clerk looked mystified.

I asked again. Louder.

He looked horrified.

I frantically pulled out my travel dictionary and leafed through. Ah! Silly me. I had been insisting he rent me a cat (*chat*) for the night instead of a room (*chambre*)!

C'est la vie.

If you're going to a foreign country and you don't know the language, a translation book is *muy importante* ("very important" in Spanish). If you're a really ambitious type, you can get language tapes to listen to before your trip to hear the pronunciation.

The basics are usually enough to keep you out of trouble: "Please"; "Thank you"; "Excuse me"; "Do you have a bathroom?"; "How much does this cost?"; "Where is this street?" After you've mastered those, let loose and get creative:

"Hey, what do you mean I'm a size 15 in a Ferragamo sandal!" or, "I'm DYING for more of that fresh parpardelle and ricotta. . . ."

Then go ahead and throw in an exotic swear word for flourish ("*bastardo!*"). The locals will think you're one of them and they'll be lest apt to pickpocket you.

As you take your crash course in a new language, beware the words that *sound* the same, but aren't. Sometimes a world of difference lives in one letter. Natasha spent two months in the former Yugoslavia eating all the cabbage rolls (*sarma*) they could make and kept telling her Old Country, babushka-wearing grannies (*baba*) what fantastic cooks (*kuvar*) they were. One kindly relative finally took her aside and corrected her pronunciation. Seems she had been calling the sweet, little old ladies prostitutes (*kurva*). Not good.

"And yet," says Natasha, amazed, "they kept cooking for me!"

911 TIP In a foreign place always ask permission to take a person's picture, says photographer Melanie Dunea. A camera is a powerful tool and some people feel it takes their spirit away, so use it respectfully. Also, don't worry if you forgot your camera at home. I take pictures with disposable cameras and they come out great.

   Emme's Tip: With a disposable camera, take pictures without looking through the viewfinder—the shots will come out with an interesting border and have more of a creative feel.

GETTING THE GOODS

When you buy stuff in a foreign country—barter, and beware of the communication gap. After a long day on a modeling shoot in Germany I went into a naturopathic store to buy bath tablets for a relaxing soak in the tub and a good night's sleep.

"Which ones are good for sleep? *Sleep!?*" I asked the salesgirl, miming a dramatic yawn. She pointed to the rosemary tablets.

Back at the hotel I drew myself a hot bath, plopped in the rosemary, then plopped myself in—plop, plop, fizz, fizzzz. I waited for the relief. Thirty minutes later I was climbing the bathroom wallpaper I was so jittery. I lay awake all night, and after three nights of this, I went back to the store and discovered the problem: lavender puts you to sleep, while rosemary gives you the jolt of ten pots of coffee. It was an innocent communication gap that cost me serious shut-eye.

If you find something cheap and fabulous—bring lots home with you.

Phil and I took a bike tour through Tuscany and swooned for the local grape. We bought a case of this fine nectar. But how do we get the wine home in time for our party the day after we land? UPS would have taken two weeks. So we did it the old-fashioned way: We lugged it home. We emptied our carry-on bags and filled them with the bottles—cushioning the glass with dirty bike shorts and sweaty socks from our bike expeditions. I'm sure the stink alone from our dirty laundry deterred customs officials from checking what goodies we might be transporting. When we got home and unpacked, not one bottle had broken. That called for a celebratory drink and a toast!

Baby, You Can Drive My Car

Altimeters, odometers, carburetors, dipsticks. This is car talk.

When I was twenty-three, I moved all my earthly belongings from L.A. to Flagstaff, Arizona—the highest point in the state—in my beloved, pea-sized, green Hondamatic (before your time). Before my eighteen-hour drive, no one bothered to warn me I'd have to adjust the "altimeter" as I drove up, up, up the mountains.

Alti . . . what?

A week later, I was driving to my new job as a TV reporter and my car started sputtering and backfiring and choking like an animal gasping for its last breath. I pulled over. Hmmm. I must have put "bad" gas in the car. This was my theory. I called a garage—picking one blindly out of the Yellow Pages—to send a tow truck. They replaced my carburetor and told me, "Your altimeter wasn't adjusting to the altitude."

Sure, fine, okay. Just fix it, please. Just make it drive.

One week later, it happened again. He fixed it. And again. And again. I kept going back to the same shop. The seventh time, it didn't start at all. It was 5:00 A.M. and I was in my driveway in curlers and TV makeup, en route to the studio to go on camera.

That's *it!* I had myself a good cry, then called a cab and a tow truck. Later that day I confronted my mechanics and they just smirked at my impassioned speech.

It finally dawned on me: *They were taking me for a ride!* I discovered they had taken my old carburetor, sandblasted it to make it look like new, and put it back in. I went to a new mechanic. He looked over my engine and, again, that familiar shake of the head.

"Lots of damage here," he murmured. "Lots of fixin' to be done."

Three days later, the honest mechanic handed me a bill for nine hundred dollars.

Moral of the Story: *(1) Know your car basics. (2) Find a trustworthy mechanic through friends, co-workers, or family.*

Girl Road Trips

There you are sitting in the driver's seat out there on the open road, the sun setting behind you, the horizon beckoning ahead—and Bruce Springsteen is belting out from the radio: *"BABY WE WERE BOOOOORN TO RUUUUUUNNNNN! . . ."*

Every good road trip starts with good road music. I pack at least ten CDs when I'm heading out for a long drive and I sing along, really, really loud.

BEST ROAD TRIP TUNES

"Born to Run"; "Pink Cadillac" (Bruce Springsteen)

"Sweet Home Alabama" (Lynyrd Skynyrd)

"Back in the USSR" (Beatles)

"Rockin' Down the Highway" (Doobie Brothers)

"Let's Get This Party Started" (Pink)

"You Make Me Feel Like a Natural Woman" (Aretha Franklin)

"Little Red Corvette" (Prince)

"Hotel California" (the Eagles)

"I Think I Love You" (the Partridge Family)

BEST ROAD TRIP FILMS

Thelma and Louise
Midnight Run
Easy Rider
Planes, Trains, and Automobiles
The Straight Story

Road trips are romantic in that philosophical, I'm-free-and-I can-be-whoever-I-want way. If I'm not the driver, I stare out the window and write all sorts of goofy, poetic, deep stuff in my journal as the road passes by me.

Gather the girls together, pick someplace kooky, pack snacks, and take off. And don't forget to visit the ladies' room before you set out. My friends Jill and Marcy and I took a winter road trip in a snowstorm to a party two hours away. We loaded up my CJ7 Renegade Jeep with blankets, music, and thermoses of hot coffee before hitting the road. We cranked the Doobie Brothers and shivered and sang all the way.

Halfway there I had drunk too much coffee, and I had to relieve myself so badly that I couldn't wait for the next gas station. We pulled over and as I did my business behind the car door with the wind and snow causing a wind tunnel, I had the quickest drip-dry call-of-the-wild experience of my life. Oh yes, the girls laughed their heads off in the car. Needless to say, it was one of my finest moments.

Girl road trips are a good time for girl talk. There's nothing like staring out at an endless road that makes a woman meditate on where she's come from and where she's going. Natasha took a five-hour drive from Toronto to Montreal with buddies Liza and Marina and they spent the whole time giving each other *Cosmo* sex quizzes.

"We learned more about each other that day than we had in five years," she chuckles. "And we laughed so much our guts hurt all night!"

The other great thing about a girl road trip is this: If you get lost, there's no guy in the car to keep you from asking the nearest gas station for directions.

> **TAKE NOTE:** *The American Automobile Association has tips on how to drive safely and they can prepare a customized map for your journey. Before you strap on your seat belts, log on to: www.aaa.com.*

Whatever trip you take with the girls is usually healing and enlightening. My most blissful thing to do with my buddies is to meet them at a spa. Hello, heaven. We get massaged, prodded, plucked, peeled, and slathered. Last time we went to the Miraval spa in Tucson, Arizona, and surrendered to the "hot oil drip" treatment. Drip, drip, drip on our foreheads. It sent us astral traveling. I felt my legs rising up, up, up and away from my body.

My friend Jennifer took six of her friends and chartered a forty-foot boat to sail around the British Virgin Islands for a week one February. They hired a good-looking captain with a sexy accent ("We called him 'The English Muffin,' " she giggles) and spent a week snorkeling, sunning, and dining on deck.

"It was a completely bonding experience," she says. "We all brought one small bag and lived in this tiny space together. We were stripped down to our bare minimum."

In more ways than one. On their final night, they docked at local pub and had to barter to win the pub's free, coveted T-shirt.

"We all dropped our bathing suits to the floor in unison for the bartender," she says. "It was quite a finale."

They got their shirts, which read: I CAME, I SAW, I GOT NAKED AT THE WILLY T!

Talk about good girlfriend exposure!

MY SPA WISH LIST
I've been keeping a list of all the spas I want to go to. And every time a girlfriend comes back rejuvenated and glowing from another spa, I add it to my list. I've only been able to cross out a few so far, but give me time . . . I'm working on it.

Destination Spas:
Canyon Ranch in the Berkshires, Lenox, MA
www.canyonranch.com. 1-800-742-9000.

Center for the Well Being at the Phoenician, Scottsdale, AZ (I had one of the best reflexology sessions there recently.) www.thephoenician.com. 1-800-888-8234.

The Homestead, Hot Springs, VA. www.thehomestead.com. 1-800-838-1766.

Solace Spa at Fairmont Banff Springs, Banff, Alberta, Canada. www.fairmont.com. 1-800-259-7544.

Top Location Spas:

Amangani, Jackson Hole, WY. www.amanresorts.com. 307-734-7333.

Enchantment Resort, Sedona, AZ www.enchantmentresort.com. 1-800-826-4180.

Fairmont Chateau Lake Louise, Alberta, Canada www.fairmont.com. 1-800-257-7544.

Hyatt Regency Kauai Resort and Spa www.kauai.hyatt.com. 1-808-742-1234.

Las Ventanas al Paraiso, Los Cabos, Mexico www.lasventanas.com. 1-888-767-3966.

Miraval, Tuscon, AZ (such a serene environment, incredible spa treatments) www.miravalresort.com. 1-800-232-3969.

Rancho La Puerta, Tecate, Mexico www.rancholapuerta.com. 1-800-443-7565.

Ritz-Carlton Laguna Niguel, Dana Point, CA www.ritzcarlton.com. 1-800-241-3333.

Ten Thousand Waves, Santa Fe, New Mexico www.tenthousandwaves.com. 505-992-5025.

International:

Chiva-som int'l Health Resort, Thailand.www.chiva-som.com.

> **TAKE NOTE:** *Check out more spas online at www.spafinder.com or pick up* Conde Nast Traveler *magazine.*

Emma

Q & A with Karen Valenti, car expert; author of *The Women's Fix-It Car Care Book*

Q: *We saw this neat scene in an old movie where a woman uses her nylons as a substitute for her broken fan belt. Is this really possible? It's so cool.*

Karen: You can do that with the older cars. But most of us don't wear nylons anymore. If you tried it, you'd have to tie the nylon in a way that the knot was really smooth so the bump in the knot would be small enough to fit in the groove of the fan belt.

Q: *What should one have in her car emergency kit?*

Karen: At the top of the list is a cell phone. Most people don't know this but pretty much any cell phone company sells a prepaid cell phone that you can throw in your kit with some batteries. On the back of the cell phone, tape the phone number of a roadside service station.

Q: *Are more women learning about what makes a car run?*

Karen: Yes, and they didn't learn it from their dads. As young women, they are realizing it's time to take responsibility and learn about this to keep safe.

Q: *How do we find a good and honest mechanic?*

Karen: It's not easy. If you are totally ignorant about cars and you find a mechanic who doesn't really know how to fix your problem, he's not going to tell you that. Mechanics in the United States don't have to have any formal training whatsoever. You could be a cook one day and a "mechanic" the next and no one would know. You've got to ask around and trust your instincts. Choose your mechanic like you'd choose your family doctor. Talk to him. Do you like him? Is he taking the time to talk to you so you understand what's going on? Don't hire somebody who doesn't talk to you, double talks to you, uses words you don't understand, talks down to you, or says things like, "Honey, just leave me the keys, I'll take care of it . . ." Ask your friends who they use. The best thing is word of mouth. If your friend has someone she's been using for ten years and her car runs beautifully, her mechanic is the one.

Q: *What should every girl know about what's under the hood?*

Karen: You've got to know the basics of your car and how it works. It's no different from baking a cake: You learn the ingredients and you know the oven has to be at a specific temperature. It's the same with a car. I'd say every woman should know what the five fluids in your car do. The oil lubricates the engine. The coolant cools down the metal parts of the engine. The transmission oil runs your transmission. The brake fluid stops the car. The power steering is a liquid that helps you turn the wheel. If you know what those five fluids do in your car, you'll be able to keep it running.

FINAL THOUGHT

Boy oh boy, how a few helpful pointers from Karen would have helped me back in my Arizona days with my broken-down Hondamatic! Knowledge is power. Without it, you are stuck in the mud or at the mercy of some pretty lowlife scammers who want to take advantage of you. When everything works well in the technical department, a road/plane/train/boat trip can be a freeing adventure—meeting new people, tasting new flavors, becoming part of a world that is bigger than your everyday life. Pack your passport and a few essentials, and take off on your cultural, spiritual journey.

party
emergency!

O ne of the best parties I ever threw cost me fifteen bucks.
It was an intimate little affair in 1987: a block of aged
cheddar, crackers, cheap champagne, and an apple. My
younger brother, Chip, was visiting me at my tiny abode in
Arizona as the sun set. Looking back, I already had all the elements of a perfect party mastered: good food, great company,
something fizzy to sip, and mood lighting.

I come by my party-giving talents genetically. Mom was a
superb party thrower and I was her faithful taster and KP
helper—scraping and dicing the carrots (on special occasions I
did curly ringlets with a radish). An hour before party time, Mom
would sit at her vanity mirror lipsticking, powdering, and per-
fuming. Then came the dramatic slipping off of her slippers (she
hostessed barefoot) and the slipping on of the party dress.

And the most important ingredient: a smile.

What makes a great party? ALWAYS have more food, snacks, and drinks than you think you will need (even if you don't put everything out). A drought can clear the house. Never try a new recipe on party night. Music is a must, especially if it is set up where tipsy guests can't play DJ and scratch your CDs. And always remember: If you're still rushing at the last minute, it's going to be a great night. It's those overplanned occasions that always bomb.—"Nevada"

Suddenly Social

It's Saturday night. I'm curled up on the couch in my bunny slippers watching reruns of *Gilligan's Island*. The phone rings.

"It's us! We're down the street! We're coming over!"

It's the gang/the family/old friends. No need to panic. My pantry is stocked with what it takes to throw an impromptu soirée that swings.

TOP TWENTY PANTRY ESSENTIALS

Canned tomato sauce

Carrots/celery

Cheese (brie, goat, Jarlsberg, or sharp cheddar)

Chocolate brownie mix

Coffee

Cookies

Crackers

Eggs

Frozen hors d'oeuvres

Frozen pie crust

Frozen pizza crust

Fruit

Olives

Onion soup mix

Salsa

Sour cream

Tonic/seltzer/margarita mix

Tortilla chips

Wine

I slice the cheese, cut up the carrots and celery, line up the crackers, and arrange all on a nice tray around a bunch of grapes. Toss tortilla chips, salsa, and cheese together in a bowl and nuke it for one minute or heat in an oven at 350 degrees for 10–15 minutes. Put out a saucer of olives. Uncork the wine. Serve pretty biscotti and coffee as a chaser.

Not bad! I just made a little party and even had time to hide my bunny slippers under my bed and do it barefoot, just like Mom. Most kitchen-challenged people don't realize they have the ability to whip up a quickie pie, brownies, quiche, or pizza within fifteen minutes and feed a group of hungry pals. Homemade pizza takes ten minutes.

Watch: Pour tomato sauce on ready-made pizza crust, sprinkle on cheese and any herbs/extras you have in the fridge (olives, smoked salmon, this morning's leftover bacon, etc.), stick it in the oven. Presto!

People get intimidated by the phrase "hors d'oeuvres." Just because it's French doesn't mean it's snooty. Slice up a cucumber, spread on cream cheese, and sprinkle a dash of paprika. Congratulations, you just made French food.

Many of the above items can last in your fridge/freezer/pantry for months at a time, so stock up and sit back and relax in those bunny slippers. You have it all under control.

---

911 TIP My sister-in-law, Liora, makes the easiest, best, fastest chicken wings in the East. It's as easy as one, two, three. . . .

1. Boil wings in water for 15 minutes.
2. Place wings in bowl and pour spicy, store-bought barbecue sauce all over.
3. Cook 'em up on grill for 10–12 minutes or bake in baking dish at 350 degrees for 25 minutes. Finger-lickin' good.

But wait.

"Any girl can throw together crackers and cheese," says my friend **Chef Sarah Bouissou,** a culinary artiste at Bernard's Inn in Ridgefield, Connecticut. And you are not anyone. You are a gutsy girl! You try new things! In that case, "Let's fancy it up a bit," says Sarah, with a wink.

CHEF SARAH'S FANCIER TOP EMERGENCY PANTRY ITEMS

1. A wheel of **Baked Brie** wrapped in puffed pastry—buy this or make it (it only takes five minutes: buy phyllo and Brie, wrap the Brie up, bake ten minutes), and store in the freezer for these sudden occasions. Warm in oven for five minutes. Serve with **Honey Mustard** or **Chutney** on the side because "it's a lot fancier than just cheese on a cracker."

2. **Canned Chickpeas** in the cupboard and **Pita Bread** in the freezer: You can whip up fresh hummus in one minute! Rinse and drain peas, add 4 tablespoons lemon juice, 2 cloves garlic, ½ cup olive oil, and puree in blender. Warm up pita bread in oven. Cut in triangles and watch your friends dip.

3. **Cumin** (an underrated herb): Brush olive oil, salt, and cumin on the pita bread and stick in oven—"you now have exotic pita chips," says Sarah. "It takes only five minutes and it's fancier than just crackers and easy to make.

   "Basically, you should keep your spice rack full because you can rev up anything with dried herbs. Dried oregano and thyme will do wonders for your impromptu pizza."

Emme

4. **Lemon and Lime**: You can make boring old water interesting when you dress it up with a wedge.

5. **Popcorn** (but you don't serve it like everyone else): Throw on some dried herbs or Italian seasoning and kosher salt and *it's more than just popcorn.*

6. **Block of Parmesan Cheese**: It stays good in the fridge for a long time, longer than most cheeses. Can use on top of pizza or in a dip or in pieces with olives. It's zingier than regular cheddar or mozzarella. Parmesan is never boring.

7. **Hazelnuts:** Great to throw in a salad or put out in a bowl when someone is coming over quickly. More elegant than peanuts.

8. **Cream cheese:** You can make a quick dip with mixed herbs, olives, and tomatoes in the blender. Cream cheese lasts longer in the fridge than sour cream, so it's a good staple.

9. **Frozen Shrimp** (see below).

10. **Frozen Berries and Ice Cream** (see below).

If your guests are still hungry after the little foods, move into a quickie main-meal mode. Try the pizza (above) or warm up a frozen quiche and serve with salad and crusty bread. Or, if you really want to make them feel loved all over, rustle up a gourmet pasta dish and a little *dolce* ("sweet") before they can say, *"Ciao, bella!"*

Eight-Minute Pasta Dish
(And a Classy Dessert)

Nuts

Wine

Frozen, whole, peeled
  shrimp

Olive oil or butter

Herbs

Pasta

Can of whole tomatoes

Bread

Salad

Frozen berries

Ice cream

Champagne

Biscotti

Put on pasta water to boil. Put out bowl of nuts and some wine. Arrange a bunch of candles on a plate and put in center of table as a centerpiece. Sauté shrimp in butter or olive oil, garlic, salt, pepper, spices, herbs (fresh basil or whatever you have growing on your windowsill or dried in the pantry). Put on pasta to cook. Drain tomatoes, chop roughly, add to shrimp, and stir. Toss over pasta al denté! Serve with bread and salad.

For dessert: Defrost berries (follow directions on bag), toss with lemon juice, serve over plain vanilla ice cream with some biscotti. Biscotti is always a good item to keep in the house because it won't go stale.

Pour some champagne and add a little cassis if you have it. DONE!

The Easiest
Sit-Down Dinner Party

*The most important thing to remember when throwing a
dinner party? Never let them see you sweat! If you are
confident, no one will know you burned this or that. Stay
relaxed. Have fun.* —CHEF SARAH BOUISSOU

Then there are times when you actually *expect* people over for
dinner. You know . . . when you actually *invite* them?

A woman isn't mistress of her household until she's invited
and gloriously fed a group of close friends around her table with
food she made with her own hands. I mean a real, honest-to-
goodness dinner party with shined-up cutlery and good china and
people who sit down at a table to dine. This isn't having the posse
over and ordering pizza. It's a dinner party Mom might throw if
she were twenty-seven, single, and cool. It's a little formal (but not
too formal) and a lot of fun. If you've never done it before, don't
worry, it's easy.

Assuming you are starting from square one, here are step-by-
step directions for the easiest, tastiest, simplest, most inexpensive
and artfully decorated dinner party for eight.

SETTING UP:

Go to antique stores or thrift stores to find:

4   large silver serving spoons.

1   cake knife.

3–4   cheese knives (smaller than regular knives).

3   sets of glass candlesticks. Clear, blue, pink—whatever
        you can find. Candlelight sets a warm, relaxing mood
        for a dinner party. Place in the middle of the dining
        room table.

3   vases, silver plated or glass (different shapes and sizes).

1   white antique tablecloth in good repair; otherwise buy a crisp new one.

3–4 interesting white serving platters in all shapes and sizes. (I like to jumble different shapes of white together. Such a fun, clean look.) You will use them over and over again when you entertain, and whatever you serve will look great. (Pottery Barn and Dansk outlets rule.) If you can find antique glass plates, they're wonderful for salad.

25 off-white (cream) 8–10" candles. After each party, replace with fresh ones. (New guests, new candles.)

2   bunches of flowers: tulips, roses, daises—whatever your fancy!

PREP WORK:

1. Clean bathrooms: Put in new paper roll, clean mirrors, bathroom floor, toilet bowl under seat and around base. Light a fragrant candle that won't set your home on fire (always tend to lit candles).

2. Vacuum rugs.

3. Wash and dry wineglasses.

4. One-and-a-half hours before guests arrive, boil pasta water, then turn off, and keep the lid on.

5. Clean kitchen—run dishwasher with pots and pans 1 hour before guests come.

6. Cut and clean flowers and put some in the entranceway, in bathroom, and on dining room table.

7. Day before: Clean lettuce (Boston, butter, and endive) leaf by leaf, dry and rip leaves into bite-size pieces, put into a Ziploc bowl, place in fridge. (I wouldn't serve iceberg lettuce unless you plan to serve it alone, cut into wedges with chunky blue cheese dressing drizzled on top.)

MUSIC: For when you are cleaning and prepping:

> TLC: *CrazySexyCool*
> Angie Stone: *Mahogany Soul*
> Macy Gray: *On How Life Is*

THE TABLE

Set the table the day before. (If you're running around at the last minute, at least you know it's done and it looks great when the guests arrive.)

> dinner plate (smack in the middle)
> salad plate (upper left of the dinner plate)
> dinner fork (to the left of the dinner plate)
> salad fork (to the left of the dinner fork)
> dinner knife (to the right of the dinner plate)
> soup spoon (to the right of the dinner knife)
> dessert spoon (above the dinner plate with face toward left)
> dessert fork (above the dessert spoon with prongs facing right)
> water glass (upper right tip of knife)
> white-wine glass (upper right, to the left of water glass)
> red-wine glass (right behind and just left of the white-wine glass)
> dining table linen
> cloth napkins
> salt and pepper shakers/dishes (placed at the two ends of the table)

This is how I learned to set a formal table, but dress your table as simple or as formal as the situation calls for. I am always open to new ways of doing things, so if anyone has a better or more correct way, I want to hear about it!

APPETIZERS:

Cheese platter: Let the cheese temper 2 hours before
serving (take out of fridge)

¼-wheel Brie, goat cheese roll, Jarlsberg wedge, green
grapes on vine

Carr's whole wheat and sesame crackers

25 mini veggie quiches (mushroom, cheese, and tomato):
Check freezer department of supermarket. Put into oven
10 minutes before guests arrive.

Lay out cheese on one large white serving platter.

Lay out quiche on another.

PREPARE SIDE DISHES:

Boiled beet and goat cheese salad: Peel and boil fresh
beets for about 40 minutes. Let them cool. Slice into
semithin pieces onto a serving platter and toss crumbled
bits of goat cheese and chives on top.

Garlic bread: Slice a loaf of good Italian bread. On stove,
melt a stick of butter with chopped garlic. Brush inside
of bread with garlic butter and pour remaining mixture
on top. Wrap in tin foil, leaving some of the top exposed
(to get golden brown). Warm slowly at 250 degrees until
it's time to eat.

GUESTS ARRIVE:

Put coats on your bed, that's the easiest. If you have a house, des-
ignate a closet next to the front door with sturdy hangers. Offer
cocktails and serve appetizers. Ask one of your friends to be in
charge of serving drinks if you need to finish up a few things in
the kitchen before joining the fun. But don't leave yourself too
much to do in the kitchen or you'll miss the party!

MUSIC: For the arrival of the guests: soundtrack to *Big Night*.

Bobbie Carle's vinaigrette salad dressing

3 tablespoons Dijon mustard
¼ cup of sherry
2 pinches of kosher salt
¼ cup of honey

Shake the above ingredients in an old jam jar then add:

½ cup virgin olive oil

Then shake again.

If you like balsamic vinegar, replace the sherry with 3–4 teaspoons of balsamic. Then pour into servers and place on table on a plate with a serving spoon or in creamers. Put one at each end of table.

- If serving red wine with dinner, uncork and place on table 30 minutes before the meal.
- Put ice water at each end of table. I collect white pitchers in all different shapes and sizes that can be used for water, juices at brunch, margaritas, or flowers.

THE DINNER MENU

Veggie ravioli
Marinara sauce
Mixed green salad with vinaigrette dressing
Boiled beets and goat cheese salad
"Bold" me over garlic bread
Wine
Green bean salad

- Light all candles on table at the start of the meal.
- While everyone is having cocktails and appetizers, arrange undressed salad on vintage glass plates you can get at any garage sale.
- Throw ravioli in hot water while everyone is eating salad.
- Throw garlic bread in oven for fifteen minutes, preheated at 400 F.
- After salad course, scrape and stack salad plates in sink. Don't run the water or wash dishes. Just put to one side neatly. If you wash, guests will feel uncomfortable.
- Heat sauce and serve in a porcelain gravy boat. (NOT GLASS! It can break!)
- Strain ravioli and serve on a big white serving platter.
- Put bread on table in bread basket, covered with a white or Tuscan napkin.
- Serve ravioli and veggies.

Remember to turn off stoves and burners and ask if anyone needs anything. Then sit down, enjoy, and LET THE EVENING ROLL ON!

MUSIC during dinner:

Chris Botti: *Night Sessions*
Miles Davis: *Miles Away*
Evan and Jaron: *Evan and Jaron*
Nelly Furtado: *Whoa! Nelly*
Gypsy Kings: All the CDs are great
Norah Jones: *Come Away With Me*
Keb' Mo': *Just Like You*
Ottmar Liebert: *Barcelona Nights: The Best of Ottmar Liebert, Vol 1*

Emme

John Mayer: *Room for Squares*
Shawn Mullins: *Beneath the Velvet Sun* (awesome CD!)
U2: *All That You Can't Leave Behind*
Pete Yorn: *Musicforthemorningafter*

I prefer beautiful background music for any at-home event, regardless of the type of affair. My favorites are Diana Krall (The Look of Love), Buddha Bar I, II, *and* III *(they have both "cocktail" and "dinner" music in each), and* Aria 1 *and* 2. *Unless it's a very large event with dancing, I prefer the elegance of background music so your guests can visit with each other, especially during dinner. I would suggest choosing more personal favorites if someone is planning a romantic dinner for two.* —Party planner **David Tutera**

THROUGHOUT THE MEAL

- Always offer water.
- Always offer seconds.
- After all guests are finished, clear the plates. Not one second before. Don't rush! Take your time, enjoy the company and conversation. Let everyone digest a bit before you make any sudden movements to clear.
- Encourage people to get up and stretch their legs.
- Have coffee preset to go on. The coffee should be special: a hearty French roast. Make decaf and don't tell anybody (they'll sleep better and they won't be able to tell the difference). Or make sinful Godiva chocolate coffee.
- Once again, DO NOT load the dishwasher or do any dishes. Make piles.
- I serve the coffee in comfy, homey mugs. We collect mugs from all over the world, and for me it makes it personal and sentimental.

MUSIC: For lingering over dessert:

A Tribute to Curtis Mayfield
Bach, Mozart, Handel
Classical guitar
Elton John: *Tumbleweed Connection*
Alicia Keys: *Songs in A Minor*
Sade: *Lovers Live*

DESSERT

Italian cookies
Italian ices
Coffee
Herbal teas

- Take dessert out and let ice cream sit to room temperature.
- Don't rush serving.
- Let conversation linger, turn down lights even more if not completely at candlelight. Dim, dim, dim.
- Once last plate of dessert is finished, bring down the lights even more so people are focused on the candles and one another.

MUSIC: To pump everyone up after dessert:

Marc Anthony: *Marc Anthony*; *Libre*
Destiny's Child: *Survivor*
Janet Jackson: *Velvet Rope, All For You*
Lenny Kravitz: *Lenny Kravitz Greatest Hits*
Pink: *Missundaztood*
Santana: *Supernatural*

Saturday Night Fever (soundtrack)

Shakira: *Laundry Service*

AFTER DINNER

Fifteen minutes after the meal, offer after-dinner drinks.

- Anisette
- Baileys Irish Cream
- Chambord
- Cointreau
- Courvoisier (Cognac)
- Crème de Menthe
- Disaronno Amaretto
- Frangelico
- Kahlúa
- Sambuca
- Tia Maria

All the above can be served either on or off the rocks, over ice cream, or in coffee.

- Load the dishwasher and put stemware aside to do the next day. Put food in Ziploc bags.
- When the girls start hanging out in the kitchen and the guys are hanging out in the living room (or vice versa— after all, these are modern times) that's the time to put on DISCO. Yes, disco. Grab a friend and start dancing.

GENERAL TIPS

- Don't push help away. If they wanna help, great. But take it slowly and enjoy.
- Buy "name swirls" to identify each person's wineglass so

you don't have to use dozens and dozens of extra stemware. You can buy these curled paper ringlets by the bunch online. Write each guest's name on the swirl and curl it around the stem of the wineglass. Log on to www.tuits.com or call toll-free 1-888-935-2865.

- Take note of who brought what to your home and say thank you!
- If you have a really good friend coming over, ask him or her to bring dessert from a favorite bakery—a tart or a deep, flourless, rich chocolate cake. It's one less thing on your mind.

Linger for a while. Share stories, play games, play music, dance a little. Next day? Eat leftovers and enjoy reflecting on a fun evening.

Ya-Ya Sisterhood: Girl Gatherings

It's great fun having the gang over or getting together with other couples. But sometimes you just need to hang out with the girls. No matter how you slice it, there is no better bonding experience than when the girls gather to make an evening of it.

Whether you spend it hitting the clubs dressed to the nines for some flirty fun or a titillating bachelorette party or lounging in front of the tube in pajamas with a box of tissues and a good chick flick, girl's night is sacred. It's where hearts are bared, secrets are revealed, gossip is spread, and sex tips are shared.

 The best bachelorette party I attended started as a sort of "Laverne and Shirley bowling night." We had made

Emme

bowling shirts for everyone attending, complete with mono-grammed alias names. We had to be these "names" all night. We presented the bride with a Polaroid camera and an empty scrap-book. She had tasks to complete all night: get married advice from three single men and three married men. Get a condom from a guy. Kiss a policeman. The night ended in the West Village at a Mexican cantina with margaritas and we put the scrapbook togeth-er!! She'll keep the memories of that night forever. —"Mary Jo"

I think it is still fun to have slumber parties. The best is a Saturday night. You start at around six o'clock having old-fashioned cocktails, like "pink squirrels" and "grasshoppers" or anything you can find in a 1960s cocktail recipe book. Then you do each other's hair and makeup real sixties style with doe eyes and pink lips, while watching a video like Breakfast at Tiffany's. *Then you go to the chicest cocktail bar in town, and have hors d'oeuvres and a cocktail, and find a great dance place. It's fine when some-one flirts with you or asks you to leave with them, because you have to go to a slumber party later. It gives you a great excuse to get a number and invite him to tomorrow's brunch. That's right. The next day you all go to brunch and invite the guys you met the night before. So five girls turns into a reservation for ten. It's just for kicks, you don't have to marry the guy whose number you get, and besides, your friend might like the guy you met and you may like hers. PS: DON'T do this if you are already married. Go to brunch as five girls. . . . HA HA.—"Alicia"*

> **TAKE NOTE: Beauty Bonding.** *For a girls' night in, get a Beauty Parlor Night Kit. The $35 kit is filled with beauty parlor goodies like mud masks, facial scrubs, manicure kits, and invitations for six pals. See www.jaquagirls.com for more info!*

After the girls stay over on a Saturday night, there's nothing better than having a scrumptious, lazy Sunday morning (not *too* early!) brunch. Let everyone sleep in and take her time. If the weather is warm, I'll set up a table outside in the backyard, throw on a colorful tablecloth, and fill a vase with sunflowers. If there's a chill in the air, I throw a log in the fireplace and put some Italian love songs on the CD player, while we all hang around the warm kitchen, sipping coffee from steaming mugs as the popovers bake. Mmmm.

NOTE: In my kitchen, I like to eat well and serve the best food I can find to my guests. Generally, I try to use mostly organic, whole, fresh foods that have little or no additives. This way most of the nutrients remain in the food instead of being bleached, stripped, or replaced for one reason or another. I also hate needing a dictionary when I read the ingredients on the side of food containers or when the first ingredient is sugar, fructose, or salt. So I've learned to look at the ingredients of what I buy and keep my food simple; then I know what I am eating. I want to be nutrient-filled instead of nutrient-deprived. I think this caused my constant hunger in the past when I was eating on the run. You can't fool mother nature!

This is how I replace what some recipe calls for (just to list a few):

- *White flour*—whole wheat, brown rice, or spelt flour (You need to add a bit more liquid to the recipe if you choose to try whole wheat or brown rice flours.)
- *Sugar*—stevia, which is a leaf and very strong so use sparingly. (www.steviaplus.com.) Or try pure Turbinado raw cane sugar (Hain Pure Foods). It's really amazing how little sugar you really need to make a recipe sweet. I usually put in ¼ of what a recipe asks for.
- *Butter*—organic butter without the hormones or steroids used in the cow's milk.

- M*ilk/cheeses*—soy, rice, organic goat's milk, and on occasion organic cow's milk. Most of the cheeses I eat are goat cheeses and the milk I use in all recipes is either soy or rice milk. I've found I don't wake up in the morning with a stuffy nose when I eat fewer cow-based products.
- *Eggs*—free range organic for the same reason as the butter.

BRUNCH MUNCHIES

Blender Popovers
Coffee Cake
Blueberry Kutchen
Kitchen Sink Omelet for 6 hungry gals
Thinly sliced smoked salmon
Bagels and cream cheese
Champagne and orange juice
Steaming cappuccino
(. . . plus, *The New York Times*)

Blender Popovers

(Given to me by my Aunt Sally Clark, her favorite recipe in The Cookbook of Houston Junior League.*)*

> 1 cup flour
> ⅛ teaspoon salt
> 1 tablespoon butter, melted
> 1 teaspoon sugar
> ⅞ cup milk (or soy milk)
> 2 eggs

Preheat oven to 450°. Butter and heat popover pan, deep muffin pans or Pyrex custard cups, until sizzling. Put all ingredients in blender and blend well. Fill heated cups ⅔ full. Bake at 450° for 12 minutes. Reduce temperature to 350° and bake for 10 minutes. Unlike most popovers, these, which are made in the blender, do not fall. Makes 10–12 popovers.

Sally's Coffee Cake

(My mom's ultimate, never-fail coffee cake.)

> 1 cup milk, scalded
> 1 cake yeast, softened in ¼ cup warm water
> 2 cups flour (about)
> 1 egg, lightly beaten
> ⅔ cup sugar
> ¾ teaspoon salt
> 4 tablespoons shortening
> Sugar, cinnamon

Cool the milk and add the yeast and one-half the flour. Beat well and let rise until very light. Add the beaten egg, sugar, salt, and melted fat, mix thoroughly, and add remaining flour. Let rise until almost double in bulk. Pour into shallow, greased pans. When light, sprinkle thickly with sugar and cinnamon. Bake 20 minutes at 400°. Serve hot.

Blueberry Kutchen

(This came from my friend Patty—it's a recipe she got from her mother-in-law, Aline.)

FILLING

> 5 cups (2 boxes) blue-
>   berries
> 1 cup sugar
> 2 tablespoons flour
> 1 teaspoon cinnamon
> Pam spray for springform
>   pan

CRUST

> 2 cups flour
> 4 tablespoons sugar
> 1 pinch salt
> 2 sticks Fleischmann's sweet
>   oleo margarine (gold and
>   green package)
> 2 tablespoons vinegar

1. Preheat oven to 400°.
2. Spray Pam on springform pan.
3. Wash ½ blueberries and set aside.
4. Mix all other blueberry-filling ingredients in separate bowl.
5. Mix all crust ingredients with hands. Spread on bottom and sides of springform pan.
6. Dump blueberry mixture in it.
7. Bake 50–60 minutes.
8. Take out of oven and pour uncooked blueberries on top.

**Note:* You can substitute peaches, plums, or cherries for blueberries, but who wants to pit the cherries? Although, bless her, Aline did.

**Note:* You can leave the sugar out of the crust and fill it with sautéed mushrooms for an appetizer.

Kitchen Sink Omelet for 6 hungry gals

INGREDIENTS

    2 tablespoons extra virgin olive oil
    ⅛ teaspoon salt
    ½ cup sautéed mushrooms
    ¼ cup diced scallions
    12 eggs divided into 6 yolks, 12 whites
    3 tablespoons of club soda or seltzer (helps make the eggs fluffy)
    1 cup shredded mozzarella, Monterey Jack cheese, or goat cheese
    1 tablespoon herbs de province
    Salt & pepper to taste

OPTIONAL INGREDIENTS:
(Use any one or as many of the following as you desire.)

⅛ cup chopped white onion
¼ cup diced ham
¼ cup asparagus
¼ cooked bacon
You name it, put it in!

In a large omelet pan with a lid (you can use a cookie sheet too), heat olive oil on medium heat, add salt. Cut up mushrooms and scallions and sauté. When cooked and browned, turn heat to low and let the pan cool a bit. Beat eggs with club soda until light and fluffy, pour into pan, and cover with lid. After 5 minutes, lift lid and add ¾ cup cheese, the seasonings, and whatever else you want. Replace cover and check from time to time to see if all ingredients have blended into egg mixture and if it has started to harden. Once this happens, you can fold the egg in half making a half moon . . . add the rest of the shredded cheese to the top, cover again for 2 minutes, and voila! A sight for sore eyes! Salt and pepper to taste. Total cooking time: 40 minutes. (The key to this recipe is in the low heat and slow cooking.)

When the Soufflé Falls

The cosmos loves to toy with us. So it's inevitable that the night company comes for your big dinner—so does catastrophe. Your cream isn't whipping, your gravy is lumping, and your guests are an hour early (what *were* they thinking?) Mishaps can be mended if you're a glass-half-full kinda gal. When life gives you lemons, make lemonade.

The first Thanksgiving I was cooking for the family, I wanted

911 SUPPER CPR with Chef Sarah Bouissou

Dear Chef Sarah:
I'm in the midst of a cooking emergency and the guests are on their way . . . WHAT SHOULD I DO IF . . .

The chocolate soufflé falls: Once it falls, there's no getting it back up again. But if it's a chocolate fondue, you can make it look like one of these new desserts, a fondant chocolate, which is an overturned soufflé. Just run a knife around the edge of the pan, turn it upside down, and serve on a plate with ice cream and powdered sugar and a sprig of mint. The taste is the same; it just looks different (and now it's got another name!).

The spinach soufflé falls: Take the garnish you would have served on the side—parsley, wild mushrooms, and put them in the center of the soufflé and drizzle hollandaise sauce over the top. So what if the puffiness is gone!

I'm out of breadcrumbs: Whip up some crackers in the Cuisinart. Or toast bread in the oven and chop into quarters. If you don't have crackers, you can use Cheerios or melba toast.

I'm out of sugar: With a lot of recipes, you can substitute applesauce for sugar. But you really have to know what you're doing when you substitute for sugar because there's usually some chemistry going on in the recipe. When in doubt, just go borrow some from next door. Sometimes you can substitute honey, but you must taste as you go along because honey is sweeter than sugar.

I overcoooked the meat: Take the juices from the bottom of the pan and turn the meat into a stew with the juices as the sauce. If you've made roast beef and had surrounded it with carrots and potatoes and garlic, take all of that out, too. Add white wine to the pan and chicken broth and mushrooms and let it all bubble up. Thicken with a bit of flour. Put all in blender, including the veggies. Then cut up steak or beef and either pour it on top of meat or turn it into stew.

My stew is too salty: That's a tough one. If it's a soup or a sauce, add more unsalted chicken stock. Or you can plop in a peeled potato, which often will absorb the salt. Don't forget to take it out before serving.

  If it's fish, you can add lemon juice to counterbalance the salt. Or make a quick salsa without any salt in it and serve on top.

My dessert mold is ruined: If it's very liquidy, serve in a bowl as a chilled soup. If you have time to put it in the freezer, it can be a frozen soufflé with whipped cream on the side or folded in, like a chiffon. Add a sprig of mint. (A sprig of mint will turn many disasters into something beautiful.)

The pancakes are flat and lumpy: Whisk or strain the batter. For flat pancakes, just turn them into a tower by stacking them. Your baking soda perhaps didn't work. Make sure to get a fresh box! In other recipes when the baking soda doesn't work, you can often add an egg.

I burned something and there's too much smoke!: Light candles and leave the doors and windows open. Flap your arms. Do anything to get that smoke out.

You're out of vanilla extract: Use liqueur, Grand Marnier, raspberry Framboise, Chambord, cinnamon, nutmeg . . . depending on what you are making.

Too spicy?: Add some fruit! If your curry sauce is too spicy, add some apple or coconut milk to help counterbalance. It's the same theory as chutney falls under.

Lumpy mashed potatoes: Add peas or wild mushrooms so the lumpiness seems intentional. With lumpy gravy, throw it in a blender.

WISE GUY

Mark Fierro, The Grillmeister

Barbecue!

I've crashed a zillion barbecues at my buddy Mark's place. He's so good with the tongs that I had a special apron made for him: THE GRILLMEISTER LIVES HERE! His barbecuing tips:

Classic bird: Mark's recipe for his famous chicken wings: "Prebake the wings until just cooked through before marinating in Tabasco sauce, honey, vinegar, finely chopped fresh garlic, black pepper and red pepper. Marinate them in a Ziploc bag overnight, then crisp them up on a hot grill and sprinkle with some dry herbs before serving."

Smoke 'em out: To get extra smoky flavor, "cut a soda can in half lengthwise to make a trough. Put in wet smoke chips, like mesquite. Set it between the burners under the rack. It's amazing how much flavor smoking can give you. I'll also take clippings from a rosemary bush, soak them, and put them under the grill rack for extra flavor."

Veggies: "Portabella mushrooms are as good as steak when barbecued. Sprinkle with good olive oil, finely chopped Vidalia onion, and pepper on the gills. A lot of the onion falls into the grill, but it creates more of that great smoky flavor when it does."

Dessert: "Yes, it's true, you can put fruit on the grill. I grill fresh pineapple . . . slice it and brush lightly with olive oil and a bit of balsamic vinegar. It makes the fruit caramelize and sweetens it up. Get some grill marks on the fruit and serve it with vanilla yogurt dip (add some vanilla and brown sugar to the yogurt and stir). Grilled peaches, pears, mangoes, and figs are also great. Split the figs and grill split-side down. Mix together some mascarpone cheese and sugar. Flip the figs sliced-side up and dollop some cheese on top . . . it will melt right in."

What a rack!: "I'll toast my garlic bread, bake potatoes and tomatoes, or finish browning onions on the top rack. Use Vidalia onions from April to September. They're so sweet . . . you can bite into them like an apple."

Ready when you are: "Don't cut into food to see if it's ready. If you do, all the juices will run out. If you're experienced, you can tell something is done by *feel* . . . by a poke with a finger or tongs. Stick a fork into a bigger piece of chicken and see if the juices run clear. If they do, it's ready."

So, HUNGRY YET???

everything to be perfect. It was time to stuff the turkey, the oven was preheated, the celery and onions were browned, I had the sage in my hand . . . but I couldn't find the breadcrumbs. No crumbs. No bread. Not even a stale, lonely, melba toast.

The empty turkey beckoned. I had to think *fast* (or the onions were going to burn). I grabbed a box of Cheerios and poured! And you know what? It was de-lic-ious. My Cheerios stuffing has since become family folklore.

My friend Donna was making homemade ice cream for dessert, but the ice cream didn't "ice." She smiled, and served it as "ice cream soup" in her best bowls and silver spoons, with fresh mint and blueberries floating on top. It was yummy, and no one knew it was born from a faux pas (someone even asked her for the recipe). Martha Stewart would have been proud of us both.

Guests take cues from you. If you're frantic, they freak. Whatever happens, keep your cool. If someone you tells you your emergency gravy is amazing—IT IS. No need to argue and go on to describe how you strained the lumps with last night's nylons. Kitchen horror stories stay in the kitchen war zone. Just smile—even blush a little (nice touch)—and say, *"Graci, bella!"*

Charm on the Cheap
(A Bash Without Blowing
Your Budget)

I have a very optimistic friend who threw a dinner party but owned no tables to speak of. As if that would stop my very creative, industrious pal. She did a round of secondhand stores the day before and bought old silver trays and platters, polished them up, and placed them on overturned crates around her living room.

Last year I went to a sit-down dinner party given by a couple whose living room and dining room were filled with boxes from their recent move. So? They turned their garage into a temporary dining salon. They whitewashed the floors, walls, ceilings, and old wicker furniture and rolled up the garage door. Fresh flowers on the table added bold color. Talk about dining al fresco. It's amazing what you can do with few resources and loads of imagination.

Just one great piece can add such class to your table. Maybe it's one terrific vase in the center or an antique butter knife you inherited from Grandma. I used to throw "white" parties where my table was filled with only white, offbeat pieces I found at garage sales for pennies.

Because I had a theme, it looked ultra-chic. Against the jumbled ivory palette, the food became art. Under the dishes, more white. I used my mother's old linens—doilies, cocktail napkins, and tablecloths—and layered them with her delicate, antique lace tablecloths. The cherries looked redder, the greens became emerald. . . .

Garage sales/secondhand stores/five-and-dimes

PLUS

Imagination

EQUALS

Charm

- Buy an old card table and paint it or throw on a colorful tablecloth. Pick up odd chairs at a secondhand store and paint funky colors.
- Shine up old, mismatched silverware and jumble them together. Ditto for glassware. Use colorful pipe cleaners or ribbons to hold silver together at each plate. Or get your five-year-old niece to make some cutlery holders with paper and crayons.
- Autumn leaves: Rinse leaves, lay them under a book to dry flat, and use as coasters or on the cheese platter.
- Make simple place cards and find pretty pebbles on the beach to lay on top.
- Missing condiment holders? Improvise. Put little dishes at each end of the table in lieu of salt and pepper shakers. When everyone sprinkles with fingers, it feels very bohemian.
- Fill the bathtub with water and float lighted tea candles.

Booze, Sex, Drugs, Rock 'n' Roll (The Delicate Chemical Balancing Act of Party Central)

WHEN GUESTS MISBEHAVE

An empty wineglass is not a bad thing. Let your guests take a breather from drinking alcohol. Offer them water (keep a jug on the table). If you know someone has a drinking problem, don't plop the bottle next to him or her. Always offer nonalcoholic drinks on the drink menu. And if someone has had too much to drink and wants to have another, ask them for their keys.

Shaken not Stirred (A Gal's Starting-out Bar)

Utensils: Martini shaker/strainer, 1 oz. shot glass, bottle opener, corkscrew, can opener, blender, ice bucket and tongs, cocktail napkins/coasters, metal or plastic ice scoop (don't use a glass to scoop ice—bits can come off into the ice and go into other drinks), swizzle sticks, a pitcher, and a bar towel.

Glasses: Short highball, champagne, red wine, white wine, liqueur, and martini glasses, and beer mugs (silver and pewter).

Alcohol: Rum, vodka, gin, tequila, vermouth, beer, red and white wine, and champagne.

Nonalcoholic: Tonic, seltzer, Coke, ginger ale, grapefruit, orange, pineapple, and cranberry juice, sour mix, nonalcoholic beer, tomato juice, and a big pitcher of water with ice.

Lingo: Straight up (no ice, water, or juice); on the rocks (with ice); with a twist (twist of lemon, lime, orange); dirty martini (with some olive juice).

Fruits and veggies: Green olives, limes, oranges, cherries, small onions, mixed nuts, and celery stalks.

One New Year's Eve, I saw a guest sliding down my couch *drooling*. I took her to another room, gave her a pillow, blanket, aspirin, water, and tucked her in till morning.

Your bedroom is a good place to let someone regain their composure, as long as it isn't occupied.

In my college years, my roommate and I often found exuberant party guests lost and squirming in the coats piled high on our beds. That's okay for college. But once you graduate you want to reach a new level of PDA (public display of affection). Now, closets, balconies, and pool cabanas may have the right kind of feel, depending on what kind of mood you're in.

A votre santé! Prost! Cheers! Salud! L'chaim!
Five Really Easy Drinks:

1. Cooler or Spritzer
1½ oz. liquor
Add ginger ale or seltzer
Serve in short highball glass. Garnish with lemon wedge.

2. Salty Dog
1½ oz. gin
Add grapefruit juice over ice
Serve in a highball glass.

3. Apricot Fizz (nonalcoholic)
2 oz. apricot nectar
1 oz. lemon juice
Mix and strain over rocks in a highball glass. Add sparkling water.
Garnish with lemon or lime wedge.

4. Hot Buttered Rum (makes 4 servings)
4 cups of hot water
4 T of butter (not margarine)
4 teaspoons of unrefined brown sugar or molasses
1 T cinnamon and nutmeg
6 oz. dark rum (optional)
1¼ T of vanilla extract or 4 T of vanilla schnapps (optional)
Blend all the ingredients together and add whipped cream.

5. Bloody Mary
1½ oz. of vodka
1 T of Tabasco
½ T of horseradish
½ T Worcestershire sauce
Pinch of cinnamon
Salt and pepper to taste
One celery stalk

Stir ingredients together and serve in a tall glass with ice. Garnish with celery stalk in drink.

TAKE NOTE:
1. If you break a glass anywhere near the ice bucket, get rid of all the ice in the bucket. Better safe than sorry.
2. Never add ice cubes to a hot drink. It most likely will shatter the glass. Be careful!
3. For frosty mugs, dip them in water and place them in the freezer for 30 minutes prior to using.

RISKY BUSINESS

Don't expect life-long enemies to kiss and make up at your table even if it's the Last Supper. True story: Natasha was once at a party and the guests included a girl, "Nadia," Nadia's new boyfriend "Martin," Nadia's ex-husband (who had found her in bed with Martin and tossed their clothes out the window), and the ex-husband's new, jealous, insecure date. All it took was one comment:

"So," said the ex to his replacement, "break up any other marriages lately?"

Punches flew. No one stayed for dessert.

PARTY CRASHER

If you're having a sit-down dinner and your invitation says "admit one" someone may still show up with their hungry cousin in from Des Moines. Smile and quickly set another setting. They should have called and asked. At a get-together at my place last year, a girlfriend called to say: "I'm madly in love with a new guy, I can't stand to be away from him for one second never mind an entire meal, I want you to meet him . . . *can I bring him along?*" OF COURSE!

Rock Till You Drop: The Music

"If music be the food of love, play on."

So writes Shakespeare, a man of melody.

Flipping on any ol' radio station as background Muzak will make your party animals snooze. Examine your specimens. Are they downtown funky? Are they jazz intellectuals? Match the music to the milieu.

Natasha's music collection consists of Frank Sinatra and the Partridge Family (she has yet to analyze this in therapy). So, "I tell my guests to bring their favorite CDs," she says. "We give each one a spin and everyone's happy. They even let me play a David Cassidy tune or two."

My friend Rich played only disco at his parties: Donna Summer, the Bee Gees, and K.C. and The Sunshine Band. After two hours, we'd start yelling at him, *"Rich, do you have anything else?!"* That wasn't his only music oddity. He also could never play a whole song in its entirety. Halfway through one tune he'd pop out the CD and say, "Oh, but wait, you gotta listen to *this* one . . . !" Our mutual friends Jill and Nick gave him a much-needed music makeover. Today, Rich plays cocktail tunes when people arrive, classical during dinner, disco for dancing, and jazz for dessert. A smorgasbord. And he tries to play each song to the end.

Volume should be loud enough to make you tap along, but low enough to allow you to hear one another debate the day's gossip. If you have talented friends, ask them to bring the guitar. Nothing like a communal sing-along to make you all warm, fuzzy, and prepped for a group hug. When midnight hits, switch tactics; stick on a dance CD, and shake your booty for an hour. It works off dessert and wakes everyone up for the journey home.

MORE MUSIC IDEAS

Jazz
Tony Bennett: *Playin' with My Friends*
Bebel Gilberto: *Tanto Tempo*
Norah Jones: *Come Away with Me*

R&B
D'Angelo: *Brown Sugar*
Craig David: *Born to Do It*
Macy Gray: *On How Life Is*
Alicia Keys: *Songs in A Minor*
Maxwell: *Now*
Shannon McNally: *Jukebox Sparrows*
Sade: *Lovers Rock*
Jill Scott: *Who Is Jill Scott*
Remy Shand: *Way I Feel*
Angie Stone: *Mahogany Soul*

Funk/Dance
Brand New Heavies: *Shelter*
Brooklyn Funk Essentials: *Make Them Like It*

Rock/Pop/Folk
David Gray: *White Ladder*
John Mayer: *Room for Squares*
Martin Sexton: *The American*
U2: *All That You Can't Leave Behind*

Ambient
Groove Armada: *Back to Mine*
Zero 7: *Simple Things*

Classics
Any Miles Davis
Any Little Feat
Any Bob Marley
Any Steely Dan
Any Van Morrison

Give Me Light!

People can't connect with one another under the blaze of a 500-watt bulb. Do you want to remind them of the high school cafeteria?

At my girlfriend's birthday party last year the food was delicious and plentiful, the music was hopping, and the lighting was bright and cheery. Guests were hanging around the edges of the room, taking cover in the shadows. I approached the party planner and offered, "I know in my heart that if we dimmed the lights near the center of the dance floor, people will move in and get dancing."

We dimmed, and the people began to relax because they didn't feel as though they were at an interrogation! Dim the bulbs, light candles, or string up those little Christmas lights along the windowsills, and your guests will warm up with the softer focus.

911 TIP **Party Picture Perfect:** "If you are taking group shots of the party gang and you use a flash, put the blondes in the back and the dark-haired people in the front," says my friend and photographer **Melanie Dunea**. "The light from the flash can make people in the front look washed out, so let the dark-haired people absorb the light."

The Company You Keep:
Who Goes with Whom

A successful party is not a gathering of every person known to the host. It's a selected grouping of like-minded folk (i.e., don't invite your prayer group if your sister is bringing her witchy friends). —"SHARON"

INVITATION ETIQUETTE
I had a beautiful baby shower and I wasn't involved with the invitations. My family didn't want to invite one particular person because she was a real downer at other parties I've thrown. I asked that she be invited, to cheer her up. Among eighty smiling women eating pink cake, this woman complained the entire afternoon like a dark cloud, friends reported to me later. Be kind, but know your limitations. If someone has proven time and again to be a party pooper, leave him or her off the list and invite the people you *like* to be around. For that same party, I wish certain neighbors had been invited because some of them felt left out and didn't speak to me for weeks. I felt bad about that.

P.S.: If you're the invitee, always, always, RSVP.

MIXING AND MATCHING
A party is kind of like a science experiment. You combine variants in a test tube and shake it up over the Bunsen burner and wait for it to sizzle—or combust. Go ahead, seat your prim Aunt Ruth next to your friend with the bellybutton ring. Seat your priest next to the girl who "sees dead people." See what happens. Make life interesting. Make your day.

Sometimes it doesn't work. I used to think that if you invited

> ## 911 TIP   What If My Guests Don't Mingle Well?
> by party planner **David Tutera**
>
> If you are entertaining at home I suggest you plan your guest list carefully. Try to mix an "interesting" group, but one that has similarities. No one knows your friends better than you, so bring together the people you think would enjoy each other's company. If you are having a larger party, then mix everyone together . . . everyone is bound to meet someone he/she will get along with. When entertaining a group of couples, I like to seat each person at separate tables. This allows for each couple to mingle separately and chat about something different. If you are forced to have an eclectic group of friends together, it is your duty as a host to make sure you introduce everyone to each other. They obviously have one thing in common (having you as a friend), so try to get a conversation going between them.

everyone you knew and had one big bash, you'd cover all your bases and it would be a blast. Not so.

At my last collection of characters one of my suburban New Jersey neighbors was sitting next to a fashion-designer friend. She came up to me later and said, "I've never met a man who could talk so long about a piece of fabric before." (It wasn't a compliment.)

Thematically Speaking

For the drama queen in everyone, throw a theme party:

Mystery party: Everyone dresses up as his or her favorite detective. Stage a pretend murder and you all have to

Emma

figure out who the killer is. Serve the food a British detective would eat (Yorkshire pudding!).

Medieval party: Everyone dresses up like characters from Camelot and eats meat with their hands while a wench serves wine from a jug.

Tea and poetry party: Everyone recites a poem he or she loves or wrote. Serve tea, scones, jam, and cucumber sandwiches.

Fifties party: Dress up like Elvis or a bobbysoxer and serve meatloaf and mashed potatoes. Play classic rock 'n' roll tunes.

Americana: Wear red, white, and blue and eat hot dogs on paper plates. Watch *American Graffiti.*

Sex and the City: Drink Cosmopolitans, wear sexy skirts, and watch back-to-back episodes of the show.

Q & A **with David Beahm,** party planner, noted in 2000 for the wedding of Catherine Zeta-Jones and Michael Douglas. He's a favorite of celebrities, socialites, and the fashion world, as well as nonprofit organizations such as the Whitney Museum of American Art, Children's Advocacy Center/NYU Medical Center, New York Hall of Science, and Carnegie Hall.

Q: *What makes a great party?*

David: Besides the guests, by far the central element to a really great party is the host. If she's not relaxed, not free to greet guests and to have fun, then how could a guest expect to enjoy the party? A host must be exactly that—not off in the pantry getting more ice for the bar. The host must be organized, prompt, attentive to "wall flower" guests and introduce them around the party (but not attach themselves to one or two people for the night), and aware of guests' needs. "Many hands make light work": If a party planner or even a caterer is not in the budget, simply ask several close friends to be responsible for just one thing during the party (one friend to watch the door, one friend to keep the ice bucket filled, etc.); a tremendous burden is taken off the host and frees him or her up to do their job of hosting. It also frees up your friends to enjoy the party, too. Oh—it's also the responsibility of the host to make sure your guests look good, too—lighting at a party is so very important. The value of professional lighting should not be underestimated . . . but when in doubt, candlelight is a tried and true friend.

Q: *Have you ever had any party emergencies?*

David: Well—proper preplanning for anything that can go wrong will make you ever the more prepared for when something actually does go wrong. However, Murphy's Law intact, keeping a calm head in an emergency is always the rule. Remember, hopefully there is no life or limb in peril—and since a party is not brain surgery, take a huge deep breath and let a calm head prevail. Accidents happen, and as host it is your responsibility to make them unhappen—*with a smile.* And for the "uh-oh—I forgot" emergencies, from posies to panty hose, you'll be surprised what you can find at the convenience store on the corner.

Q: *Can you suggest some inexpensive party decor?*

David: The value of candlelight for the ambience of a party cannot be underestimated. For home parties, install dimmers, and light candles—the dust bunnies magically disappear and the old furniture suddenly seems brand new! To create a funky atmosphere, change all your lightbulbs to pink, lavender, or gold—you can also alternate in with red bulbs. Do not use blue or green light; it is not flattering at all.

Also—don't forget about all the other senses. Make the room feel warm by paying attention to not only what your guests see, but what they smell—perhaps have a sheet of cookies baking when your guests come in the door—or even some onions and garlic sautéing on the stove top emanate a feeling of home and comfort—instantly your guests are relaxed and smiling. Comfortable chairs or even pillowed sitting areas on the floor are important, too. Use what you have the best way you know how.

Q: *Any far out ideas for a party?*

David: We once made a tunnel using fifteen thousand Animal Cracker boxes for the Whitney Museum of American Art Gala. Everyone loved it—and the staff of the museum had Animal Crackers for all the children in their neighborhood for a really long time.

There are now a few companies that have performers that are encased in stretch fabric who become living, moving statues. It's very interesting, effective, and unexpected. One company we use airbrushes performers' bodies to mimic the surroundings—they totally blend in—it's wonderful to watch a guest's face when a picture or a wall moves.

Q: *Any good party tricks?*

David: The secret to a good party is no trick—it's simple: Preplan, preplan, and preplan for a beautiful and comfortable atmosphere, good people, good food, and good drink.

FINAL THOUGHT

I love entertaining with a passion. I love to have candlelit parties and see my home filled with people we really care about. I love setting an ambience. The food tastes better, the conversation flows, and the evening takes its time. When the holidays roll around I love the contrasts of snowy evenings and warm, cozy fireside gatherings. The smell of the candles and dinner cooking on the stove makes me feel full and complete. Can you tell I'm a true Cancer? I love David's suggestion of baking cookies before guests arrive. I'm definitely going to try that!

romance
emergency!

Men!
They smear our lip gloss and gulp milk from the car-
ton and break our hearts into a zillion pieces. But one
good kiss and we forget the crummy stuff the last guy did and fall
head over heels with the new Romeo.

Men can drive you batty and they can also rock your world.
That's just a man's job. They'll send you flowers, sing you songs,
hold your hand, and melt your heart.

They'll make you laugh with joy and burn with passion. And
the right guy can make life feel complete—but finding your soul
mate can be a long and sometimes painful pro-
cess. You really do have to kiss a load of toads
to find a prince—so pucker up and I'll tell you
my tales of woe and romance along the rocky
road of loooove . . .

Hello Hormones!
(Love vs. Lust)

It's not the men in my life that count; it's the life in my men. ——MAE WEST

As a young woman, I was in a constant state of dis-hormone-y. Hormones surged through my body at a mile a minute but my brain and heart never seemed able to keep up. What was I suppose to do with these physical impulses? I honestly didn't have a clue.

The more mixed up I got about sex, the clearer boys seemed to get on the subject. They seemed to understand horniness from the get-go and didn't let their emotions get in the way of what they wanted—and they knew exactly what they wanted: SEX—and plenty of it, thank you very much. No confusion there.

Today, women have definitely caught up and are smarter and more savvy in the ways of lust and love. But still, sometimes, there is that same age-old, head-heart-horny tug of war that can yank us every which way but loose.

Every time I felt heat for a guy in college, I thought I was "in love." I had no idea that it was just plain, good ol' fashioned lust.

I remember dating a dear guy who lived out of town. When we were apart we'd write, call, and have these incredible rendezvous (see more about long-distance romance later in the chapter). But then, without warning, I'd meet some hunky guy at a party and be like, "Oh my God, why is my heart throbbing?!" It confused me to no end. I had no idea what lust was about, other than when it was contained in a loving relationship. Why did it pop up when-ever it wanted? It made me doubt a few of the relationships I was in because these strong feelings were so new (I guess I was a late bloomer in this area) and they came (I thought) out of nowhere.

Emme

There I was, breaking up with a great guy just because my bod' was acting naturally.

My poor boyfriend. I must have broken up with him at least six times in three years. He, on the other hand, being a little older, had all this lust stuff squared away; he knew he wanted ME and not another "experience." He finally got sick of the moronic/hormonic mood swing roller-coaster ride I was taking him on and he bailed—and I don't blame him. It took me a long time to realize that my body was being taken hostage by primal forces: female hormones.

Wow, what a revelation it was when it finally dawned on me that I didn't have to let my hormones run my life. I mean, I could actually care about one person and *still feel attraction* for other guys. And just because I lusted after a guy didn't mean he was The One.

But then, what is this lust?

Lust is when your heart races and your temperature rises and all your senses are shooting sparks as though you've got your finger jammed into an electrical socket. All you can think is: *I must have him.*

Love?

Love is like that great, tasty, Saturday-morning breakfast at your favorite diner: cheese omelet, bacon, cappuccino, croissants with jam. It's comforting and dependable without ever being boring. It's exactly what you want. And, especially when served hot, it's so, so, satisfying. It's nourishment for the heart and soul.

If love is the hearty meal, lust is the mouth-watering spice sprinkled on top. If you can combine the two and whip up a sizzling entrée using the best of both ingredients, you've won the lotto.

I knew I was in lust *and* in love with Phil a few months after we began dating.

After a night of merriment, he'd leave my apartment in the morning to go to work . . . but it took us half an hour to say goodbye because we didn't want to be apart. He'd descend the stairs like a doomed man who would never know love again, turning back to look at me from each step, begging me to throw him one more farewell kiss as I stood in the hallway clutching my nightshirt and smiling from ear to ear.

It was so Romeo and Juliet; parting was such sweet sorrow . . .

Wham, Bam . . . Is This Love? (Or Am I Just Happy to See Him?)

Okay, ladies. I posted the Love vs. Lust question on my website and here's what you had to say:

"You know you're in love when the thought 'I need some time alone' never enters your mind. You know you're in lust when that special someone's touch almost carries an electrical charge, and when their smell is downright intoxicating." —**"Sarah"**

"I'm 57 years old. I still haven't figured it out. I've been married and divorced twice . . . Nearly every guy I see, I lust over, until I get to know them!"—**"Mathilda"**

"I was in love with my previous boyfriend and knew it by the feeling of innate peace and calm I would have when I would wake up next to him—and by how much I loved having his smell on my sheets."—**"Liz"**

"I'm in love when his absence leaves a hole in me."—**"Leah"**

"I knew I was in lust when I felt like I had no control over anything in my life . . . it was like PMS, but more intense. I knew I was in love when I saw my whole future life flash in front of my eyes; when I looked at that person and didn't worry about what he was thinking or where the relationship was going—I just wanted to be where I was, enjoying our time."—**"Naomi"**

"In love, you feel safe enough to confess your worst flaws and biggest dreams."—**"Cloe"**

"Lust is that 'can't eat' butterflies in the stomach. Love is full and warm."—**"Lorrisa"**

Avoiding Mr. Wrong

Mr. Right is out there . . . waiting for you.

He's sensitive yet strong, smart *and* humble, ambitious but patient, serious while silly, handsome but definitely not pretty. A real guy's guy who shoots hoops with the boys in the afternoon but loves reading poetry to you in the moonlight.

WOW. Where *is* this guy?

He's standing behind about one hundred Mr. Wrongs. Like I said earlier, you've got to pucker up for a lot of toads before you find a real Prince Charming. You're going to have to navigate through a murky swamp of hellish dates before reaching that distant shore known far and wide as the land where the great guys hide.

But thankfully, Natasha and I have hosted enough girl-talk sessions to come up with a few guidelines that should help keep the Mr. Wrongs at bay and keep your toad kissing to a minimum. You've seen that *Seinfeld* episode where Elaine is conserving her contraceptive sponges and has to decide which of her suitors is "sponge worthy"? Well the guys described below don't even make it to that stage.

Men Who Are Not Second-Date Worthy

MR. ENRIQUE SUAVE

He's got the moves and grooves that will make you feel like you're the most irresistible woman on the planet. Rose petals line the hallway to the bedroom, proclamations of love are made on the first date, his gaze penetrates deep into your eyes and soul. Problem is, he does this with all the girls—even the cashier at the dry-cleaner. And he checks them out, too, while he's on a date with you. No such thing as "the love of one good woman" to this Romeo. If you want him, be prepared to share him.

MR. BEAUTIFUL

He's beautiful, yes. An Adonis! People stop him on the street and ask him if he's the guy in that half-naked, billboard-size Calvin Klein underwear ad in Times Square. He loves it when they do that. You'd better have two bathrooms when you date this guy . . . he'll take longer than you to get ready and he'll use up all your hairspray. If you want him, you'll have to get up an hour earlier than him every morning to put on makeup before he sees you! Forget that.

MR. MARTYR

He has a laundry list of things to do for other people and puts himself (and you) last on the list. At first you think he's really nice and big-hearted. Then you realize he's just avoiding his own life and his own problems while he tries to fix everybody else's. If you want him, understand that one day when your car is stuck in a snowbank and you're freezing your butt off, he'll be out shoveling someone else's driveway.

MR. KNOW-IT-ALL

Ask him, he knows everything. Or at least he thinks he does. At first he comes off as really smart and assertive. Quantum physics? He did his thesis on that and he'll tell you all about it in detail. Again and again. Somewhere between splitting the atom and the theory of relativity, you realize you haven't been able to get a word in at all. And, God forbid he should ask you about *you*. If you want him, you'd better be a listener with no opinions of your own. There's no room for two brains in this relationship.

MR. BUDDY

He goes to girl movies and wants to know all about your feelings and your friends' feelings. He's an expert at this stuff 'cause he grew up with, what, ten sisters? At first, it feels great to have a guy

who *understands* you. But soon it feels like you are dating yourself. And he's not all that into sex, either. If you want him, be prepared to toss out your romance-novel ideas of relationships and invite him to your girl dinners.

MR. CONTROL FREAK

Wow, he's so organized! What a change from those guys who leave their underwear on the floor. He's got everything timed perfectly . . . his meals, his appointments, his life. He's so in charge. But it won't take long for you to see that he clings to his schedules because of his fear of change and because he cannot adapt to new situations. Can you imagine this guy taking care of the kids for a day? Don't ever throw a surprise party for him—he'd hate it! If you want him, be prepared to act as his secretary for the rest of his life.

E ven with all our advice, we know (you can't fool *us!*) you will still date the wrong guys sometimes. Don't sweat it. It's in our gene pool. It's something we have to get out of our system.

"I have too many friends who go for the wrong guys. It's like smart women have some sort of wiring snafu that sends them straight into the arms of Mr. Wrong. But after trying to prevent more than one from getting sucked into a bad situation, I have developed a theory: If you have a friend who is in LUV with a bad man, you cannot deter her. She may LOVE you, but she LUVS that man, and the LUV will always trump the LOVE. I'm not talking about abuse; if my friend is being abused, I'm getting her out of there even if she hates me for it. I'm talking about smart women, foolish choices. The best thing that you can do for that friend is be there for her when the LUV is gone."—"Sharon"

"I told my best friend from college that her new boyfriend was 'vanilla' (the kindest thing I could muster . . .) Well, they are now married and I hardly ever see her . . ."—*"Nancy"*

"Once, in the hall of a friend's house, her boyfriend seductively asked me to join him in his assigned room. I said NO, but never told her. He was drunk, and they are happily married now."

—*"Karen"*

The Safe-Dating Game

In our parents' day, dating was simple: He asks you out, he picks you up, he pays for dinner, and maybe he gets a good-night peck on the cheek, if he's lucky. Those were the standard rules. Today, the rules are . . . well . . . What rules? We don't need no stinking rules! Out the window they go.

The dating game has become a complicated and confusing test of wills and won'ts and dos and don'ts. Do you kiss him good night? Do you pay half the check? Do you give him your phone number? Are you being too aggressive? How soon is too soon to have sex? Should you be carrying a condom in your purse? Will he respect you in the morning? What about STDs? . . . HOLY SMOKES! What's a girl to do?

When it comes to playing it safe—take no chances. Yes, bring a condom if you expect or hope the date will end doing the dance of the two-backed beast. Don't ever count on a guy to bring one to the party. He may, but most guys don't think about wearing a raincoat indoors. You have to look out for your own safety: Insist on protection.

As far as how far you should go—that's a call you have to make

WISE WOMAN

Mavis Leno, chairwoman of the Feminist Majority's Campaign, and wife of Jay Leno

Soul Mates

Finding love is a two-part process. The first part is to find the right person. The second part is to BE the right person. It doesn't matter how perfectly you've chosen if you have a lot of things you haven't worked out about yourself. The best preparation for finding the right person to spend the rest of your life with is to work really hard on becoming a very together, responsible, capable person yourself. I believe relationships can't be pursued directly. You have to do Zen pursuit. You have to sit in one place and grow stronger and stronger within yourself.

I met Jay in a comedy club. He was so different from the men I had picked before that it took me a while to think of him in that way. I knew I was besotted with him and infatuated with him, but I have always been able to differentiate between that and being in love with someone and thinking that would be a person you want to spend your life with. We really knew what was what by the time we ended up with each other.

Jay and I work really well because we have identical emotional natures. Whenever I say something seems bad or good or right or wrong, it is exactly the same as what he means when he says it.

He is so easygoing and calm about things and I get so worked up about things. That works really well for us. He just jokes me out of it. It's brilliant.

on your own. The key here is never to allow yourself to feel pressured into doing something you are not ready for or aren't sure of. If you don't want to—don't. Save it for when you feel it's right. Remember, it's your choice. Any guy worth having is going to respect your wishes—if he doesn't, don't waste your time.

He Says, She Says

Sometimes—a *lot* of times—I feel like my husband and I are from different planets. I'm not alone in this theory. My friends think their husbands have been abducted and replaced by aliens, too.

"It's like we speak a different language," we complain, in unison.

Guess what? You do. Your man can look out the window and say, "Oh, it's cloudy out there." You might look out that same window in the same direction and see sunshine. But you were both looking at the same sky, right?

Right. But you each assimilate what you see and express yourself differently. The sooner you know this, the better. Because then you and your guy can figure out ways to bridge the communication gap and find a common dialect.

Here's an example from my household:

I'm usually late. Phil is never late.

When Phil tries to say things that he thinks will speed me up, they only slow me down. Let's say we're going to a party. He'll see I'm not dressed yet. He'll come into the bedroom and say, "So . . . are you going to wear the red dress?"

In his mind, he's trying to help me choose. In my mind, he's slowing me down and he's telling me that the blue dress doesn't look good on me. And what does that do to me? It makes me want to go even slower just to spite him! Okay, this is not the most mature reaction, but it IS my reaction. And he was only trying to help, but I took what he said to mean something completely different from what he meant or what his intentions were.

I recall with way too much detail the time I was standing in my lacy underwear, ten minutes to party time, when I discovered to my absolute horror that the dry-cleaner had sent over the wrong dress. At this point, Phil was yelling from the living room those

oh-so-familiar words: "You should have *planned ahead*!" (This is the exact reason why you should have at least two favorite LBDs hanging around. You never know when one might not be able to perform that evening. Pull out your trusty second and off you go.) I got angry, he got impatient, and we arrived at the party late and on edge. After a few of those tense, preparty moments we found a way to meet in the middle. I put a watch in the bathroom where I'm doing makeup so I can be aware of the time, and I have a few outfits ready to go. He promises to leave me alone and not to say or do anything that would distract me.

Natasha and her hubby, Steve, have another variation of the language barrier/running-late issue. Here are his and her (very different) versions:

Natasha: "He always thinks I'm late, but really, I'm ready before he is and I'm waiting for him . . . he just won't admit it. I'll be ready, then I'll see him busy at something so I'll start doing something else while I'm waiting for him."

Steve: "I'm always ready first and I don't say anything to pressure her. I try to keep myself busy until she's ready . . . I'm waiting for her. . . ."

If they're supposed to leave at 2:00 P.M. and it's 2:30 P.M., one of them will finally yell, "Honey, *c'mon*, when will you be *ready*??!!"

And the other will say, "What are you talking about? I've been ready for half an hour! I'm waiting for *you*!"

After a few months of this, Natasha came up with a solution:

"Now, fifteen minutes before we're supposed to leave, one of us will call out, 'I just want you to know, we have to leave in fifteen minutes!' Then when it's time to leave, one of us will say, 'I just want you to know, it's time to go and I'm READY. So we can leave whenever YOU are ready because I am now READY. I'm going to sit here and watch TV until YOU are ready, *so let me know when you are* because I'm prepared and want to leave as soon as that minute arrives. Once again, just so it's clear, I am indeed *ready to go when you are. . . .* ' "

Yessiree. LOUD and C-L-E-A-R!

Both Natasha and I try to adhere to that don't-go-to-bed-angry rule. Very rarely, it could be as late as 4:00 A.M. and I'm on the couch, refusing to go into the bedroom, and Phil will come out and say, "Okay, I'm sorry. But I don't agree with you."

"I don't agree with you, either," I reply. "I love you."

"Now what?" he asks in his flummoxed, boyish way.

"We agree to disagree. We're married, aren't we?"

PMS Lifesavers

For most of the women in our lives, once a month, the sexual communication gap widens as large as the Grand Canyon. My girl-friend Caroleigh sent me this over the Internet and I thought you'd get a kick out of it:

> Every "Hormone Hostage" knows that there are days in the month when all a man has to do is open his mouth and he takes his life in his hands. This is a handy guide that should be as common as a driver's license in the wallet of every husband, boyfriend, or significant other.
>
> **Dangerous:** What's for dinner?
> **Safer:** Can I help you with dinner?
> **Safest:** Where would you like to go to dinner?
>
> **Dangerous:** What are you so worked up about?
> **Safer:** Could we be overreacting?
> **Safest:** Here's fifty dollars.

Dangerous: Should you be eating that?
Safer: You know, there are a lot of apples left.
Safest: Can I get you a glass of wine with that?

Dangerous: Are you wearing THAT?
Safer: Gee, you look good in brown!
Safest: Wow! Look at you!

Dangerous: What did you DO all day?
Safer: I hope you didn't overdo it today.
Safest: I've always loved you in that robe.

TOP 12 Things PMS Stands For

1. pass my shotgun
2. psychotic mood shift
3. perpetual munching spree
4. puffy mid-section
5. people make me sick
6. provide me with sweets
7. pardon my sobbing
8. pimples may surface
9. pass my sweatpants
10. pissy mood syndrome
11. pack my stuff
12. permanent menstrual syndrome

and:

Q: How many women with PMS does it take to change a lightbulb?
A: Only one! And do you know WHY? Because no one else in this house knows HOW to change a lightbulb! They don't even know that the bulb is BURNED OUT!!! They

would sit in the dark for THREE DAYS before they figured it out. And, once they figured it out, they wouldn't be able to find the lightbulbs despite the fact that they've been in the SAME CUPBOARD for the past 17 years! But if they did, by some miracle, actually find them, 2 days later the chair they dragged to stand on to change the STUPID lightbulb would still be in THE SAME SPOT!!! And underneath it would be THE WRAPPER THE STUPID LIGHTBULB CAME IN!!! BECAUSE NO ONE EVER CARRIES OUT THE GARBAGE!!! IT'S A WONDER WE HAVEN'T ALL SUFFOCATED FROM THE PILES OF GARBAGE THAT ARE 12 FEET DEEP THROUGHOUT THE ENTIRE HOUSE!!! IT WOULD TAKE AN ARMY TO CLEAN THIS HOUSE!

I'm sorry, what did you ask me?

Technical Difficulties

My "first time" was at Syracuse University with this cute jock. It took three months of sweaty, hot 'n' heavy make-out sessions for him to persuade me to Just Do It.

He said it'd be great, so freeing, so fabulous and fun! Sounded like spring break in Fort Lauderdale. I booked my ticket, bought sexy briefs, and prepped for fireworks—the kind Tom Cruise ignited in *Top Gun*.

So we got to the hot and heavy stage, and then went further.

The condom broke. Fumble, fumble. We put on a second. Huffing and puffing. Then it was over.

Wait a minute (and I mean a *minute*). Somehow, I missed the Big Bang.

Such a buildup, such a letdown. I mean, it was *nice*, I grant you. But it was more Judy Blume than Judith Krantz. The waves didn't crash against the shore, the earth didn't quake, and I'm sure I didn't see stars or hear music. Was there something wrong with me?

The reality is: Most girls don't have the "Big O" the first time. Some women have *never* had one. Somewhere in between is the majority. What's the deal?

First, you have to feel comfortable with your body. I have a buddy who always walked out of the bedroom backward after having sex so her partner wouldn't see the backs of her thighs. She pulled this trick off for two months until he surprised her one day in the shower when her back was turned. He didn't seem to notice what she was worried about because he was enjoying being with *her*. Unfortunately, she never enjoyed sex because she was too busy looking down, worrying her tummy was sticking out. Sadly, my friend is not alone in this thinking.

Personally, when it was two weeks past my baby's due date and I needed to have sex to help labor along while weighing 265 pounds, I think this gave me a boost and a new perspective on my body image. Beyond laughing really hard, I saw myself then as a large, but incredible ecosystem. I know this sounds so corny, but I feel that I now have more of an appreciation for what I do have, and this has definitely positively affected what goes on in the bedroom.

Second, the grey matter between your ears needs to relax and not judge. Mind over matter.

Maybe all it's going to take is a little extra work and patience. Be honest with each other and let each other know what works and what doesn't. Remember how sensitive an issue sexual intimacy is, so try not to sound frustrated, annoyed, or judgmental. We all have fragile egos. Reflect on this: If you like a man enough to get naked with him, you should like him enough to stick with it until you both get it right. Draw a road map for him and have fun getting lost.

Having said that, I want to include an addendum and put my money where my mouth is—right on the kisser. If the eyes are the windows to the soul . . . the lips can be the door to the hot spot . . . and kissing is the key to the door.

The Big Smooch!

Guys kiss like their personalities.

One football player I dated kissed like he was going for the touchdown. He had passion, but he lacked poetry . . . and I swear that under his breath he was muttering, "Go, Orange!"

Another guy—the sweet, romantic type—smooched like he was Rudolph Valentino in a silent movie. He'd take me into his arms, gaze soulfully into my eyes, and then dip me like he was doing a swan dive. I had a backache for months.

If you don't like the way a guy kisses, you're not going to like how he does *other* stuff. What to do? Like I said, if you like him it may be worth your while to stick around . . . attempt to retrain him—but again, be tactful. I once scolded a messy kisser. I was dying to say to him what was on the tip of my tongue: "What are you, a Saint Bernard? Stop shoving your tongue in my face!" He must have heard me telepathically because he never called me back (just as well). Or maybe it was the look of horror on my face after he slobbered all over me.

If the smooch situation doesn't improve after your best efforts, throw in the towel and get outta there, girlfriend! Don't bother taking things to the next level. Life is too short to never be kissed good again. Find a guy who kisses like Kevin Costner in *Bull Durham*, remember that?: "I believe in the soul . . . and in long, slow, deep, soft, wet kisses that last three days."

Hubba-hubba.

> **TAKE NOTE: Movie Kisses We Love:**
>
> Gone with the Wind: *The scene where Rhett asks Scarlett to marry him.*
>
> From Here to Eternity: *Burt Lancaster and Deborah Kerr on the beach (classic!).*
>
> Somewhere in Time: *When Christopher Reeve and Jane Seymour meet on the staircase.*
>
> The Way We Were: *When Hubbell and Katie do it for the first time and he's drunk, but gooood.*
>
> Ghost: *When Demi and her ghost kiss before he has to go to heaven.*
>
> City of Angels: *When Meg and her angel kiss for the first time.*
>
> Tequila Sunrise: *Mel Gibson and Michelle Pfeiffer in the hot tub!*

The Size of His Hands

Speaking of anatomy. Eve probably told Adam size didn't count. She lied (sort of). Some people have to work at "fitting" together well. If you're petite in the nether regions and dating a guy whose nickname is King Kong—and it's an *understatement*—honey, this is trouble. Every pot has its cover, and while his lid is for a large Italian pasta pot, you are a little French saucepan.

A friend of mine who is big, bold, and beautiful once dated an actor known for his macho brawn on the silver screen. Tall and hulking, she expected the same below the belt. Not so. Tab B did not fit snugly into Slot A. Needless to say, she was disappointed— "We just couldn't click together," she reported later.

What to do? Get creative. Those guys who say size doesn't count also claim it's how you use it. Let's test-drive that theory. Try different positions. Pick up one of those erotic sex books and have a marathon weekend of Tantric twisters. Take a trip to the naughty sex store and buy funky toys that come in plain brown packaging—batteries not included. Do a *9½ Weeks* feast on the kitchen floor. Make some popcorn and rent a dirty movie. Sometimes, all it takes is a little encouragement and experimentation.

The "Big O"

By age fourteen, Natasha was reading *Cosmopolitan* magazine. After just a few issues, her vocabulary included "G-spot." Every month, *Cosmo* had a new and improved story on how to "Get the Orgasm You Want! Ten Easy Ways!" Natasha was a Cosmogirl-in-training.

I, on the other hand, first learned about the birds and bees from some generic romance-novel excerpt. When the heroine *did it*, she heard angels singing and he presented his "throbbing man-

---

Kim Cattrall, actress, author of the book *Satisfaction: The Art of the Female Orgasm*, Warner Books

People often ask me if I'm anything like the characters I play. Some people have even said that they assumed that for me to play a sexually open character, like Samantha Jones on HBO's *Sex and the City*, I must have had fabulous sex most of my life. Well, the truth is that until three years ago, most of my sexual experiences were unfulfilling. I talked with friends, read books written by sex therapists, and sought professional help. I stood naked in front of the mirror learning to get in touch with my body. I turned forty. I'd gone through two decades of unsatisfactory sexual relationships. I had convinced myself that I just wasn't a sexual woman, and like my mother before me, I began to feel that sex really wasn't that important.

Then, in January of 1998, I met my husband, Mark. Since then, I have learned many things about communication, sexuality, and honesty. I was quite surprised to discover how quickly my body responded to being touched in the right way.

hood" and she had milky-white thighs and a "sweet spot" and she trembled for two whole pages.

Oh, yes. The Big O.

Better than they were before—better, stronger, faster.

I wanted to know: When was I going to get mine?

I have a friend who can have one when she's in her car, stopped at a red light, just by squeezing her thighs together. Take heart. This is rare. Most of us have to work at it.

In Da Mood: Music to Get the Juices Flowin'

Bryan Adams: *Best of Me*
Shawn Colvin: *Whole New You*
Marvin Gaye: *What's Going On*
Al Green: *Al Green—Greatest Hits*
Alison Krauss: *Forget About It, Now That I've Found You*
Maze with Frankie Beverly: *The Greatest Hits of Maze, Vol. 1, Greatest Slow Jams*
Aaron Neville: *Ultimate Collection*
Sade: *Lovers Live*
Barry White: *All-Time Greatest Hits, The Ultimate Collection*

Bad Boys
(The Call of the Wild!)

Ever since Natasha saw *Gone with the Wind* at age ten, she understood immediately the magnetic force of the Bad Boy. Ashley Wilkes was nice . . . nice and *boring*. Rhett Butler was, in his own words—"*not* a gentleman." He was, in Scarlett O'Hara's words—"a nasty dog." But he was passionate and exciting. Natasha wanted Scarlett to choose *him*. She wanted Cathy in *Wuthering Heights* to choose the dark and brooding Heathcliff over the pale and whiny Edgar Linton.

Marlon Brando, Mick Jagger, Russell Crowe, Sean "Puffy" Combs—and the guy you went out with last week who tossed you on his motorcycle, kissed you like a madman, then never called. They are all Bad Boys. What's the allure?

Blame the oppressed rebel in you.

In fifth grade, there was this boy, "Jeffrey" who used to smoke cigarettes behind the school. He'd tell me to bring smokes, so I'd sneak Marlboros from my mother's purse. Then he'd make me smoke as much as him, threatening to tell my parents *everything* if I didn't. After I got home, I'd shove a spoonful of peanut butter in my mouth to kill the scent. I kept going back for more. God forgive me, but there was something irresistible about my little Marlboro man. He made me feel reckless. He made me test my barriers. He helped me get in touch with my Bad Girl within.

In college, I dated a guy who had way too much for his own good. On top of it all, he was handsome, so the world was his oyster. We did have a great time for a short while. He'd whisk me away on a private, single-engine plane to Florida for a quick dip in a fabulous swimming pool. He taught me how to cook scallops just right, then eat them with a glass of wine in bed. He tested every limit in existence—especially speed limits, recklessly wrapping his car around a telephone pole after a few drinks. He was a rebel without a cause.

At first, speeding on the back of the motorcycle ride of his life made my head spin. Even though I knew he was wrong for me, I played Bonnie to his Clyde. He made my predictable collegiate routine very exciting.

But after a few months, I got dizzy with the whirlwind (and not enough sleep). I wanted *my* life back. The real me. One morning, I woke up and told him it was over. I had to go. I got on my gray Schwinn and rode back to my dorm apartment, crying all the way. I was in and out of tears for two weeks. But I knew I needed to rescue myself from him.

My take on all this is that Good Girls want to "save" Bad Boys. They believe Bad Boys are just misunderstood Good Guys! If we love them, we can fix them—we're *that* good! But there's a reason why no other woman could perform this miracle before us. A Bad Boy can't turn good *unless he wants to.*

And after a while, the thrill of a man who doesn't call, has no job, and cheats on you gets a little bit thin and you begin to see him for who and what he really is: insecure, maladjusted, and immature.

Hello! The emperor has no clothes.

Say goodbye, burn some sage, and find yourself a guy who doesn't hate his mother and likes to cuddle.

Sex and Self-Power

Cleopatra, Queen of Egypt, knew the power of sex.

She wasn't a typical beauty but she could conquer kingdoms with a glance of her almond-shaped eyes. She also conquered Julius Caesar and Mark Antony—two of the all-time most powerful men in the world, who happily fell to their knees before her.

Monday mornings in the college cafeteria was always an all-girl postweekend kiss 'n' tell session. And it was as detailed and raunchy as any porno show—not that I'd ever seen one of those. I'd hear classmates boast about their Friday and Saturday night conquests in the same way guys would boast about their sexual triumphs while hanging out in a locker room.

I was sure their escapades were dramatized. Still, I used them as my measuring stick and I sure fell short.

But so what? I decided. There's power in doing it, and there's power in *not* doing it. Every woman has a sex goddess within who knows what's right for her. Do not abuse her.

> ## 911 TIP If You Have a Dud Date and You Want to Ditch Him
>
> ### Tell Him:
>
> "If I don't take my lithium by 9:00 P.M., my parole might be revoked."
>
> "A family member is ill," which I felt sooo guilty about, but it always worked.
>
> "I have to go home and walk my dog, because he can't hold it." (He can.)
>
> "I've got the most *volcanic* period of my life . . . really, I'm hemorrhaging."
>
> "Does this mean we're gonna get *married*?"

PROTECT YOUR SEX GODDESS WITHIN!

Every woman has her own pace. Don't compare yourself to others. Don't do anything you don't want to do. Your body and brain are smart. If they are saying No—listen. If you give away little pieces of yourself against your will, you will damage your self-esteem. Every woman has the right to say No.

I remember when a potential paramour crashed at my apartment one night during a spectacular rainstorm. I didn't feel ready to have sex with him so I told him he could share my bed, "But, buddy, keep your underwear on and stay on your side!"

I let him know from the start that my goddess within wasn't coming out to play that night. (Note: He made her acquaintance at a later date—I married him!)

Long-Distance Romance

Billy Crystal speaks the truth in *When Harry Met Sally* when he explains why his fiancée doesn't meet him at the airport. He says

something like, "Because one day, she'll stop meeting me at the airport. And I never want to have to say, 'You never meet me at the airport anymore . . . ' "

Long-distance romances are delicious agony: furious airport embraces, impassioned late-night phone calls (dirty talk!), and poetic e-mails.

The adrenaline-filled first stage of courtship lingers—a happy drug that keeps on giving. It's that honeymoon phase that never lets him hear you fart. Then the honeymoon is over. Some say that distance makes the heart grow fonder . . . but I think it just makes the heart a bit forgetful after a while.

Natasha once had a long-distance romance with an undercover cop living in Paris. Okay, right away, this sounds romantic and dangerous all rolled into one. But there was a *seven*-hour time difference and only a one-hour window where they were both awake and near a phone at the same time. Yes, sure, he made admirable use of those sixty minutes like any decent Frenchman schooled in the arts of romance would, serenading her with Edith Piaf and wooing her with promises of picnics at Jardin de Luxembourg.

It lasted three months. Who could keep that up? It wasn't real. Why? Because you do not see how the person is day-to-day. It was like a fictional romance in a paperback novel . . . it gives you what you want but it doesn't last long.

Years later Natasha married a great guy (Steve!). But in the first part of their relationship and well into their marriage they lived an hour's plane ride away from each other. Again with the long distance! They visited each other back and forth for years and it was physically, emotionally, and financial exhausting. Their phone bills were astronomical.

After three years, they finally merged in one city (*hers!*—New York).

"Before then it was kind of like a Stepford relationship—

everything was beautiful every time we were together—I can't recall having a single argument," she says.

"We never wanted to fight about anything because we had so little time together—but it wasn't real and we were holding a lot of stuff back—things that might have been bothering us were tucked away.

"So when we finally did move into one apartment and had our first fight, it was a dilly. Sure, it was a shock to suddenly be arguing with each other—but boy it felt good to know we had a real, normal, healthy, honest-to-goodness relationship."

WISE WOMAN

Trisha Yearwood, singer

Togetherness

If you can avoid long-distance relationships, avoid them. A lot of being married or being a couple is about being together. When you have a long-distance relationship with someone who is on the road as much as you, you're together to be apart. And that is really tough on a relationship. I was married to a musician who was touring as much as I was. Chances were, when I was home for a few days, he wouldn't even be there. He'd be on the road. When you do finally get together, you spend a day or two adjusting to having another person in the house. I went through the phase of thinking you can have it all. But eventually you have to make a choice that your relationship is going to have priority over the other things in your life. That's when it has an opportunity to work. I spent my twenties saying my music is the most important thing in my life. I don't regret that. I just regret that I tried to make my marriage work when it wasn't really my priority. That's a lesson I wish I had learned in my twenties. Because I wouldn't have gotten married then. If you're not in a place where you're willing for your priorities to shift, don't jump the gun to be in a relationship when you're not ready one hundred percent to commit to what it takes to do it.

Phil and I had tons of fun during my early modeling days when I traveled a lot. We'd meet in different cities around the world and have a romantic rendezvous when my work was done. When we were apart, we had our little rituals to keep us going—things like when I'd arrive at a new hotel, there would be a faxed letter waiting for me and, if he was especially amorous, bunches of red roses.

Temporary separations can be dealt with. They may even make the heart grow fonder—for a while. But if you want the romance to grow and endure, you've got to get (it) together.

His Cheatin' Heart

Natasha was sure her boyfriend was cheating.

She confronted him, but he denied it so sincerely. She needed proof in black and white. When he was out of town on an assignment, she went to his apartment to feed the (loyal) pet and feverishly sifted through his boxes of negatives for clues.

Bingo! A self-portrait of him in a hotel room with a girl "and his tongue down her throat," she recalls. The swine had the gall to use a self-timer to snap the incriminating photo. She borrowed the negative and made an 11 x 14 enlargement—"*poster*-size!" she says, gleefully.

The next day, as he professed his undying devotion, she handed him the plain manila envelope.

"His face went gray," she says. They broke up.

When someone cheats on you, it's a kick in the gut. Every woman I know has tales of heartache and drama, usually made worse by the fact that she found out from someone else and not the louse in question.

Strangely enough, if your guy cheats, it could be a blessing in

911 TIP Her Cheatin' Heart: *What if your guy cheats on you . . . with your friend? Do you dump them both?*

Then your friend might be what **Jan Yager, Ph.D., author of *When Friendship Hurts,*** calls the "Double-Crosser." In her book she discusses twenty-one types of potentially negative friends:

> The "Double-Crosser" gives friendship a bad name. One of the expectations about a friend is that she will be kind and reliable, not a double-crosser who betrays you. In the 180 surveys on friendship I analyzed for *When Friendship Hurts*, the betrayal ranged from inappropriate flirting with a friend's spouse, to stealing, to sharing confidential information without permission, to emotional betrayal, to causing someone to get fired.
>
> *Why might someone become a Double-Crosser?*
>
> Her parents or siblings may have betrayed the Double-Crosser during her formative years so, in adulthood, she is treating others the way she was treated. Your friend may need outside help to understand, and change, her behavior. But if you do decide to end your friendship with the Double-Crosser, try to do it in a low-key way. You want to avoid the wrath of the Double-Crosser; you do not know what she might say or do behind your back to cross you.

disguise. First, it might mean there are problems in your relationship that need looking at and now you must work on it. Second, this guy is a creep and you finally see it and you finally have a great reason to dump him. And three, you never know what good will come out of it.

When Natasha was tipped off that another boyfriend was cheating ("I know, I know," she moans, "I can really pick them!"),

Emme

she needed to hear it from the horse's (or in this case, the no-good, low-down dog's) mouth.

She asked him straight out: "Are you cheating on me?" "Oh no, darling," said the lying SOB. Now Natasha did what any true blue American girl would do—she said, "I believe you, dear," and then went straight to the *other* horse's mouth . . . the other woman. She had found out who the girl was and where she lived through a friend and was soon knocking on her front door.

"Are you seeing my boyfriend?" demanded the teary-eyed Natasha.

"What? *Your* boyfriend?! Come in, honey. My name's Silvia. We really need to talk."

The gals soon discovered that the heel was two-timing both of them, so took matters into their own hands by simultaneously dumping him! After a good cry, a good laugh, and a bonding toast of vino, Natasha and Silvia became fast friends and remain bosom buddies more than a decade after ditching the guy who brought them together.

"It doesn't even occur to us anymore how we met," says Natasha. "I don't think we've even mentioned his name in six or seven years."

Q & A with Dr. Bonnie Eaker Weil, Ph.D., author of *Make Up, Don't Break Up* and *Adultery: The Forgivable Sin*

Q: *Why do we lust after Bad Boys?*

Bonnie: The Bad Boy is a challenge. We all want high drama, excitement, and what we can't have. That again is the lust and the chemicals. They rev up when you can't have something. The adrenaline pumps. We are all attracted to the not-knowing, the not-having.

Q: *Tell us about Love vs. Lust!*

Bonnie: Love is responsibility, caring, and commitment for someone. Lust has to do more with chemicals going on in your brain—endorphins, like a runner's high. I call lust a form of craziness. Chemistry takes over and the endorphins do all the work, so it's like a vacation versus work. Love is work. Lust is no work—it's a honeymoon stage where everything seems great.

Q: *Can you forgive the scoundrel after he cheats?*

Bonnie: Forgiveness is a gift you give yourself. Tell him you want to forgive him someday. Not now. Now you're too angry. First, give yourself permission to be angry. Then, look at the part you played in it. It's not your fault, but you played a part. That way, you will be less of a grudge-holder and it will be more of a wake-up call. He must stop the affair immediately, you must set that boundary, and he must show remorse. That has to happen. The other woman represents something he's missing with himself or with you or in his childhood.

Q: *How do you have a heart-to-heart about intimate stuff without fighting?*

Bonnie: The first thing to do is start off positively. Start off with the little things you love about him. You think he's a terrific, wonderful lover and person and you are happy on so many levels. Then tell him you want to feel comfortable enough to talk to him about things that are bothering you. Both of you need to put on your "bulletproof vest" for the conversation and agree not to take offense at anything you say to each other when you are honestly bringing up issues in a loving way. Make it safe for each other to say whatever you need to say. Once you feel safe, say what you need to say. Then ask him to repeat to you

what you said so you know he heard you correctly. You'd be surprised sometimes how a man can misinterpret what you are trying to say. Keep saying it until he has it right.

FINAL THOUGHT

Romance is a tough thing to sum up—just saying, "Men! Can't live with 'em, can't live without 'em," doesn't quite get all the nuance. I remember reading this story in Plato's *Symposium* that takes place at a drunken guys' night out—yeah, they even had them twenty-five hundred years ago—where the topic of love and romance was being hotly debated.

One of the hiccuping guests tried to explain why men and women were attracted to each other in the first place. He claimed that at the beginning of time, men and woman were actually one being joined together at the back. They traveled everywhere together by doing head-over-heel somersaults. Each step was made in perfect unison as they moved through life together with grace and in perfect harmony.

That is, until the gods got jealous and split them in two. Ever since, the story goes, men and women have been desperately seeking their other half . . . and according to Plato, only those who find it are truly happy in this world. Hey, it's definitely one way of explaining the confusion between the sexes and the thrill of that exciting, much-anticipated first kiss, warm embrace, or proclamation of love.

family
emergency!

As the saying goes, you can choose your friends but you can't choose your family. Even if you could, do you think we'd all pick a 1950's utopian household to grow up in like *Leave to Beaver* or the insanely understanding and patient Huxtable household on *The Cosby Show*? A world where your greatest childhood problem would be sneaking a cookie before lunch, the biggest crime about borrowing the family car and staying out too late?

Get real. Even if those families did exist in the real world . . . your family and the issues that come along with them teach you about life.

Real-life families aren't and shouldn't be so quiet and quirk-free. Real-life families are imperfect and *alive*!

To use one of my mother-in-law's favorite Yiddish expressions, every family has their own "*mishegas.*"

WISE WOMAN

Emme

Judy, my mother-in-law

Mishegas!

My mother-in-law, Judy, is the rock of the Aronson clan. She's brought up three sons, hand-held two daughters-in-law through many ups and downs, and lavished three grandchildren with love. Here is her advice on bringing up family:

Yes, every family has their own *mishegas*. That means a crazy or silly little thing that, to an outsider, would seem really absurd. The most important glue that keeps a family together is love. You should also be able to talk about anything. I always try to make myself approachable for my kids so they can talk about any problem they have.

Family members don't always fit together like a puzzle. You have to realize that everybody is different and they can't always do what you want them to do when you want them to do it. You have to give people space and you should try not to be too judgmental of your family. I say this, and of course, I don't always do it myself! And you should give people their privacy. My mother, a real matriarch, used to say: "If you're not going to invite me into the bedroom when you make love, then don't invite me in when you're fighting." Meaning, I will help you any way I can, but don't put me in the middle of your quarrel!

Put Up Your Dukes! (How Your Family *Discusses* Things)

Shout it out. Hold it in. Ignore it. Don't make waves.

Unlike the Cosbys, not every family sits around the dinner table and calmly discusses their problems as they pass the potatoes. The way your family communicated sticks in your psyche like gum to the bottom of your shoe. If it wasn't so great, it takes a lot of work to scrape it off.

In my family, we didn't show our anger. If you were angry or disagreed with someone, you just didn't talk at all. Zilch. Phil's family is the opposite. They yell, they make noise, and they don't let you get away with *anything*. In the early days of our marriage it freaked me out because it was so . . . so foreign to me. Say out loud what I'm feeling inside? What a concept! Who invented this?

Phil's family knew they could express their anger, get it off their chest, and then hug each other and make up in the next millisecond. Everything was out on the table and it felt *much* healthier. Being angry wasn't the end of the world—or the relationship.

Hmm. In the early nineties, I tested this theory at a family debate on a current news topic. A topic I had mixed feelings about, a perfect discussion piece. It was about partial nudity. In the United States, you can't sunbathe topless without causing an uproar, while abroad, it's natural. So here it was. . . . Seven women from Rochester, New York, were arrested for the petty offense of "exposure." The charge asserted that they violated New York Penal Law sec. 254.01, which (according to this case) prohibits exposing "that portion of the breast which is below the top of the areola" except for purposes of breastfeeding or "entertaining or performing in a play, exhibition, show, or entertainment." These women were apparently exposing their breasts as, "part of an effort to dramatize their opposition to the law." Basically, if they were men taking off their shirts in the park, it would not have been against the law.

"I admire the women," I said boldly. Well, that started a loud living room dispute; me versus my hubby and his two brothers. The guys all felt I was being contradictory in my feelings—"So why don't you back off on topless bars then?!" they shouted. We had a heated discussion, which in the past would have overwhelmed me and I would have just kept quiet and burning inside. However, the newer, more confident me, believed my voice counted—*especially* my female voice with all that testosterone around me! I rose to the occasion with passionate words.

"These women are fighting for lib-er-a-tion you guys! Topless bars are about degra*da*tion!" Our heated debate lasted at least an

hour and everyone in the house got into it. Finally, we agreed to dis-agree, and then . . . we kissed and made lunch. Don't get me wrong, I don't judge women for dancing topless, it's just that I feel the envi-ronment just seems so compromising to a woman's self-esteem. Yes, I know, to each her own! (By the way, the charges against the women were dropped but the law continues to stay on the books.)

And I learned that I could disagree and yell out my opinion, and the world wasn't going to end. Whatever style of expression you learned growing up, it may not jive with who you are today. You can unlearn with an open mind and learn differently, with practice.

Daddy's (or Mommy's) Little Girl

You're a modern girl but your parents are from the Dark Ages. Or in Natasha's case, the Old Country. And they packed those strict, Old Country ethics in their baggage. Natasha never discussed boys with her father (except briefly in high school when she was told she wasn't allowed to date. *End of conversation*).

Skip ahead fifteen years.

Natasha is thirty years old and her steady, out-of-town suitor, Steve, thirty-five, comes to town to visit.

"Where is he going to sleep?" Dad inquires.

"Um, at my apartment," she replies, hoping to sound noncha-lant. (After a decade of dating, five years living on her own, and at least two long-term boyfriends, Natasha figured it was safe to assume that Dad knew she was . . . you know . . . a *woman*.)

She figured wrong.

"WHAT?!!' yells Dad. He demands a man-to-man meeting with Steve—that no-good low-down rotten scoundrel. Natasha sends the unsuspecting Steve over to her dad's place "just to say hi and get to know each other a bit over a cup of tea." Before the kettle had even begun to warm up, Natasha's dad was boiling over.

"You may be a fine young man, although I really don't know that because I don't know a thing about you—so I have to ask you WHAT EXACTLY ARE YOUR INTENTIONS?"

Gulp . . .

"Well, sir . . . I love your daughter very much and I want to spend the rest of my life with her and—"

Bang! Natasha's father slams his hand down on the table, sending the sugar cubes scrambling.

"WELL!" Hand banging the table again. "That is all fine and good. Nevertheless . . . [*bang*!] THIS [*bang*!] PREMARITAL [*bang*!] SEX [*BANG*!] HASGOTTOSTOPDOYOUUNDER-STANDME!!! (*Bang bang bang bang bang.*)

Later that night, when Natasha eagerly asked her hubby-to-be how the meeting went, Steve reported that the operation was a success, but the patient died. "Your dad and I had a long inform-ative talk, a strong and bitter cup of tea, and I told him not to worry—that I'd never sleep with you again even after we were married. *He scared the hell outta me!*"

Steve took the patriarchal third degree pretty well and never said a bad word against Natasha's dad (they eventually became good pals).

But Natasha and her dad didn't speak for months—and she didn't bring Steve around for the next two years. The incident cre-ated a real rift between dad and only daughter. Her father wanted her to stay a little girl, and she didn't know how to make him understand that she was an adult living a different lifestyle in a different era.

There were other factors at play here, too. Natasha's mom had passed away two years earlier and she was the one who had been the emotional touchstone in the family. Natasha had confided in her mother about everything, and Mom always understood every-thing Natasha was doing and was always there to love and support and encourage, no matter what it was.

Her mom would have loved Steve to pieces. Instead of banging the table, she would have covered it with her finest linen tablecloth and laid out a beautiful home-cooked Macedonian feast. Instead of yelling at this new beau she would have and hugged and kissed him until his cheeks were beet red, saying, "Welcome to our family . . . now eat and tell me all about yourself, you handsome boy!"

But her death had changed the family dynamic forever. Natasha was expecting her dad to be like her mom—but it just wasn't to be.

"Suddenly I expected my dad to be Mr. Modern and Mr. Sensitive. He did the best he could but our views on this particular subject were so different, I wish we could have found a way to meet in the middle. We were so angry at each other I thought we'd never speak to each other ever again." Nearly a year later, they were talking again. But they never, ever discussed *that*. They never discussed *that* again until a few months ago. Natasha called him up and they had a heart-to-heart. "I was taken by surprise, I think, at the time," her dad confessed to Natasha about their disagreement seven years ago, "and there I was—trying to be mother and father. I was worried about you but I didn't know what to do. I wish we could have talked about it at the time but I was too upset." They agreed that if they ever came to such an impasse again, they would put anger aside and talk until they reached an understanding. They never again want to lose precious time holding grudges.

One of the duties of being a parent is to give advice. Even when we're all grown up, our parents still treat us like we're sitting at the kids' table. My mother-in-law, Judy, is a master at giving counsel and I utterly adore her for it.

However, sometimes it's just a bit *too much*. (This sounds familiar. It's a taste of my own medicine because I do the same thing. Read on!) You're having a party? She's got the perfect recipe. You need a doctor? She knows the best. You have a problem? She's got the solution times ten. She knows when it's going to rain. She knows what we should bid on the house. She just knows. And she's usually right. Moms have been around the block and seen it all.

But it can get overwhelming. I've had to tell her point-blank, "Listen, I can't handle this barrage of information right now. When I'm ready, I'll let you know!"

But beating around the bush isn't her style. When I gave her a rough first draft copy of this book to get her opinion, she was honest: "It's boring." And you know what? She was right! Many rewrites later, I am happy she was honest. But I couldn't see that at the time. All I could do was get weepy.

"Couldn't you at least put a silver lining on it?" I asked.

I reminded myself once again that other families have different ways of communicating.

"You don't have to do everything she says," my much-enlightened hubby explained. "You just need to *listen* to what she says, then do what you want!"

So now, she calls me up and says, "Okay, I'm going to tell you this piece of advice and you can use it or not, it's up to you. But at least I'll feel good that I've told you. . . ."

Marcia, Marcia, Marcia! (Sibling Revelry and Rivalry)

So moans Jan Brady, the notorious middle sister in *The Brady Bunch*, about older sister Marcia. She gets all the attention, all the awards, and all the boyfriends. Sibling rivalry is as old as Cain and Abel. And the psychological effects of your birth order are totally valid.

As the eldest of three kids, and because my mother passed away when we were young, I always felt I had to act as stand-in

mom for my younger siblings, Melanie and Chip. To this day I have to fight the urge to take over (too much) and make everything okay (too much) in their lives.

My sister, the youngest, called me up the other day to say she had to find a new apartment. My immediate reaction: "I'll drive right over and we'll start looking."

She didn't ask—I just bulldozed right on ahead. Sometimes my sibs just want to have a chat with me—not a pep talk or a therapy session or an Emme-made solution. But there I am, advising ad nauseam while their eyes glaze over and they slip into a coma.

"Why don't you tell me to *shut up* sometimes?" I ask Mel.

"Well, I sure want to," she admits, "but I don't want to hurt your feelings."

As adults, my sibs and I are learning to deal with one another as just that—adults. Not the middle child, the older one, or the baby of the family. You can break the patterns—but it takes work, honesty, and communication.

Four Weddings, a Funeral, and a Turkey . . . (Staying Sane at Family Functions)

Hi, dear, aren't you married yet? Are you still in that same old job? Boy, you sure are filling out. . . .

Family get-togethers: Who thought this up? The insults! The food fights!

Potent with undercurrents of ancient feuds, critical eyes, and crying children—by the time the turkey's carved you're ready to disown the whole bunch. Still, ya gotta love these crazy people. Take a deep breath and dig in. Appreciate the good stuff (Baba's cabbage rolls) and take the rest with a grain of salt.

911 TIP Can You Spot Your Family Troublemakers?

The Gossip: They tell you wild stories about other family members that are difficult to believe. (Chances are, they tell wild stories about you, too.)

The Cynic: You say "It's a beautiful day!" and he says, "It's gonna rain."

The Know-It-All: You're a brain surgeon, but they've been reading *The New England Journal of Medicine* and have a few things to point out to you.

The Victim: It's *never* their fault!

The Martyr: It's *always* their fault!

If you have a gripe with a family member, the time and place to air it is not at Thanksgiving, Hanukkah, or Christmas dinner. Timing is everything so time it away from family gatherings . . . PLEASE!

We all have relatives who: wear too much perfume or cologne making it close to unbearable to sit next to them, chew their food for all to see, continue to release farts when they think no one will notice (but, believe me, we do), talk so loudly that it is impossible to hold another conversation in the same room, or, last but not least, do not know how to say thank you or keep their mouths shut when appropriate.

Natasha used to skip family functions when she knew the Official Family Gossip would be in attendance.

"As soon as someone walked out of the room, she'd make up some awful fabricated story about them," says Natasha. "She's caused hurtful and long-running family feuds for no reason. It took the rest of the family years to catch on. Once we did, we realized she was just terribly insecure. Now when we she starts up we all just exchange glances and feel sorry for her."

911! Stupid Things Family Members Say to You (And Brilliant Things to Say Back)

STUPID THING 1

You walk into a family gathering. You've put on a few pounds since the last one and the first person you see is your eternally skinny aunt. She looks you up and down. You know what's coming next.

She: "Oh, you've gained weight!"

You: "Oh, thanks! Doesn't it look great! Marilyn Monroe was a size 16, you know. . . ."

STUPID THING 2

You've just broken up with your boyfriend and you're feeling the pain. All you want is some comfort. You walk into the room and your Family Cynic sees you.

She: "You're gonna be an old maid. . . ."

You: "Thanks, that's really nice of you to say. And how is your third husband?"

STUPID THING 3

You've taken a new job that you are really excited about. It will be a challenge because you are moving up a level. Your Family Downer approaches you.

She: "You're never going to be able to do it!"

You: "Wanna put your money where your mouth is?"

Q & A with Dr. Jane Greer, on handling family get-togethers

Q: *How do we break out of our classic birth-order role in the family?*

Dr. Greer: You have to roll out of a role. First you must be aware that you are acting in that role and being perceived in that role—the baby, the jokester, the black sheep. You must realize what role you were cast in as a child. But . . . you are no longer a child! You can now make conscious choices about how you interact with your siblings as well as your parents. So what if you're the baby and it's Thanksgiving dinner and the family starts teasing you. . . .

Keep things light and humorous if you can. Say something like, "Oh, so nobody wants to see I'm one of you now . . . that I've arrived! That I'm no longer operating at a seven-year jet lag!" Poke fun at it so you make the point but nobody gets defensive or offended.

Q: *How can we handle family get-togethers?*

Dr. Greer: It's holidays, but they should be called "hell"idays. Holidays are overloaded with expectation for good times. Also, people come into them dragging around a lot of residual resentment and bitterness and disappointment and rivalries over unresolved issues from the past because lots of times families don't know how to put issues to rest. So at holiday time, with the expectation to have a great time on high burn and feelings of previous disappointment and hurts on high burn, it's a Molotov cocktail for disaster. You want to be able to put the fire out as opposed to fanning the flames. If anybody brings up an old issue, you don't want to engage. You want to observe and say, "Look, obviously you have some bad feelings from before, and I want to talk about them and work them out with you, but not today. Let's put them aside and we'll revisit them later." So you are acknowledging where the other person is coming from.

The other recipe for disaster is people are always drinking at holidays, so stuff you never think you're going to talk about just pours out. You pour the liquor and you pour out your feelings. And then nobody has the impulse control or the better judgment to monitor what he or she says or how he or she says it. So then the gloves come off and everybody is duking it out.

Emme

Losin' Your Religion (Not!)

The beauty of this country is the way people are able to adapt to different cultures and religions. When there are different religions within your family, you learn how to adapt and blend.

Maybe your Greek Orthodox family wouldn't dare consider circumcising baby Stavros . . . unless of course your brother is married to a nice Jewish girl. Time for the *bris*! And you're expected to be there applauding. It's not your child and not your decision to make, so attend with a smile, shut your eyes at the *snip* part, and when it's all over—have a little Manischewitz.

I was raised Christian and my hubby is Jewish.

In our household we sort of blend the two together. But for a long time, before we got married, the question on his side was: Will she convert? I told Phil's family: "I come into this marriage as I am but I'm open to seeing things in new ways."

I certainly threw a cog in the wheel.

One of the first conversations I had with Phil's parents began with their asking us how, if we got married, we intended to raise our children. I went through a whole religious reevaluation (his family watched closely) about how I felt about organized religion.

When it came right down to it, I believed in a more inclusive kind of faith that encompassed all religions. I like and agree with what psychic medium John Edward, host of TV's *Crossing Over*, said to Natasha once: "Religions are like airlines. They may all have different names, different foods, different seats—but they're all taking you to the same destination."

I told Phil I wanted to bring our kids up Jewish, that I would even consider converting, but at the same time I didn't want to give up some of my traditions like my Christmas tree. I studied the Torah for months with my mother-in-law as a way to understand what being Jewish was about. It turned out to be a wonderful bonding experience for us. I loved what I learned and I found it profoundly interesting.

Every so often on Friday nights, we light our shabbat candles, say our prayers of thanks and have a family meal. However, when the holidays approach, Phil whips up tasty latkas with sour cream and applesauce and we gather around for our Festival of Lights on Hanukkah and say our prayers of thanks. The whole house is a happy jumble of dreidels and chocolate coins (gelt) and Hanukkah songs.

A week later or depending on when the holidays fall I throw a fabulous Christmas Eve dinner for our family and friends, and the house smells like pine needles and I put on Bing Crosby crooning "White Christmas." Phil insists on putting up the wreaths and picking out the Christmas tree.

Sharing the holidays with friends of different religions is what I feel that season is all about. We each get a chance to see what the other does, find out what is different, what is similar.

Last year, my buddy Marlene and her two daughters came to our house for the first of many tree-picking and tree-trimming afternoons with hot chocolate and cookies near the fireplace. We sang Hanukkah and Christmas songs, laughed, and strung ornaments on our tree. We had such a good time together.

Beginnings

Of all the family functions, you have to have nerves of steel sometimes to handle the little emergencies that pop up out of nowhere before the Big Day—your wedding. Something happens, I swear, the moment after you are proposed to. You feel it in the air. There's a tingle in your stomach and an exciting undercurrent running through your veins. But something more environmental sets things into motion that you have no control over. If you just accept it and

work around the silly things that could make you cry, you'll be the better for it. If your goal is to have a smooth sailing, perfect wedding, I warn you to consider a slight adjustment. Leave room for error. Remember all the planning you are doing is for ONE DAY. I repeat, ONE DAY. An important day, I admit, but all I ask is that you keep it all in perspective. The hard work will take place ten years down the road or when times get tough. So cut yourself some slack, take the pressure to perform away, and do what you and your honey want. No one expects anything but happiness from both of you. Above all, wear your sense of humor on your sleeve and you will have your mother, caterer, florist, and whomever else you will be working with, eating out of your hand and doing whatever is necessary to make you happy. You can only imagine the stories they have to share.

For the sake of hitting this point home, let me share some of my big-day plans with you:

Emergency 1: I wasn't able to pay (traditionally the wife's parents pay for the wedding) for a wedding. A really nice intimate dinner at our two bedroom condo for immediate family and no friends was about all we could do then.

Solution: Phil's father saved the day.

"Listen, kids," he said. "I'm going to give you twenty-five thousand dollars as a wedding present . . . you can do what you want with it. You can take it and run. Or, you can use it to pay for your wedding. It's totally up to you."

Slack-jawed, I almost fell off my chair. A down payment for a home, a small wedding with family and friends . . . it was all very tempting. We had a family meeting. I got emotional . . . then I realized exactly what I wanted.

"You know what?" I declared in front of all assembled. "I always wanted to have a wedding and I can't imagine myself not having one. Do you mind? I want to be a bride! I want to walk down the aisle.

"Okay, it's decided. We're gonna have a wedding!"

Emergency 2: My mom was no longer alive and I was in a strange place having to plan a wedding without her.

Solution: In steps my amazing mother-in-law! "I'll do it with you, Emme!" Thank God! Judy rolled up her sleeves and got to work choosing flowers, food, and taking care of all those details, including finding me the most beautiful wedding dress.

Emergency 3: My mother-in-law draws up a guest list of nearly three hundred. I look at the list. "Oh my God, this is out of control!!!" I panic.

Solution: I bow to my mother-in-law's need to have a big wedding and she compromises by cutting the list back by fifty.

Emergency 4: We had to find a rabbi who would marry a nice Jewish boy like Phil to a big blond shiksa like me. And not only that—he had to allow my uncle Walter, my godfather, who is an ordained pastor in the Episcopal Church, to be involved in the ceremony.

The orthodox rabbis would have no part in this: "We will not marry you," they told us.

Solution: We called dozens and dozens until we finally found wonderful Rabbi Fass, a reformed rabbi, who would perform the ceremony and let Uncle Walter officiate as well.

Emergency 5: We had to change the wedding date to fit the schedule of our rabbi. This would be the FOURTH time we had changed it. Oy!

Solution: We changed it.

Emergency 6: I forgot to check with Uncle Walter before signing off on the new date. So when I excitedly called him up to tell him of the new schedule, he was crestfallen. He couldn't make that date. The bishop was coming to his church that day (a high honor) to perform the confirmations and Uncle Walter *had* to be there.

"But, Uncle Walter," I cried, "I've already put down the deposit!

The caterers have been paid! The Inn doesn't have any other weekends available until two years from now."

Solution: Uncle Walter understood. He said, "Honey, don't worry about it. We'll do something special just for us at another time." This was really not a solution or something I felt at peace with, but it was what it was. Not good.

Emergency 7: I was really, really upset that Uncle Walter was not going to be there to represent me and my mom at the wedding since he was so close to her growing up.

Solution: I took my mom's beautiful, embroidered linen tablecloth from Trinidad and used it as a *huppah* ("canopy") over our heads during the ceremony. It was beautiful, with the detailed embroidered lace cascading down the four sides being held up by poles the four groomsmen were holding. When the light shone through it, it made me feel like Mom was with us, taking part.

The End (*or So We Thought*)

SKIP AHEAD TEN MONTHS

Phil and I are visiting Uncle Walter and Aunt Sally in my mom's hometown of Sharon, Connecticut. Walking around outside, we pass my mom's old church. It was lovely and peaceful and had a pretty, white, picket fence.

I stopped walking.

"Walter, I have an idea . . ."

He smiled. He was thinking the very same thing.

He took us in and he blessed us alone in the church, with Aunt Sally as our witness. Phil and I were wearing shorts but Uncle Walter says even in our casual garb, it was "pretty official." On Saturday, September 8, we renewed our vows in the church my mother went to every Sunday when she was young with Uncle Walter officiating. Phil and I were so happy!

So get your massages, work on deep breathing, and enjoy the

journey of planning a wedding, you never know what will pop up around the corner. But whatever it is, know you will be able to handle it.

> ▶ **TAKE NOTE:** *Big, Bad, Bridesmaid Dresses*
> *I am guilty of this underrated crime. My eyesight must have been impaired by prewedding bliss when I picked out those awful, evergreen, tea-length frocks with puffy Cinderella sleeves for my dearest friends to shell out $200 a pop for and wear at my side. My sister, who is nine years younger than I, fixed it up later and wore it to her junior high prom. Along with the dyed-to-match green shoes! Now I call that innovative and brave!*

Endings

Other family gatherings where long-buried grievances and suppressed emotions suddenly erupt are funerals.

Sometimes people choose funerals as the time to settle scores or assign blame for family rifts, or argue over money and estates—that's not only bad taste but a bad, bad idea. Funerals are emotional and what's said there can stick forever. Also, it is a time to grieve and show respect for the dead—not a time to give a piece of your mind to Aunt Tilly, no matter what's she's done or how long she's had it coming.

But the most common emotional problem I see people experience around death is emotional numbness. Feelings freeze up and people don't know what to do, what to say. My best advice is to say or do *something*.

If you can't be there, send a card or flowers or make a phone

WISE WOMAN

Ellen Goodman and Patricia O'Brien,
lifelong friends and coauthors of *I Know Just What You Mean:
The Power of Friendship in Women's Lives*

Friends for Life

It amazes us now to look back and see what we've been building: the story of our friendship is the story of our divorces, our children, careers, loves, losses, remarriages, knee injuries, and even our differing opinions on such earth-shattering matters as pickles and olives. At a dozen times, we might have taken a different course without each other's advice—wrecked a love affair, accepted the wrong job, or made the wrong decision for a child. We knew precisely how important this ongoing conversation, this running commentary, was to the person each of us had become. But it was a bit of a jolt to recognize that we had become the joint owners of a respectably long and grounded friendship. We had moved from youth through middle age with each other, becoming stronger than we would have been alone. We had talked and talked and talked, and finally talked our way through a quarter of a century—and in that time, we had become fluent in the language of female friendship. . . . Friendship matters to women; it matters a lot; women today—with lives often in transition—depend on friends more than ever.

call. A small gesture speaks a thousand tears. Natasha and I both remember the people who reached out and comforted us during our moms' illnesses (both had cancer)—and funerals.

When my mom died I was in a state of shock for many years.

I was a young teenager and had no idea how to handle it. I decided I had to be "strong" for everyone.

"I'm a big strong girl," I wrote to one family friend. "No need to worry about me!"

I didn't show emotions and I didn't deal properly with her passing. I needed help and I didn't know how to ask for it or how to accept it. What made matters even more difficult was that my mother hadn't wanted a funeral, so I had no ritual to help me say good-bye. There was no memorial service. No finality and no closure.

This was a time when I got help outside the family circle. When you don't have anyone to lean on in your family, your friends become the people who love and support you unconditionally.

After Mom passed away and I went back to boarding school, I had a hard time and my school friends really reached out to help me even though I wasn't aware I was shutting them out. I had shut down my feelings because I didn't want to deal with the emotions surrounding her being gone.

But one friend kept trying to get through to me—she knew I needed to connect with someone. She telephoned me constant-ly—inviting me to the movies or for a bite at the cafeteria. I never returned her calls, so she'd knock on my door. When I didn't answer, she'd say from the hallway, "Hey, how about coming out for some burgers?" I had closed myself up tight but her constant kindness finally brought me out of my shell and back into the world. I will always be thankful to her for not taking "no, thanks" as an answer.

I have another friend who excels at listening when I have a problem. I can feel her nodding sympathetically from hundreds of miles away whenever I telephone her with my crisis du jour. I can call her up at 4:00 A.M. from wherever I am when the rest of the sane world is sound asleep, and I know she'll patiently listen to my hysterical ranting.

She interrupts only when I say something so whacked out she's certain it's time to call a taxi to send Dr. Freud over . . . but 99 percent of the time she just says, "Uh-huh, uh-huh, uh-huh . . . I hear ya."

She doesn't smother me with advice because her girlfriend meter tells her that what I really need is to let loose and ramble on and get stuff off my chest. She's my truest sounding board, and just knowing she's on the other end of that phone line is exactly

OLDER & WISER

I wish an adult had pulled me aside and told me it's natural to grieve, to cry, and to feel sad. I wish someone had helped me talk about what I was feeling and to *feel* it. I wish I had asked for help. I wish I had accepted people's willingness to help me through this. I remember one old friend came to our door to express his condolences and I just stood in the doorway. I didn't even invite him in! I didn't know what to do. I CLOSED EVERYTHING OUT. I wish someone had told me it was okay to feel angry and vulnerable. It would have helped me a lot.

what I need to figure out the problem on my own.

When I had a miscarriage a few years ago I was devastated. I phoned her right away and was sobbing so uncontrollably I could barely say her name, let alone tell her what had happened. She soothed me with just a few simple words: "Tell me all about it, honey. . . . I'm here for you, I'm listening."

Even though someone isn't related to you by blood, he or she is still "family" because you are connected by love. The family you make with your friends can be just as strong and everlasting.

I am blessed to have rekindled a very special relationship in my life with a couple that I knew when my Mom and I lived in New York City when I was two to five years old. Having not seen one another for thirty-two years, I reached out to make a connection, and joyfully, over the last six years, we have become very close and important to one another. Today Phil and I consider Bobbie and Eric Carle family and as another set of grandparents to my daughter, Toby. Bobbie and Eric are not blood relatives, but because of the feelings we have for each other, we are family in my book.

Life's rituals—christenings, graduations, and funerals—tell

us one stage is ending and another is beginning. I didn't deal with my mother's death until a decade later.

During the year Phil and I were engaged, we went to nine *shivahs*. Sitting shivah in the Jewish tradition taught me how important it is for families and friends to be together and support one another when someone dies. It helps the grieving to take place.

Twenty years after my mother's death, I visited her ashes with my sister and we did a little ceremony of our own for closure. I learned that the ritual is important for healing. And so is letting out the emotions. So whenever I'm with people who are in mourning, I encourage them to let it all out, not hold it in.

FINAL THOUGHT

I am so lucky to have a family that I love so dearly, that supports my career and shows up at book signings in the middle of nowhere just so I can have people there to ask questions. Who cares if the loud guy at the back is your brother-in-law?!! My mom gave me so much, I thank God I had her for the short time I did. I think she would be so proud of me, my brother, and my sister. Now it's my responsibility to pass down the emotional nuggets I received to my daughter so she can effect positive change in her life and in the world. There are people I call "my family" who don't share the same bloodline. Out of a yearning, I sought them out. I have friends who have crossed my path and offered a kind word or a place to stay or gave me a helping hand or came to my rescue. Maybe your family sometimes makes you want to jump over the edge. But before you do, leave a number where you can be reached and let them know when you'll be back. You don't want them to worry too much!

10 spirit emergency!

On your mark, get set . . . GO!

The alarm clock rings at 6:30 A.M.—you leave before having breakfast, fight people and traffic to get to work, sit behind a computer all day, maybe get yelled at by the boss/client/customer and your mother, who can't understand that you've been *too busy* to return her calls . . . work an extra three hours to catch up so you don't get fired, dash off to the grocery store, the dry-cleaner, and the pharmacy while arguing on your cell with your boyfriend who is whining because you're *too busy* to see him . . . you stumble home by 9:00 P.M., pop a frozen dinner into the microwave because you're *too busy* to cook something real, and you pass out in front of the tube watching infomercials. . . . The alarm goes off at 6:30 A.M. and you jump right back on the same crazy, daily merry-go-round. When the weekend rolls around, you're too exhausted to enjoy it. Forget about going out— you barely have the energy to do your laundry and scrub that disgusting mold off the bottom of your bathtub. . . .

WISE WOMAN

Mariska Hargitay, actress, *Law & Order: Special Victims Unit*

Serenity

My surefire, guaranteed-to-work, absolutely best prescription for de-stressing is swimming with wild dolphins off the Kona coast in Hawaii. Sure, it takes some planning and not a small amount of cash, but if you have the opportunity, jump at it. Being in the presence of something that heartbreakingly pure, beautiful, and free could change your life.

But, hey—you're a woman of the world, right? Of course you're *busy, busy, busy.* I mean—you're trying to make your mark in the world! To get noticed, to forge a career, and to be a successful upwardly mobile whatever. Busy is good, right?

Sorta. Busy is good only if it's balanced with a needed dose of *not* busy. Believe me. I've been on the treadmill of life and it's a run that will take you to burn-out—fast, if all you worry about is getting through one hectic day after another with no thought to your inner soul.

A wise man once said, "Man does not live by bread alone."

Well, a wise woman might put it like this: "Girl . . . your soul is starving. You need to feed your spirit before you disappear into nothing."

A big part of being a healthy woman is making sure that every part of you is well nourished. And that means your body, mind, and *spirit.*

Food for the Hungry Soul

You can't see it, but it's there—inside of you.

Your soul—the driving force in the center of your being that is the essence of who you are—needs to be nurtured in a very real and primal way.

It needs nurturing in the same way as you feed your body, in the same way as you exercise your muscles, in the same way as you test your intellect.

How? For many, that nourishment is found in song or prayer at church, temple, synagogue, mosque, or other place of worship. The fact that millions of people subscribe to an organized religion tells you how fundamental our spiritual needs are. For others, that nourishment is found in meditating every morning as the sun rises or walking in the woods or soaking in a hot tub or ladling soup in a homeless shelter.

Everybody must find her own tool to fix a spirit that is off-kilter.

Often, spirituality is the gateway for creativity.

By opening yourself up to the spirit within, you are opening yourself to all the creative powers of the universe. Just think of all the artistic people you know personally and I bet you'll see they all have one thing in common—they are connected to their spiritual selves.

Take the world's most famous rock 'n' roll band—the Beatles. They didn't sit on their guitar strings after they became super-successful—no sir. They flew off to India to seek spiritual enlightenment and then they produced the best music of their lives and changed the world. Today's rock band Creed is a good example of a group of musicians known for their spiritual connection.

Even the doyens of the fashion business are getting in touch with their inner as well as outer beauty. Model Christy Turlington practices Yoga and takes spiritual retreats to strengthen her spiritual connection. She has even developed a Yoga-inspired line of clothing and the Ayurvedic skin-care line Sundari as an extension of her spiritual journey. Fashion designer Donna Karan hires a Yoga instructor before her fashion shows to give her models a pre-runway stretch-and-breathing class, and designer Diane Von Furstenburg practices Yoga on a regular basis.

The examples are endless but certainly not restricted to the rich and famous. And the ways in which people nurture their souls are also varied. Some are small, some are big, some are life changing—but all, in their own fashion, are paths to inner peace.

Take this day not so long ago: I was preggers out to here with Toby, my back ached, my feet were killing me, and I was working like a dog. Besides all the normal crazy workday chores—Phil and I were deep into the launch of our new line.

It was one of those days where there was too, too much going on and soon my head was spinning, my heart was pounding against my ribs, my chest was tightening up, and I was breathing shallowly.

But my world kept demanding attention—the phone was ringing, the fax machine was spitting out orders and contracts that needed to be addressed and signed, a deliveryman was leaning on the doorbell. *Breathe*, I kept telling myself. BREATHE.

I put my hand on my belly and wondered what all this stress was doing to my baby. And that's when it hit me, a moment of totally clarity when all my priorities that had been bouncing around trying to spell success suddenly came into alignment. My spirit was sending me an S.O.S.

ENOUGH!!! I marched straight downstairs—let the fax fax itself senseless, someone else could open the door, and the phone could ring off the hook for all I cared. I needed to close out the world, slip into my own personal universe, and give my strained spirit an emergency injection of tender lovin' care.

I shut the bathroom door, lit some candles, ran a steamy hot bath with lavender and vanilla bath oils, and slid into heaven. I did deep breathing exercises I had learned years before. . . . I focused my attention on the steam rising from the bathwater and began sending myself positive messages: "I am healthy, my husband is healthy, and a beautiful healthy child is about to come into our lives—business is only business, let it go." I repeated that phrase out loud again and again in a quiet, soothing chant that became a kind of spiritual mantra that crystallized everything wonderful and honestly important in my life. Suddenly I felt the tension draining from my body, my breathing became deep and relaxing and a sense of peacefulness enveloped my entire being.

Now that was a bath! Forty minutes alone in the tub had rejuvenated my ultra-frazzled spirits. When I emerged from the bath-

TAKE NOTE: TARA, president and director of TARA Spa Therapy *(www.taraspa.com)*

Water Therapy

We have a need to cocoon and seek refuge so we can replenish and rejuvenate and restore. More so nowadays because we used to stop and rest on the weekends to catch our breath, sip some tea. Not so anymore. Taking a spa bath is about nourishing ourselves and finding a balance when we feel depleted.

Make your bathroom as spalike as possible with smells, lighting, water temperature, plush towels and slippers, and sound/music. Throw everything that reminds you of clutter in your bathroom into a box. Toss some dried rose petals into the bathwater and add a few tablespoons of olive, almond, or apricot oil. Place aromatherapy

room I was ready to take on the world once again—but this time the world wasn't going to get the better of me.

Everybody who knows me knows a long, hot bath sends me to nirvana. I visited a friend once at the beach after a week of energy-depleting work. As we sat in the kitchen while I rattled on about my exhaustion, she excused herself from the room. She called out to me from the bathroom ten minutes later having filled the tub with bubbly, steaming water and bath salts and lit the candles. *Nirvannnnaaaa!*

Taking baths has become one of my favorite ways of going on a spiritual vacation. It calms and centers me and resets my mood. It's like a watery rebirth. After my soak, I top it off by smoothing on rich and luxuriant lotions from head to toe.

Now, finding forty minutes in the middle of a hectic day for bath time just isn't possible in my life or the life of most other working women I know. But I still make it a non-negotiable point to set aside at least ten minutes most nights for my steamy, relax-

---

candles on the countertop near the tub and next to the sink . Put on some music: New Age, easy jazz, something with a relaxing slow beat that is soothing and comforting. Something to slow you down, not rev you up. Soak for at least twenty minutes.

Complete the ritual by having a cup of herbal tea.

De-Stress
12 drops of lavender
4 drops of clary sage (do not use this item if pregnant)

Serenity
10 drops of lavender
4 drops of bergamot
2 drops of orange

ing bath. It's my alone time—after the baby is asleep, after work is done. It is a date with my spirit—and I've learned from experience not to stand it up.

Other tools I have used over the years to make that essential body-spirit connection are mediation, yoga, and prayer. All three are things you can do just about anywhere at any time. They don't cost money, but the payback can be phenomenal. Even five minutes a day gives your soul a little snack.

Sometimes stealing away from your desk for ten minutes to dip into a favorite novel or book of inspirational writings may be just the ticket you need to refresh your soul in the middle of a busy day. Go for it—a few minutes spent with yourself away from work will help you do your job better, leaving you feeling physically invigorated and mentally sharp.

The Nature Connection

My love of nature began when I lived in Saudi Arabia as a child. The vast desert with its sand dunes and mirages always fascinat-

WISE WOMAN

Linda Ellerbee, TV producer

I've learned I need a certain amount of natural beauty in my life. It's as crucial to my spiritual and emotional well-being as a good night's sleep or eating right or getting to the gym. I need to be out in nature. I need to see trees and flowers and meadows. I go out every year on my birthday in August for a week alone in the wilderness just with what I can load on my back. During that week, I'm able to stop my brain long enough to listen to the world around me and see the world around me. It gives me a spiritual gift that nothing else can give me on my birthday.

ed me. I was connected in a strange way to the void of it all. To me, it was all so big, yet very close to God. Anytime I camped under a tent as a Girl Scout, I always made a point to spend some time with my friends under the stars. Talk about the vastness of God, you have never seen anything like this before.

Thankfully, I have found a partner who connects on this level.

Phil and I have often found a surefire way to give our spirits a much needed lift is to just get out of the house and into nature. A favorite hiking spot is the amazingly beautiful Shawangunk Mountains in New Paltz, New York. It's a place that resonates with the beauty of unspoiled Creation. The rocks and trees and birds transport us to a time when the world was new and pure.

Not only do the sounds and sights of such a beautiful place elevate our souls, but also the wilderness continually teaches us many wonderful life lessons.

I remember seeing a tiny pine tree—just a sapling really, that had taken root in a hairline crevice deep in a huge rock. "How can it grow like that?" I wondered. It just didn't seem possible that something so beautiful could emerge from something so hard and unyielding—but there it was right before my eyes! It made me realize that no matter how difficult and challenging the place in which we find ourselves—with enough will and determination, we can all choose to find the light and grow toward it.

Nature really is a wonderful classroom for life lessons and a great place to connect with your spirit. For some people nature is like a gorgeous cathedral—a holy place where a beaten spirit can be reborn, inspired, and set free . . .

Phil and I love orchids and have many of them in our home. One favorite type of orchid is the white Phalaenopsis—it never fails to inspire us. It can sit dormant and seemingly lifeless for months, looking to the entire world like a dried-up twig ready to be tossed on the backyard bonfire.

In fact, we often give this wonderful plant to friends as gifts, only to find out later that they had thrown them out after the flowers fell off—completely convinced the orchid was dead. Little did they know this resilient little fellow was quietly gathering its energy and nutrients—preparing to burst out as a radiant flower when the time was right.

I think people are the same way. We may think we are dried up spiritually, that there is no connection, but really, deep down inside, our spirit never stopped growing strong—it's just waiting patiently for us to slow down enough to be able to be felt and heard.

Natasha once met an extremely beautiful girl who at a very young age became a sought after and highly successful fashion model. She moved to New York while still a teenager and began living the fairy-tale life so many young girls dream of—a huge bank account, a posh Manhattan apartment with closets full of gorgeous clothes, a stack of invitations to celebrity parties, and long a line of handsome suitors lined up at her door.

She was in heaven—at least that's what she thought, until her beautiful blond hair began falling out by the fistful.

"I thought I was happy and then it hit me like a thunderbolt— I was totally cut off from everything that was true and real and important to me—my spirit was dying!!!"

In short order she quit what she had once believed was her dream job, sold her apartment, gave away most of her clothes, packed what was left in her car, and headed west. She ended up buying a remote piece of land where the prairies meet the mountains, adopted a few animals, and pitched a tent. That was more than a decade ago.

It's where I live . . . more important it's where my spirit can live. Ten years ago, I thought I had it all, but really I had nothing—work began consuming me. The parties I went to

were as phony as the men I was meeting . . . and wherever
I went I was standing on concrete.

I needed to feel the earth under my feet and see the stars
when I looked up—I needed space and peace and quiet to
reflect on who I was, what was important to me, and what
my place was on this planet we all call home. It might not
be for everyone, but I needed to feed my spirit and Mother
Nature became my pantry.

When I touch the earth it's like touching God. I know
how corny that may sound—but my heart is at peace 24/7
and I have never been happier.

> ▶ **TAKE NOTE: Getting started—Suggested
> Spiritual Readings from My Bedside Table**
> The Seven Spiritual Laws of Success, *by Deepak Chopra*
> As You Think, *by James Allen*
> The Power of Now, *by Eckhart Tolle*
> You Can Heal Your Life, *by Louise L. Hay*
> The Road Less Travelled, *by Scott Peck, M.D.*
> The Tao of Pooh, *by Benjamin Hoff*
> A Return to Love, *by Marianne Williamson*
> Manifest Your Destiny, *by Wayne W. Dyer*

The People Connection

Remember my thoughts on the pine tree sprouting from the rocks,
seeking the light? Many people have similar experiences.

If you weren't brought up in family that valued religion or spirituality, you may never have placed any importance on your own
spiritual well-being. Maybe you think spirituality is something you
learn only in Sunday school or from yogis sitting cross-legged on
some far-off mountaintop with no relevance to your life whatsoever.

Emme

Mavis Leno, chairwoman of the Feminist Majority's Campaign

Rising Above

I have never met an Afghan woman, no matter how fresh she is from the grasp of the Taliban, who doesn't already have a voice. These are really smart, really outspoken women. It really is strange, but . . . when that burkah comes off, there are no little, submissive, mother-hen-looking women underneath it. What you see are these beautiful, hawklike warrior faces full of intelligence and force. They've been forged in fire just to survive and keep their family members safe.

These women in Afghanistan are much fiercer and more realistic about life than women are here. After you've lived in such terror and depravation and imprisonment, and fear that in your lifetime you might not see schools open to girls again and you have daughters and you are frantic—it makes people very tough and basic. Their attitude is, if I die I die.

They are an extreme demonstration of the truth of the endurance of the human spirit. They really were deprived of everything that constitutes human life. They basically lived under house arrest. Almost all of the women in Afghanistan defied the Taliban in some small way. Anything from wearing makeup under their burkahs to congregating together. Congregating together was very popular. More than three women were forbidden to congregate together. The Taliban was pretty aware there could be a female revolution. They would defy that and congregate anyway.

Maybe you think if you haven't made a spiritual connection by now, it's too late for you, you've missed your chance. Well, if you do think that, I've got to tell you I think you're wrong. I truly believe that the spirit will always find a way to let you know it's there and it wants to thrive.

Natasha's husband, Steve, has a powerful story that really illustrates how a long-ignored spirit can spring when you least expect it and turn your world upside down:

"When I was first starting out as a reporter I landed a job at a large daily newspaper in the Midwest. My first boss, Max, had been a top-ranked editor for decades and was known throughout the business as being about as hardboiled as they come. You expect to meet jaded people in this business, but Max was really a piece of work. He was a workaholic who never seemed to leave the newsroom. And he seemed to live for bad news. Every day he'd scream out across the newsroom, 'Bring me murderers, find me victims, I want suffering . . . a plane wreck is good, a tornado is better. If it bleeds it leads and I want blood.' You get the idea; this was a guy without a whole lot of compassion or spiritual enlightenment.

"Then one day I saw him reading a story I'd written about a homeless man who had frozen to death on the street in the dead of winter. The fellow had been robbed of his shoes shortly before he died. For some reason, the fact that the man had died barefoot in the snow really got to Max.

" 'They stole his shoes—why would they do that?' he asked me, thrusting the paper at me and jabbing a finger at my story as though I was somehow responsible for what had happened.

"It struck me as odd that this tough-as-nails old editor who lived for tragedy would pose such a sentimental question to a cub reporter.

" 'I guess whoever stole the shoes really needed them. There are lots of people like that in this city,' I said.

"Max fixed a long, hard stare on me, shook his head, and walked away in disgust.

"I didn't see Max for a long time after that. He stopped coming to work shortly after our conversation. Someone told me he had taken an indefinite leave for personal reasons.

"Later I found out Max had taken early retirement so he could work full-time at a homeless shelter. That was his day job—most nights he could be found delivering food and clothing to people living on the street.

"I thought Max's tale would make a great human-interest story and tracked him down to see if he'd agree to be photographed and interviewed.

" 'No way,' Max said. 'You make me look like some kind of hero and the truth is I'm exploiting these people. Whatever I do for them I get back a hundredfold. The hours are worse than at the paper and I don't get paid a dime but I've never been happier. It's the first time in my life I've come home at the end of the day and actually felt good about what I do—end of story.'

"While Max tried to pass off his work with the homeless as something he did to make himself feel good, I didn't buy it. I always sensed he hated being little more than the bearer of bad news and had been waiting for a chance to give something back to the world. It took a dead man with no shoes for Max's true spirit to awaken.

"The story never did make it into the newspaper, but I never get tired of telling it, especially to someone who says people can't change."

Steve's story about Max is a great example of how your spiritual life can be enriched by helping others. The old parable of doing unto others as you would have others do unto you is a terrific recipe for spiritual awareness.

So do what you can to make this world a happier place—visit an elderly aunt, volunteer to mentor an underprivileged child, drop a dollar into the cup some poor soul is holding out to you.

Don't worry about being labeled a do-gooder or hopeless optimist, by helping someone else, the bigger picture of life is being served.

> **TAKE NOTE:** *Charity work is an excellent way to get involved in your community. Whether it is a cause that is near and dear to your heart, or helping others who are less fortunate, or giving back to a group that helped you out in your young life, like a school or university, it can bring you together with other people who have similar good souls. What better way to meet people with big hearts, a drive for community service, and the desire to make the world a better place to live? If you are single or looking for more depth in your life, find your passions and search for the right group to donate your time to www.networkforgood.org*

Q & A with Marc Allen, author of *A Visionary Life* and *Stress Reduction & Creative Meditations for Work and Career* (Audio); president of New World Library

Q: *How do spirituality and ambition/business mix? Can we have both at the same time?*

Marc: One of the main causes of the problems in our lives is that most of us have been taught to separate the spiritual from our everyday lives. We set aside one day a week—or an hour, or nothing at all—to recognize things of the spirit, then we forget it completely as we go about our daily lives. Our spirituality and ambition and careers and business lives are all intertwined, and if we remember to acknowledge our spiritual side, we will make career choices that are deeply fulfilling. We can even aspire to riches and do it in a spiritual fashion.

Q: *What is the relationship between spirituality and the creative force?*

Marc: We all have a creative force surging through us at all times; our creative force moves through every level of our being: physical, emotional, mental, and spiritual. When our creative force is aligned with our spirit, we experience the highest levels of inspiration we are capable of.

Q: *Do you think society in general is looking toward spirituality more so in this new millennium? And if so, why?*

Marc: The more problems there are in people's lives and in the world—the more frustration, pain, suffering, anxiety—the more people gravitate toward the spiritual. For many, it is their last hope, because everything else has failed them. And if we're fortunate to find the right spiritual books and guidance, we discover that turning toward the spiritual solves every problem we have.

One of the greatest and oldest spiritual books of all time is The Bhagavad-Gita—"The Divine Song." It tells us there are four types of people who turn to a spiritual path: (1) Those who are in pain, physically or emotionally; (2) those who wish to improve their lives, have greater wealth or security, and be more successful; (3) those who have discovered that the spiritual path is in itself the single best possible goal, because once we have understood our spiritual nature, all of our other problems dissolve.

The Gita states very clearly and simply that the spiritual path will fulfill all the needs of these three types of people. The fourth type, it says, is very rare: (4) those who have attained deep and constant understanding of their spiritual nature. These people have no needs whatsoever, and so don't need even the spiritual path to improve their lives in any way. You can't improve on perfection.

Q: *How can people realize their "deepest dreams" using their spirituality?*

Marc: When you get down to it, our highest and deepest dreams are spiritual. What do we really want to do with our lives? It's very good to ask that question and to follow the answer through. We may think we want to be a rock star or make a million dollars. All right—ask yourself why you want that. When you get down to it, it always has something to do with living a life of ease and lightness, and with making some kind of lasting contribution, not only for yourself but for your family and even the whole of humanity. That's what we want underneath it all, isn't it? And that is a spiritual impulse, which will only find its fulfillment when we become aware of our spiritual nature, and live in accordance with it.

Q: *How can a person tap into his or her spirituality?*

Marc: Many of us can tap in to it just by understanding it is something we already have. It is an essential part of ourselves, though we often forget because we are so busy focusing on our bodies, emotions, and thoughts. We can nurture it through prayer ("Ask and you shall receive"!), meditation, quiet times in nature, or any other kind of activities that take us out of the stream of our constant thoughts. Meditation and Yoga are excellent.

Q: *How does helping others help us?*

Marc: Helping others helps us in countless ways, many of which we don't even realize consciously. When we do it, we become more powerful, and we realize that we receive far more when we give than we're ever able to give back. There is a wonderful and mysterious principle at work in the universe: When we give to others, and when we respect and love and work in partnership with others, our lives are enhanced in innumerable

ways. The things we do and say become more aligned with spirit, and every moment of our lives becomes easier, happier, and more peaceful. It is only by giving that we can find true fulfillment and satisfaction.

Q: *How can people reduce stress in their daily lives? At work?*

Marc: Meditation and Yoga are great stress reducers. So is aerobic exercise and even just deep breathing. Whenever you're feeling stress throughout the day, take a deep breath and, as you exhale, let all tension and all thought go—just let go of your stress and your problems, let go of all thought, for one moment, one breath. That little bit of meditation is very effective at reducing stress. The more you can remember to do it through the day, the better. If things are really stressful, take a break. Get outside if possible, or even just into a bathroom or any other place you can be alone. Hot baths and massage are of course great stress relievers, as well. Valerian tea and other calming herbal teas are excellent, too—nearly everyone in our culture can benefit from them. So many of us have coffee, soft drinks, sugar, and other stimulants throughout the day—balance it out with some valerian tea and you'll find yourself far more relaxed. Another simple and effective thing to do is to repeat an affirmation to yourself that counters stress. Here's a good one: "Every day in every way, I'm getting better and better."

Q: *How can we help others, friends and family, explore their spirituality, too? How can we help the world in general evolve spiritually?*

Marc: The best way to help others explore their spirituality is to fully explore and understand our own. Let's ask ourselves this essential question: What is our purpose in it all? It seems to me our greatest purpose in life is to personally evolve into a more loving, more expansive, and light-filled being, and to help the world evolve into societies that respect, support, and love every person in the community and nation. As Riane Eisler shows us so brilliantly in her new book, *The Power of Partnership*, the best way to grow as a person and to help others is to learn to live and work in partnership with everyone—without domination, exploitation, or fear—creating loving and supportive relationships, first of all with the many aspects of ourselves, and then with our intimate family and friends, workplaces and communities, our nation and our world, and with nature and spirit. A great teacher of meditation in India, Ramana Maharshi, summed it all up beautifully: "The end of all wisdom is love, love, love."

FINAL THOUGHT

Need a break from the noise? Want to make a major change in your work or personal environment? Want time to devote your energy to a dream? Sit somewhere quiet, turn off the bright lights, and light a candle. Take a few deep breaths. I find it shocking how I forget just to breathe sometimes. When I stop for a moment and do some deep breathing, it relaxes me and helps me concentrate on what I'm doing, where I'm going, and how I'm feeling. You don't need to pack up your life and go to India to find spirituality. If you look inward, you can find it in your heart, wherever you are.

A Last Word

So here we are, right smack in the middle of an incredible time of change.

People are reprioritizing. Families are coming together and counting their blessings. Executives are leaving city jobs to live slower lives in the country. Small-towners are moving to the big city and risking it all to finally follow their lifelong career aspirations. There's been a shift. Everyone is becoming more connected with their souls and their dreams.

Writing this book has made me look back at all the funny, crazy, and sometimes heartbreaking "little emergencies" I've had as I tried to connect with myself and the world and people around me.

What I learned is this: The small ups and downs of dating and friendship and careers and everything else are all part of LIFE. Life's little emergencies keep life interesting! If you take care of them with a sense of humor, you can focus on enjoying the big things, the little things, and everything in between.

And if they make you have a little scream or cry or fit every once in a while, so be it! Let it out, baby! Just know that you are not alone—the rest of us are going through the very same emotions.

In life, as in all things, we must make the effort, embrace the challenges, and open our hearts. Just one move in a positive direction can change your entire life and the lives of the people around you.

I hope all of our experiences can help you out along your journey. Try to stay connected to the people who mean the most to you in your life. Keep them in a safe place in your heart. With them you will do just fine. Above all else, have fun and share what you learn.

Thank you for joining me on this ride!
Stay in touch!

Emme

XO

Desiderata

I have this incredible work hanging in my guest bathroom and have made numerous copies for friends over the years. The ageless advice and simple message of peace within is, in my opinion, a perfect way to leave you. Enjoy!

Go placidly amid the noise and haste, and remember what peace there may be in silence. As far as possible, without surrender, be on good terms with all persons. Speak your truth quietly and clearly; and listen to others, even to the dull and ignorant; they too have their story. Avoid loud and aggressive persons; they are vexations to the spirit. If you compare yourself with others, you may become vain or bitter, for always there will be greater and lesser persons than yourself. Enjoy your achievements as well as your plans. Keep interested in your own career, however humble, it's a real possession in the changing fortunes of time. Exercise caution in your business affairs, for the world is full of trickery. But let this not blind you to what virtue there is; many persons strive for high ideals, and everywhere life is full of heroism. Be yourself. Especially do not feign affection. Neither be cynical about love; for in the face of all aridity and disenchantment, it is as perennial as the grass. Take kindly the counsel of the years, gracefully surrendering the things of youth. Nurture strength of spirit to shield you in sudden misfortune. But do not distress yourself with dark imaginings. Many fears are born of fatigue and lone-liness. Beyond a wholesome discipline, be gentle with yourself. You are a child of the universe no less than the trees and the stars; you have a right to be here. And whether or not it is clear to you, no doubt the uni-verse is unfolding as it should. Therefore be at peace with God, what-ever you conceive him to be. And whatever your labors and aspirations, in the noisy confusion of life, keep peace in your soul. With all its sham, drudgery, and broken dreams, it is still a beautiful world. Be cheerful. Strive to be happy.

Resources

BODY-IMAGE/EATING DISORDERS

1. National Eating Disorders Association: *www.nationaleatingdisorders.org*. Information and Helpline: 1-800-931-2237. I am the Ambassador chair for this incredible organization. Confidentiality is a top priority.
2. Harvard Eating Disorders Center, c/o Massachusetts General Hospital, 15 Parkman Street, Boston, MA 02114. Phone: (617) 726-8470 *http://www.hedc.org*.
3. National Institute of Mental Health (NIMH), Office of Communications and Public Liaison. Public inquiries: (301) 443-4513. Media inquiries: (301) 443-4536. E-mail: *nimhinfo@nih.gov*. *http://www.nimh.nih.gov*.
4. *Dying to Be Thin: Understanding and Defeating Anorexia Nervosa and Bulimia—A Practical, Lifesaving Guide* by Ira M. Sacker, M.D. and Marc A. Zimmer, Ph.D. New York: 1987. Warner Books. *www.heedfoundation.org*. 1-877-729-4333.
5. *Intuitive Eating* by Evelyn Triboli, M.S., R.D., and Elyse Resch, M.S., R.D. New York: St. Martin's Press, 1996.
6. *Wasted: A Memoir of Anorexia and Bulimia* by Marya Hornbacher. New York: Harper Flamingo/HarperCollins *Publishers*, 1999.

7. *The Beauty Myth: How Images of Beauty Are Used Against Women* by Naomi Wolf. New York: Anchor, 1992, and *Promiscuities: The Secret Struggle For Womanhood*. New York: Random House, 1997.
8. *The Adonis Complex: The Secret Crisis of Male Body Obsession* by Harrison G. Pope, Jr., M.D., Katharine A. Phillips, M.D., and Roberto Olivardia, Ph.D. New York: Free Press, 2000.
9. *Making Weight: Men's Conflicts with Food, Weight, Shape, and Appearance* by Arnold Andersen, M.D., Leigh Cohn, M.A.T., and Thomas Holbrook, M.D. Gurze Books, 2000.

FASHION

1. Talbots' online style guide provides a wonderful list of fashion terms and their meaning. *www.talbots.com/styleguide*.
2. *The Pocket Stylist* by Kendall Farr. New York: Gotham, forthcoming 2004.
3. *Stylenoir: The First How To Guide to Fashion Written with Black Women in Mind* by Constance C. R. White. New York: Perigee, 1998.
4. *Style* by Elsa Klensch with Beryl Meyer. New York: Perigee, 1995.
5. *Plus Style: The Plus-Size Guide to Looking Great* by Suzan Nanfeldt. New York: Plume/Penguin, 1996.
6. *The Fine Art of Dressing: Make Yourself a Masterpiece by Dressing for Your Body Type* by Margaux Tartarotti. New York: Perigee, 1999.
7. Travel sewing kit: Austin House Sew and Stow. *www.containerstore.com*.
8. Swiss Army knives. *www.swissarmy.com*. For the little threads that need clipping on the road.

BEAUTY PRODUCTS/HELP

1. Bumble and Bumble. Travel hair products and their thickening spray for thin hair is great! Can't purchase online but can help you find store nearest you. *www.bumbleandbumble.com*.
2. Charles Worthington has two products I love. Beautiful Hair conditioner and his travel Results take aways. Take aways can take you through a week's worth of daily pampering while on the road and don't take up too much room in my suitcase. *www.charlesworthington.com*.

3. *Bobbi Brown Beauty: The Ultimate Beauty Resource.* New York: HarperCollins, 1997, and *Bobbi Brown Teenage Beauty: Everything You Need to Look Pretty, Natural, Sexy & Awesome* by Bobbie Brown, et al. New York: HarperCollins, 2000. See also *www.bobbibrown.com.*
4. *Real Beauty* by Sonia Kashuk. New York: Clarkson Potter, 2003.
5. *The Mane Thing* by Kevin Mancuso. Boston: Little, Brown and Co., 1999. *www.themanething.com.*

FLOWERS

1. 1-888-Orchids.com. Orchid plants, also offers pots and supplies and orchid-care and pronunciation guides. *www.1888orchids.com.*
2. Beautiful Orchids.com. Winner of the *Wall Street Journal* orchid retail comparison test. *www.beautifulorchids.com.*
3. Chestnuts in the Tuileries. Incredible arrangements. Worth every penny. *www.chestnutsinthetuileries.com.*

TRAVEL INFO

Passport/Visa help:

1. Zierer Visa Service, Inc. Twenty-four-hour turnaround approximately three times the cost of two-week standard processing but could be worth it! *www.zvs.com.*
2. Travisa Visa Service Inc. Same as above applies. Been featured in Yahoo picks and *Forbes* magazine. *www.travisa.com.*
3. *The Woman's Fix-It Car Care Book: Secrets Women Should Know About Their Cars* by Karen Valenti and George Mair. Worcester, MA: Chandler House Press, 2000.

SEX

1. *Satisfaction: The Art of the Female Orgasm* by Kim Cattrall and Mark Levinson. New York: Warner Books, 2002.
2. *Lesbian Sex Secrets for Men: What Every Man Wants to Know About Making Love to a Woman and Never Asks* by Jamie Goddard and Kurt Brungardt. New York: Plume Publishing, 2000.

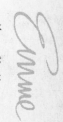

SPA PRODUCTS

1. TARA Spa Therapy: *www.taraspa.com*. 1-800-552-0779.
2. *Naturally Beautiful: Earth's Secrets and Recipes for Skin Body and Spirit* by Dawn Gallagher and Melanie Menagh. New York: Universe Books, 1999.

SPIRITUAL/INSPIRATIONAL

1. *The Ten Percent Solution* by Marc Allen. Novato, CA: New World Library, 2002. See also *www.marcallen.com*.
2. *One Last Time.* New York: Berkley, 1998, and *Crossing Over*. San Diego, CA: Jodere Group, 2001, both by John Edward.
3. *Yoga for Meditators*—John Friend. This is the video that best captures John Friend's clear, spiritually inspiring approach. Available at *www.anusarayoga.com*.
4. Yoga Zone. Introduction to Yoga and other products: *www.yogazone.com*.

PUBLIC SPEAKING

1. *The Quick and Easy Way to Effective Speaking: Modern Techniques for Dynamic Communication* by Dale Carnegie. Pocket Books.
2. *The Overnight Guide to Public Speaking* by Ed Wohlmuth. Philadelphia, PA: Running Press, 1990.

MANNERS/ETIQUETTE

1. *The Amy Vanderbilt Complete Book of Etiquette: A Guide to Contemporary Living* revised and expanded by Letitia Baldridge. New York: Doubleday, 1978.

PARTY PLANNING

1. *America Entertains at Home* by David Tutera. Stewart Tabori and Chang, 2003.
2. *Domestic Bliss* by Rita Konig. Ebury Press, 2002.

If you have funny or interesting stories about motherhood, relationships, entertaining, and everything in between and would like to share it with me, please e-mail me at *emmemail@emmestyle.com*.

Or write me:

Emme
c/o Sarah Hall Productions
670 Broadway
Suite 504
New York, NY 10012